Away with the Ferries

Away with the Ferries

Ferry tales from ten years of
Island-Hopping

STUART CRAIG

LINDSAY PUBLICATIONS

First published in 1999 by
Lindsay Publications
Glasgow

ISBN 1 898169 00 0

A CIP record of this book is available from the British Library

Designed and typeset in 10/12pt Berkley
by Creative Imprint, Glasgow

Front cover: Designed by Creative Imprint, Glasgow

Printed and bound in Finland by Werner Söderström, Osakeyhtiö

CONTENTS

Dedicated to Clare
who happily puts up with my peregrinations
and to my children
Julia, Philippa, Fiona and Tony,
who wanted to hear all about them

Dedication

I thank Alan Caplan for looking after my patients for me while I traipsed around the islands each year. His wonderful adlib to them, 'Stuart is away with the ferries!' gave me a very appropriate title for the book

INTRODUCTION

'Are you doing anything the third week in May? I've got a week's holiday!' Gibbie shouted to me across three back garden widths.

'Why?' When I'm suspicious I always answer a question with a question.

'There is a new ferry service from Islay up to Oban starting that week!'

Thus an idea was sown and the third week in May has never been the same since.

When my friend and neighbour Gibbie Anderson and I set off on a three day trip around the Western Isles in May 1989 we did not intend to start an annual pilgrimage on the ferries that would last for ten years. But by the time that Ian McLaren joined us a year later on a similar trip, that was exactly what we were doing. Our Annual Island Hop had begun and it became obvious that someone was going to have to write about it. That had to be me. So ten years on, here it is. The full unadulterated account of ten years of Island Hopping; tales of ferries, stories about characters met on the way and the continuing saga of three ship-spotters traipsing from one mode of transport to the next – usually a ship of some shape or form.

As the years unfold some repetition in the places visited or the ships sailed on is inevitable but care has been taken to spare the reader any tedium. It is really the story of three chaps, wandering, not quite aimlessly, for three or four days each May around the islands of the Clyde, Hebrides and Western Isles on the ferries, small ships and boats that serve them. It is a book for the modern day steamer enthusiast or for those who have a love of the islands. It is not a travel guide book, a ferry identification manual or a tourist brochure. There is a heavy slant on the ships. Much has been written about the old steamers that graced these waters but not so much about the modern scene. As these newer ships and ferries were an integral part of our journeys then it is inevitable that accurate accounts of their movements and design are included in the story. In fact, some boring ship concepts now follow as it is deemed necessary to explain briefly how the Western Isles shipping scene works.

Ferry services on the Clyde and in and around the Hebrides and Western Isles are run by Caledonian MacBrayne. This company was formed in 1973 as a state subsidised amalgamation of the two great steamer companies whose names it carries. Throughout the book, Caledonian MacBrayne has been shortened to 'CalMac'. The term 'fleet' refers to CalMac's fleet of ships (about thirty at the start of our travels). The twenty-four hour clock is used to relate the passage of time and the schedules we have to meet. Finally the term 'Western Isles' refers to the Outer Hebrides and it may be useful to consult a map of the West of Scotland, although maps are dotted about the text describing our journeys. Some concepts are important. Firstly, although all the ships are totally integrated, the Clyde and Western Isles services are largely independent from a geographical point of view i.e. there are no services sailing round the Mull of Kintyre from the Clyde into Hebridean waters.

Secondly, the ferries are divided into about a dozen large ships and a larger number of smaller vessels. Whereas some have served the same routes for years, others change around from time to time.

Thirdly, most of the services to the Hebrides and Western Isles depart from the main ports of Kennacraig, Stornoway, Mallaig and, most important of all, Oban. Therefore many of our journeys had to start from these ports.

Our first trip or, as far as we knew at the time our only trip, was to be centred around the new Wednesday service from Kennacraig, on West Loch Tarbert, to Islay, Colonsay and Oban. Indeed the main reason for undertaking the trip was because Gibbie and I had discovered this new, long route in the summer timetable and were keen to try it out. We had often sailed together on the ferries of the Clyde but had never sailed further afield and would in fact be inaugurating this new service as it commenced in the third week of May 1989, the intended week of our trip. All other planning was based around this sailing and the trip became expanded into a three day jaunt based on how to get to Islay, and how to get back from Oban, with one or two diversions on the way.

Islay had for years been served from the terminal at Kennacraig on the western shores of the Kintyre peninsula. Colonsay, on the other hand, had been traditionally served from Oban. However the new 1989 timetable showed that this summer, and only on Mondays and Wednesdays, one ship would serve both islands. There would be a sailing from Kennacraig to Port Askaig (Islay), Colonsay and then, on the Wednesday only, on to Oban. The ship would then retrace her route south calling at the same ports.

The reason for this 'new' route was fairly obvious. CalMac had just reduced their Oban fleet of big ships from three to two. The *Columba* and *Caledonia* had been sold and the *Claymore* re-deployed. The new *Isle of Mull* and *Lord of the Isles* had taken their places. This resulted in major juggling with the timetables in order to maintain services as two ships instead of three as before now had to provide the same service to the islands. To aid one of these new, hard worked ships, twice a week the Islay vessel would be used for two of the three weekly runs to Colonsay. On a Wednesday, instead of stopping at the island, the vessel would continue north to Oban to provide the vital link with the important West Highland town. This was what originally attracted us.

We would have to get to Islay the day before, to avoid a very early start on the Wednesday, and the best way to do this was to use Arran as a stepping stone. At the other end of the trip we planned to sail over to Mull – the idea of crossing to Iona and Staffa came from Gibbie and was an eleventh hour decision. We would return to Glasgow from Oban by train but all connecting bus journeys on our route were left to chance and not booked in advance. Indeed, although we booked our first night's accommodation at the Port

Askaig Hotel the second night was left to chance also. On future Hops most modes of transport and certainly all accommodation were booked well in advance.

At the time of our first trip services in the Western Isles were being altered for the 1989 summer season. The new *Isle of Mull* was starting her first full season as Oban to Mull ferry (having been lengthened the previous autumn to cure her dead-weight problem). The even newer *Lord of the Isles* was not due to take up service until two weeks into the summer season and so her duties were to be maintained meantime by the *Claymore* on the Western Isles routes and by the *Iona* on the Coll and Tiree services. With the *Pioneer* starting the Mallaig to Armadale service on the first week of the season it meant that the Islay service, and thus the inauguration of the Wednesday Islay to Oban route, would be left to the *Glen Sannox*. When we set out on that first day, however, we were not aware which vessel would be taking us on those first few nautical miles to Oban.

The kind of route planning and booking of accommodation that were used in 1989 were utilised for our second trip in 1990 and for subsequent Island Hops.

The descriptions of the islands in the book are largely drawn from our own experiences, past and present. Usually I have good things to say about them but any derogatory remarks are not meant to offend anyone. If this book lures you to the islands then accept the invitation and go to see them for yourself.

Finally, none of this would have been any fun without my two ship-loving companions whose humour, camaraderie and flexibility, to the extent of buoyancy, were always a joy to behold – even on Scalpay.

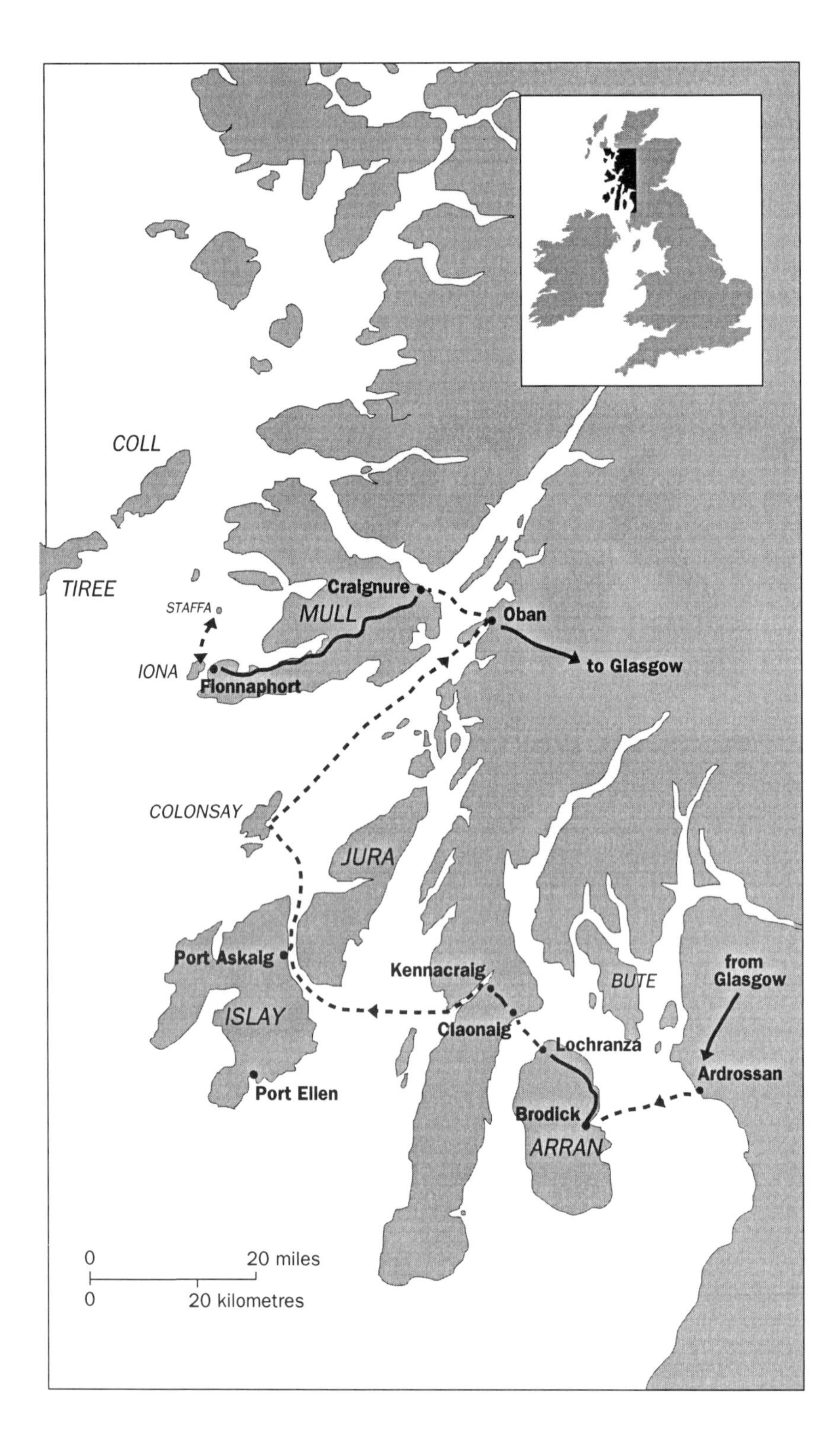
COLL
TIREE
STAFFA
IONA
Craignure
MULL
Oban
to Glasgow
Fionnaphort
COLONSAY
JURA
Port Askaig
ISLAY
Port Ellen
Kennacraig
Claonaig
Lochranza
BUTE
from Glasgow
Ardrossan
Brodick
ARRAN
0
20 miles
0
20 kilometres

1989 The First Nautical Miles

Day One – *Re-united with an Old Lady*

Tuesday 16 May 1989 and with a feeling of 'stepping into the unknown', Gibbie and I join the 0803 train at Pollokshaws East station, bound for Glasgow Central and our connecting train to Ardrossan Harbour. We are supposedly travelling light but our bags are crammed with cameras, film and numerous timetables. Little do we know that we are embarking on a series of journeys that will become so successful that they will still be taking place ten years later. Just what have we started? I had sailed no further than Rothesay and Brodick before this!

On arrival at the harbour our first ship the *Isle of Arran* is waiting at the linkspan, her bow visor gaping, like a beached whale lying with its mouth open. She is the largest car-ferry to have served the island of Arran, entering service in April 1984, having taken over from the under-sized *Caledonia* and the under-powered *Clansman*.

Gibbie announces that this is going to be his first ever trip on her. This comes as a surprise to me as she has been servicing Arran for some five years now but he explains that in his younger days they were a 'Rothesay' family. He elaborates:

'Glasgow was divided into two kinds of people; those who went to Dunoon and those who went to Rothesay – the toffs went to Arran.'

I get the impression that he thinks this explains everything.

We join the ship for the 0945 crossing to Brodick, glad that we do not have to worry about joining the queue of cars waiting to embark. Instead we can watch the queue being swallowed up into the open bow from the relative calm of the forward deck where, to Gibbie's delight, there is a clear view of the proceedings. Gibbie believes that it should be a mandatory design feature that all passenger ships should have a 'view over the bow'. He is thus immediately endeared to the *Isle of Arran*.

We sail on time in beautiful weather and descend for a guided tour of the ship's accommodation and that ultimate parameter for judging a ship's catering standards – sampling the quality of the bacon rolls.

I first visited Arran in 1974 and was then immediately struck by the unspoilt beauty of the island as a whole and the mountainous north-eastern corner in particular. I spent hours walking in the hills that year, wearing sand-shoes and carrying nothing but a packet of chewing-gum. I can recall springing my way up the sinister Glen Rosa and making an ascent of The Saddle only to be horrified by the steep descent that I had to negotiate in order to get down the other side into Glen Sannox. As I scrambled down apprehensively in my sand-shoes and chewing my gum I met hill-walkers proceeding systematically in the opposite direction with boots, rucksacks and even ropes, inching their way gingerly up towards me.

In that year I got to know the mountain geography fairly well but no amount of searching could locate the famous 'sleeping warrior'. Looking from the mainland, at a distance, the mountains of the north-eastern corner of Arran are reminiscent of the sleeping form of a human figure. The comparison is somewhat fanciful ! The appellation 'sleeping warrior' has become a maxim for that whole upland corner of the island.

A year later, in that glorious summer of 1975, I was back. This time, with hired bicycle and Mars bar, I was off on a cycle around the north circular road from Brodick to Blackwaterfoot, Pirnmill, Lochranza and back to Brodick again. Today Gibbie and I are taking the leisurely route to Lochranza – by bus.

Numerous holidays and excursions to Arran followed over the years. I sailed over on various ships: *Caledonia, Clansman, Glen Sannox* and *Isle of Arran*. My favourite 'steamer' memory, however, was at the September week-end holiday in 1976 when the *Clansman* could not cope with the departing hordes and the grand old *Queen Mary* was despatched south to fill her decks with sodden and tired Arran revellers.

Arran is publicised by the Tourist Board as 'Scotland in Miniature'. A fairly apt description as the landscapes of this large island are varied and contrasting: mountain and moor in the north, sea-cliffs, farmland and conifer forest in the south. For the holidaymaker who likes a bit of the 'outdoors' Arran takes some beating.

Finding a bus is easy on Arran. They congregate at the pier to meet the arrival of each ferry and then set off to circumnavigate the island in a variety of directions. Presumably they meet each other half way around the sixty mile perimeter road. We are soon ashore and on the North Circular bus to Lochranza, at the top of the island.

We are literally using Arran as a stepping stone across the Clyde estuary. With a ferry link to Kintyre at its northern tip we can use the island as a short cut to our next ferry terminal. As early as this we are finding that our visit to a particular island is all too short, although we enjoy the fifteen-mile bus journey along the north-eastern side of the island and, in particular, the pantomime on the narrow, tortuous road through the picturesque village of Corrie, as we encounter several cars coming towards us, and have to squeeze into the side of the road to allow them to pass. I am just glad I am not having to drive. The cars dance and cajole past the bus with centimetres to spare and we are soon on our way again.

As we reach Lochranza the ferry *Loch Ranza* is ready to depart but we have time on our side and choose to wait for the next one. We stroll off to see what this most northern Arran community has to offer the intrepid island-hopper who has only an hour to spare.

Lochranza is a very picturesque little village built around the shores of a small round sea-loch. Inland it is surrounded by hills and mountains. In fact the north facing Lochranza is so hemmed in by mountains that it has the unenviable reputation of being the least sunny village in Britain – from November to mid-February the sun's rays fail to clear the tops of the mountain ridges.

Lochranza has a castle, which is our first target. Nothing like Glamis or Balmoral but a much more modest affair. It looks a bit like a half-built tenement sitting out on a spit of shoreline that juts out into the loch. It dates from the thirteenth century but has been much rebuilt over the centuries. The north-eastern corner of it is still in ruins, having been destroyed in a storm in 1897. I can understand why nobody has bothered to repair it. We do not go inside, of course, we are not real tourists. In any case the door is locked. Instead we descend to the stony little beach where Gibbie gives me a lesson on the aerodynamics of stone-skimming. To my surprise he is able to put his considerable theories into practice as various flat 'chuckies' are spun across the still waters of the bay.

Lunch is in the cafe as we wait for the ferry to return and discuss the first problem we have encountered in our journey. On arriving at Claonaig on Kintyre we will have no means of getting across the peninsula to Kennacraig where the Islay ferry leaves from. We do not have a lot of time to get across, by whatever means, as the ferry to Islay leaves at 1445 and the *Loch Ranza* does not reach Kintyre until 1355. There are no buses and the five mile walk is not an attractive option.

Our thoughts are put to the back of our minds as we become involved in conversation with an Australian couple. They are on a different kind of touring trip and between us we practically organise their entire itinerary for them. What we fail to do is to ask them for a lift across Kintyre from the eastern side to the west to where our Islay departure will be waiting. On reflection, maybe a request for a lift would not have gone down too well after Gibbie's fairly acerbic comments about 'Neighbours'. Instead I phone ahead for a taxi to meet us at Claonaig. We will make our Islay connection as long as the taxi turns up.

The *Loch Ranza* returns and after a photo session we board. This twelve car ferry is one of four almost identical vessels built in the mid 1980s to replace some of the eclectic bunch of ageing small ferries. They resemble black and white cardboard boxes with a wheelhouse on top, painted in the red and yellow CalMac colours in a fanciful attempt to create something that resembles a funnel. The car deck is enclosed by a lounge along each side, one for the crew and one for the passengers. This gives considerably better accommodation than on the previous small ferries. These little ships have been quite a success on the routes from Largs to Cumbrae, Colintraive to Rhubodach on Bute and this route – the back-door entrance to Arran.

The half-hour crossing is exciting as the south-westerly swell which has been dominating the seas around this part of Scotland for the past week becomes apparent. The ferry pitches and rolls her way across the Kilbrannan Sound which is still bathed in sunshine. Some travellers are not too keen on a ship whose decks are constantly rising up to meet you and then falling away again but both Gibbie and I like to feel that we really are on a boat.

At 1355 we are arriving at Claonaig on Kintyre and we are delighted to see our taxi drawing up at the slipway. There is nothing of any interest at Claonaig. In fact there is nothing at all at Claonaig, which is why we chose to use up our time on the Arran side. It was either that or crossing over here on the earlier ferry and spending an hour and a half chatting to the sheep.

The taxi-driver is very interested in our journey and this seems to be reflected in his fare. He has driven twelve miles from Tarbert to meet us and then carries us six miles back across the Kintyre peninsula for £3. A real bargain, we feel, for what was the missing link in today's journey. As it happens we are at the Kennacraig ferry terminal on the west side of Kintyre half an hour before the 1445 scheduled sailing to Port Askaig on Islay.

The Kennacraig ferry terminal is built on a small islet linked to the shore 50 metres away by a man-made causeway. The result is a terminal that blends well into the environment, a sort of 'green terminal'. Originally the base for sailings to Port Askaig by Western Ferries, CalMac started using Kennacraig terminal in June 1978, thus moving their operations from West Loch Tarbert Pier further down the Loch to these deeper waters. CalMac eventually purchased their new base in 1979 and when Western Ferries eventually gave up their Islay sailings CalMac took over as sole providers of the service to Port Ellen and Port Askaig. In those days the *Pioneer* was the vessel used. Today we had anticipated that the *Claymore* would be in operation but as we look down the beautiful West Loch Tarbert, upon which the Islay ferry plies, we are surprised to see that the vessel in question is not the *Claymore* but that grand old lady *Glen Sannox*. This is a delightful surprise, for at this stage we are unaware that the *Claymore* is helping out with the Outer Isles sailings at Oban.

The *Glen Sannox* is to my mind almost unique among car-ferries in that she possesses a spacious promenade deck, similar to that found on traditional turbine or paddle steamers. The car has all but taken over in recent years and passengers are tucked away into awkward corners of ships as if they are an encumbrance to the real duty of the ship – carrying vehicles. Not so on our ship this afternoon. She had been built in a time when the real steamers still plied the Clyde and this shows from her more than adequate layout.

Built in 1957 for the Ardrossan to Brodick service she has in more recent times been employed outwith the Clyde estuary at Oban on services to Mull and various relief duties. In the late 1970s she had the triple function of peak time Clyde ferry, relief vessel and Clyde cruise ship. She had her car-deck adorned with deck-chairs and parasols for her latter function, which made her look like mutton dressed as lamb. She was not a success in her cruising role and only survived a handful of seasons. Now, as we sail on her, she is in her last two months of service for Caledonian MacBrayne. Appropriately she is having an auspicious end to her career. On 8 April she had given a special farewell cruise on the Clyde from Gourock, calling at her old haunts of Dunoon, Largs, Brodick and Campbeltown. I had in fact joined her that day for the homeward stretch from Brodick to Largs. She had then spent two weeks on her original route – Brodick to Ardrossan – while the *Isle of Arran* was being overhauled. On 10 May she was back in West Highland waters for a cruise from Oban around Mull. Thereafter she was assigned to the Islay roster, where we find her, to our surprise, today. Her final sailing will be in June for the Govan Shipbuilders, an annual event. After that she is to be sold to a Greek shipping operator. Today, as we watch her arrive, the deep purr of her diesel exhausts are evocative of many trips in my youth to Dunoon and Rothesay.

The *Glen Sannox* sails past the end of the pier and then swings her stern around to dock at the linkspan. Our cameras click furiously. Now thirty-two years old she is laden with commercial vehicles and a varied collection of the same wait to load. It looks as though they are going to take some time to disgorge. Indeed it is one and a half hours before she is reloaded. One driver is using a cab to take off the arriving trailers and load the departing ones with a skill and judgement that is entertaining to watch. Gibbie and I look on from the ship's spacious deck in almost total silence. As we prepare to leave the familiar territory of the Clyde and the waters around Kintyre we now feel that we are on a real Hebridean adventure. We are in no hurry to leave and the crew of the ship seem in a similar frame of mind. Again, we are particularly happy that we do not have a vehicle to load.

Eventually, at 1545, an hour late, we sail for Port Askaig on Islay. The crossing on the calm sea will take two hours. We zig-zag our way down the still waters of West Loch Tarbert, past seals sunbathing on the rocks and rafts of guillemots on a loch cruise of their own. Out into the open sea and then a gentle curve into the strait separating the islands of Islay and Jura. Known as the Sound of Islay this stretch of water is frequently turbulent due to a tidal stream racing down the half mile wide strip of water that separates the two islands. Today the captain takes the ship well over to the Islay side of the Sound. He heads directly across the Sound towards the lighthouse at MacArthur's Head before turning to starboard and then hugging the Islay coast to try to avoid meeting the rushing tide head on. We cruise in and out of every small bay. The tide would have retarded the ship even further. The manoeuvring attracts interest among the passengers and a small crowd assembles at the front end of the observation lounge as we approach Port Askaig.

The tiny village of Port Askaig on Islay is hidden out of sight in a small bay at the bottom of a wooded hill. It overlooks the Sound of Islay and the towering Paps of Jura on the neighbouring island. It suddenly, and almost unexpectedly, comes into view and at 1740 the ship docks.

Our hotel is only a few yards from the pier and within ten minutes we have checked in and are sitting in the garden clutching a welcome pint of beer and watching the old lady re-load again for the trip back to the mainland. The view over to Jura is stunning and seems to be getting better by the sip. In fact it is so stunning that we decide we have to go there as well. Our sailing is therefore not yet over for the day.

Suitably refreshed we jump aboard Western Ferries *Sound of Gigha* for the eight-minute crossing to island number three. I have never been on Jura before and the reason for our briefest of visits requires to be explained to the baffled crew as we quickly get back aboard the ship before she leaves us stranded on the bare shingle, raised beach.

Gibbie astounds me by claiming to have spent a two-week family holiday on Jura some years ago in which it never rained once. Whether that means it never rained once or never rained at all I am not sure.

We are soon back on Islay again enjoying a bar meal which is lubricated with no less than three peaty malts for which the beautiful island of Islay is renowned. Laphroaig, Bruichladdich and Lagavulin are the chosen ones. We give Caol Ila a miss as Gibbie cannot pronounce the name.

I fall asleep that night reminiscing on past holidays to the island, sorry that our visit here is so brief. Islay has so many lovely corners and golden beaches which on a tour such as this it is almost sacrilegious to pass by. However, tomorrow is the day of our big sail up to Oban, aboard the same ship that brought us here today. Let's hope the weather keeps up.

Day Two – *The Old meets the New at Oban*

The following morning is a relaxed affair in Port Askaig. The *Glen Sannox* is due in at 1030 and we will sail up to Oban via the island of Colonsay, another island I have never been on. As we wait in the hotel garden our attention is drawn to the spectacle of the *Sound of Gigha* struggling across from Jura. The current is flowing strongly in a southerly direction and the ferry has to point her bow at a 45 degree angle to where she is heading in order to compensate and reach Islay at Port Askaig instead of two miles downstream. She looks like a giant red crab scuttling sideways to meet us.

Port Askaig is slowly and lethargically coming to life around us, in true island style. It is a tiny little hamlet – not big enough to be a village – nestling under the cliffs. A hotel, garage, booking-office and a couple of shops are all there is. As the time of the ship's arrival nears the place begins to come alive. A gradual build up of vehicles and a slow gathering of potential travellers are the only clues that something is about to happen. The peace is soon interrupted by the deep purr of the *Glen Sannox* coming up the Sound and swinging into Port Askaig. The loading is again interesting to watch. As there is traffic for both Colonsay and Oban the arrangement of vehicles on the deck is critical. We are, of course, witnessing the first day of this innovative route.

We set sail at 1145, nearly forty-five minutes late, with almost a full complement of cars and lorries. Port Askaig recedes from the stern as we steam onwards up the Sound of Islay towards Colonsay. The waters seem calm now and the sky is a clear blue. Most of the ship's passengers seem to be out on the deck with us to watch the stunning scenery pass by: on our port side the distilleries of Caol Ila and Bunnahabhainn in their own little bays on Islay and to starboard the vast emptiness of the island of Jura. The side of Jura visible to us is completely uninhabited, the shoreline one long, scalloped raised beach running almost the length of the island. The calmness of the Sound is, however, deceiving. On rounding Rubha A'Mhail at the northern tip of Islay the south-westerly swell, though barely discernible, begins to affect the motion of the ship. On clearing Islay the *Glen Sannox* starts to roll and pitch quite considerably. It becomes impossible to walk along the deck in a straight line. Some of the faces of our fellow passengers develop frowns but ours positively gleam in delight. Now we feel that we really are at sea. Gibbie reckons that I will not be able to carry two pints of beer along the deck without spilling any. A challenge too good to refuse. And so we enjoy one of the best hours I have ever had on a ship. Our fellow passengers seem to be enjoying it too. Next to us are a retired couple from the south of England who tell us that they regularly sail in the Western Isles. The man is cradling a little white poodle under his jacket which also seems to be enjoying the experience.

The twin islands of Oronsay and Colonsay approach and the rolling of the ship lessens. The two islands are linked by a mile of golden sand, The Strand, which can be crossed at low tide only. Oronsay, to the south, is named after St Oran, a disciple of Saint Columba, and still has the remains of an Augustine priory on it. It is a privately owned three square miles of peace and tranquillity. We are heading for its bigger sister, however.

Colonsay measures seven miles by three and has a population of about 130. The only village, Scalasaig, is half way up on the eastern side, and that is where the ferry will dock. To call it a 'village' is grandiose as there are only a couple of shops, a post office and a handful of cottages. The island's only hotel sits snugly in a little hollow a few hundred metres straight up from the pier. It is now coming into view as the ship slows and then reverses in to dock. As we only have about twenty minutes here, on island number four, I am volunteered to be the one who runs around the bay with shoulders full of cameras to photograph the ship at the pier.

Colonsay is served by ship only three days a week, by the Islay vessel on Mondays and Wednesdays (today), and by the Mull vessel on a Monday evening and on Friday. Miss the boat now and I will have to wait for two days to get off the island again. Of shipping interest is the fact that in 1989 Colonsay has been served on occasions by the *Isle of Mull, Glen Sannox, Iona, Pioneer, Lord of the Isles* and *Claymore*. It is obviously a good place for the ferry equivalent of the train-spotter. But then, I can feel already that Gibbie and I are in danger of turning into that genre.

Gibbie has set foot on Colonsay before when he and his wife, Janette, visited on one of CalMac's *Columba*'s 'Mini-cruises' around the Hebrides. His main recollection is trying to find his way back from the hotel to the ship in total darkness. Fortunately the route between the hotel and the pier is a straight line, which is fine as long as you can walk in a straight line.

By the time that we depart Scalasaig to head north again we are only twenty-five minutes late. The sail up to Oban will last about two and a half hours and I decide to see if I can spend some of that time on the bridge of the ship. The necessary captain's permission is forthcoming and I scale the steps marked 'No Passenger Access' with a confident swagger.

The bridge of the *Glen Sannox* is surprisingly small. The most appealing features are the old-fashioned magnetic compass and the traditional wheel.

The mate assures me that despite her age the old lady handles extremely well. They seem to be coping well enough up here so I only stay for five minutes.

To make up for lost time and because the tidal conditions are favourable the ship is steered east of the Garvellach Islands (instead of the usual west) and Insh Island. As we pass close to the former, a jagged chain of rocky ridges rising out of the sea, a pair of golden eagles flap up from the cliffs. The Garvellachs are uninhabited but for the golden eagles and the sea-birds.

We have islands all around us now and a map is consulted to help in the interpretation of the vista in front of us. Jura dominates the view to the east, with the dome shape of Scarba at its northern tip. Between them, too distant to be seen or heard is Corryvreckan Whirlpool. Further on, with Jura still to our starboard side, we pass another vessel of interest, the sailing ship *Malcolm Miller* which is used in these waters as a training ship to teach young people the skills involved in sailing a schooner. Everyone on board her looks as though they are enjoying themselves and I watch with a touch of envy as she swishes past with the sails on her three masts billowing and looking like she has just sailed out of the 'Onedin Line'.

We pass numerous other islands on the remainder of the journey to Oban: Lunga, Luing, Seil, Easdale and finally, on the port side Kerrera. The last leg involves cruising up the narrow channel between Kerrera and the mainland. At times we seem perilously close to the rocks as if the ship is a thread of silk and the channel ahead is the eye of a needle. When we finally dock at Oban pier we are only twenty minutes late. The *Glen Sannox* is a fast ship and well capable of making up time.

Back on dry land, I fairly race up Pulpit Hill overlooking the pier with my camera equipment for the all important photographs of the *Glen Sannox* at Oban pier. This will, after all, be my last chance of such a picture. As she loads for the return journey the *Isle of Mull* rounds the northern tip of Kerrera, coming in from Mull, to give me my first ever look at her. She sits out motionless in the sheltered bay, awaiting the departure of the older ship before she herself can dock. My last ever view of the old and my first view of the new. I cannot make up my mind if it is the end of one golden era or the start of a new one. While I wait at my high vantage point I can see Gibbie take up his camera position on the pier.

Soon the *Glen Sannox* leaves and sails off down the Sound of Kerrera, quickly disappearing from view. I feel rather sad as I know that not only will I never sail on her again but this will be the last time that I see her. Why do ships fill us with such nostalgia? I think of all the times I had watched her at Rothesay and feel that she is sailing away with a bit of me aboard her. What a smashing sail we had had on her today.

By complete contrast this is my first ever view of the *Isle of Mull* and I am about to take my first sail on her. My initial impression is that she looks enormous, especially when seen along side the *Glen Sannox*.

Big she is, but beautiful she certainly isn't. Boarding her is like boarding an aircraft, via a large enclosed walkway that needs a gantry of its own to hoist it up. The fitted carpeting, smart upholstered seating and spacious lounges make her a class above anything else I had ever sailed on. The *Glen Sannox* suddenly seems old and from a different time. This is definitely the shape of things to come and we are both impressed.

The *Isle of Mull* has had an interesting start to what is likely to be a long life of sailing between the isles of the Hebrides. She entered service in April 1988 with her owners already aware that she was seriously over-weight. Agreement was reached, however, that following the summer season she would sail to Middlesborough to be lengthened at British Shipbuilders' expense. Here, in October 1988, she was literally cut in half and an extra seventeen feet of ship added. Suitably stuck together again, and now the longest ship in the fleet, she re-entered service on the Mull route on 6 December. Her increased length had the knock-on effect that the piers at Oban, Craignure and Colonsay had to be altered. These are her main calling points and she was quickly to prove a great success on these services – especially with her improved accommodation and 1000 passenger capacity.

So after a stop-over of only one hour at Oban we are off again, across to the island of Mull aboard the ship named after it. Past the southern tip of the island of Lismore with its lighthouse on one side of us and the imposing Duart Castle on Mull on the other. We arrive at Craignure, the main ferry terminal on Mull, at 1640. This is my first visit to Mull in thirteen years but Craignure seems hardly to have changed. There was not a lot there to change in the first place. A few craft shops, a garage and an Inn nestle cosily below the green hills around the bay and the whole place has that peaceful, island feel about it that can be felt at many such places around the Hebrides.

Gibbie positions himself with his camera in order to photograph the rear end ('blunt' end, he calls it) of the ship as she departs. His idea of ship aesthetics is somewhat contrary. The resulting picture, later to grace many a slide show, is one of which he is particularly proud.

During this photographic session we spot the *Iona* sailing down the Sound of Mull, coming in from Coll and Tiree and also heading for Oban. We are sorry that we would not be able to witness the ensuing race for Oban pier with the *Isle of Mull*.

Photography completed, the next thing on our minds is to find accommodation for the night. Gibbie is not sufficiently dressed for us to consider the nearby Isle of Mull Hotel and so we take more humble lodgings at a small guest house. Next is dinner at the local Inn.

We later decide to honour the Isle of Mull Hotel with our presence by sampling an appropriate beverage on the patio. In fact we somehow manage to lock ourselves out on the patio with only the midges for company. The sight of Gibbie in his knee-less Levis hauling at the patio doors from the outside raises a few eyebrows on the faces of hotel guests on the inside, as they look at each other, wondering who should be first to rush to the phone to call the local police and report an intending intruder. We decide to bide our time and wait until somebody lets us in and while we wait we discuss our plans and options for the following day.

One idea is to cross over to Morven by the Fishnish–Lochaline ferry but the high cost of taxis on Mull dissuades us. Gibbie suggests that we could visit Iona and, if the timing is right, we could perhaps take the trip out to the outlying island of Staffa. Our bus timetable suggests that we can indeed make such a journey, bearing in mind that tomorrow we have to return home. An independent operator, Gordon Grant, runs trips out to Staffa, with time ashore, on a daily basis. If we reach Iona, where he is based, we will try to find him and see if a sail out to Staffa is possible.

After forty minutes of this chat we are becoming rather distressed as we are being bitten alive by the insect night-life. Worse still – our glasses are now empty. Just as we are discussing which of us should go round to the front entrance someone unlocks the patio door – so we decide to stay for another dram.

Day Three – *In Felix's Footsteps*

The following morning, Thursday 18 May, we catch the 0850 bus to Fionnaphort on the western extremity of Mull. The forty-mile journey takes an hour and we sit back and enjoy the splendid scenery of this large unspoilt island.

Mull has, I believe, been treated as the poor country cousin of Skye in the tourist attraction stakes. Skye is often the first choice for visitors wanting their first 'Hebridean' experience. If they like what they see and it doesn't rain too much they may try Mull next time. All this is a bit unfair on Mull. It is every bit as wild and spectacular as Skye (with the exception of Skye's 'Quirang') as anyone who has driven along the western shore road will testify.

Our bus is heading across the island from east to west to the village of Fionnaphort on the south-western extremity. The road climbs up from the encroaching sea-lochs into Glen More, which as its name suggests is pretty big. From there it follows the southern shores of the longest sea-loch of all, Loch Scridain, which separates the long thin southern arm of Mull, known as the 'Ross', from the more mountainous north.

Favourable weather conditions will be essential for our intended trip to Staffa and the seas during the previous two days have been far from calm. Today the sky is overcast with a hazy horizon and a gentle breeze blowing. We are hopeful.

At Fionnaphort the Ross of Mull abruptly ends with a view across the Sound to the neighbouring island of Iona.

Iona lies just a mile over the water from Mull and yet is geologically unrelated. A glance at the map reveals a small island, four miles by two miles, with the only village, Baile Mor, at the side facing Mull. A further examination of the map shows it to be full of wonderfully evocative and romantic Gaelic place-names. *Camas Cuil an t-Saimh* (The Bay at the back of the Ocean) and *Port na Curaich* (Port of the Oracle). The island is full of names which relate its turbulent history, or did someone just make them up for the fun of it?

Iona is of huge significance to the Christian world as the landing place and home for thirty-four years to Saint Columba, who is credited with helping to bring Christianity to Scotland. All this took place from AD 563 to 597, when he died. Iona became the centre of Christianity in Europe. The contrasting turbulence came in the form of invasions and raids by those nasty Norseman at various times after Columba's death. Those scrapping Scandinavian scallywags could always be relied upon to locate and then spoil a good party.

The monastery that Columba founded still exists, in a much modified and restored form, on the eastern side of the island and is now the scene of a different kind of pilgrimage and invasion each day in the shape of hordes of tourists and day-trippers. Our pilgrimage is of a different kind again, more of a nautical one. We have to find the Mr Grant who is hopefully going to take us to yet another island.

We board the *Morven,* for the ten minute crossing to the sacred isle of Iona. This is one of the 'Island Class' ferries and a 'new' vessel for both of us. She looks like a 'landing craft' but we don't have to wade ashore from the beach.

After interrogating several islanders we eventually find Mr Grant on top of a roof. With claw-hammer in hand he confirms that he will indeed be sailing out to Staffa this afternoon, and that we will be back in time for the bus back to Craignure, that in turn will connect with our ferry sailing to Oban and the train back to Glasgow. Staffa to Glasgow in one day! This is good news. Island number seven beckons from ten miles away out in the Atlantic Ocean.

The boat for Staffa will leave from Fionnaphort in just over an hour's time. Being fairly familiar with the geography of the area and the likely nature of the two and a half hour return journey ahead of us we make for the nearest shop to stock up on provisions: drinks, sandwiches, chocolate, sea-sickness pills, sou-westers, oilskins and a couple of inflatable life-rafts – that sort of thing. Then we make our way back across to Fionnaphort on the *Morven.*

The *Fingal of Staffa* is the boat on which we are to embark for the trip to Staffa. She is a sizeable and sturdy-looking launch which seems well equipped and well capable of undertaking such trips out into the open seas. We are greeted by our skipper, Mr. Grant junior, who informs us that we will leave on the arrival of a pre-booked party of twenty American tourists who are coming across from Craignure. They are on the popular 'Three Isles Tour' from Oban. (The three islands being Mull, Iona and Staffa). After a few minutes their bus arrives and out they spill, down to the jetty, a clamour of spangled excursionists, adorned with cameras in a wide range of lens sizes. One of them thinks I am the skipper and offers me a ten pound note. As we set out from Fionnaphort their lack of lunch and lack of preparation for the journey ahead is made apparent to us when one of them asks us: 'Is there anywhere to eat on Staffa?'

'Just a few sheep,' I reply.

The trip is totally exhilarating and the apparently calm sea belies the continuing south-westerly swell. The boat rises and falls considerably and our skipper admits that on the previous day's trip three of his passengers were sea-sick. He is optimistic about making a landing on the island but it depends on the sea conditions around the landing site.

The island is a mile and a half by half a mile and is an uninhabited (save for the sheep) raised table of volcanic basalt which, when it cooled, crystallised into the famous hexagonal pillars of the seam that forms the Giant's Causeway in Northern Ireland. There is definitely nothing to eat there except grass !

The name Staffa is derived from the Norse word for 'pillar'. The most famous and dominating feature on the island is Fingal's Cave. There are several caves on the island but Fingal's is the most famous. It is a basalt-framed hole on the southern face of the island and is of cathedral proportions. Many famous tourists have visited the island and the cave over the years: Sir Walter Scott, Keats, Wordsworth, Queen Victoria, David Livingstone, Jules Verne and RL Stevenson, all within sixty years of each other. The most affected visitor has to be the German composer Felix Mendelssohn, who visited Staffa in 1829 and was sufficiently inspired to write his haunting overture 'Die Hebriden' which became known as 'Fingal's Cave'.

As we approach the island the seas look pretty rough to us and we glance rather anxiously at each other as we are informed that the pile of flattish rocks coming into view to the right of the famous cave is actually the 'jetty'. A landing looks hopeless as heavy seas pound over the shore. Suddenly the boat's loudspeaker erupts into life as 'Die Hebriden' issues out in a kind of aural assault which make the gulls and guillemots stare in astonishment and would have poor Felix turning in his grave.

With considerable skill and control, coupled with an eagerness to make our journey memorable for us, the crew edge the boat closer to the rocks and between waves manage to take it against the 'jetty'. At each brief encounter we are man-handled onto the island during lulls in the swell. It seems rather dangerous but the crew know what they are doing. We have half an hour on the island while the *Fingal of Staffa* backs out into the safety of deeper water. I secretly fear that she may not be able to get back in again. The vision of twenty-two Robinson Crusoes, all but two of them not wearing high-heels or stetsons, enduring the rest of the week in collective solitude springs to my mind. The sheep population would be decimated.

A rope-guided walkway leads us along the black pillars of rock a hundred yards or so to the mouth of the great cave. Its grandeur is awe-inspiring. Waves crash deeply into the cave which rises to sixty-five feet high. We stand in the entrance and marvel at this truly wild place. The sound of the waves is loud but I cannot hear the 'music' that so inspired Mendelssohn.

Time moves on and we retrace our steps cautiously over the slippery basalt and then climb up onto the flat, grassy plateau which forms the top of the island. It is easy to see why so many people have taken the trouble to get to this empty place over the years. This has to be the highlight of our little Hebridean journey. It is hard to believe that we will be back in Glasgow in just a few hours time.

The *Fingal of Staffa*, much to my relief, is able to reach the jetty again and we clamber back on board. By now the American contingent is positively starving and as Gibbie and I surreptitiously munch our sandwiches we are eyed enviously in the same way that a pride of hungry lions would size up a couple of zebra.

As we land back at Baile Mor the business acumen of Gordon Grant becomes apparent. As the hungry hordes race each other up the jetty towards the only restaurant we notice that Mr Grant also owns this! It is now three o'clock in the afternoon and the appetite of his diners is assured.

We stay aboard the *Fingal of Staffa* and are kindly taken back across to Fionnaphort where our bus connection is waiting. We are very grateful to the crew who have helped to make our afternoon so memorable.

Back at Craignure the *Isle of Mull* is waiting at the pier but we have time on our side and decide to delay our departure until the next sailing as this later one will connect with our train. As the ship prepares to depart we are allowed to give the pierhands a helping hand and, with considerable dexterity, I slip the stern hawser off the bollard when given the appropriate nod. From a metre away her huge bulk then slides past me.

After another visit to the Inn for a meal we eventually leave Mull on the 1900 sailing and sit out on the raised stern deck to bask in the glorious evening sunshine. From there we obtain some interesting photographs of other members of the CalMac fleet. We pass the *Eigg* sailing out of Oban Bay, with a lorry, on a special sailing to Lismore. At the railway pier the *Iona* lies tethered. No sign of the anticipated *Claymore,* however, she is out on Western Isles duties.

The train back to the big city leaves at 2030 and, apart from us having to put our fingers in our ears to escape the dreadful squealing of the wheel flanges on the tight curves of the track, the journey is uneventful.

We reflect on our trip. Seven islands have been reached: Arran, Islay, Jura, Colonsay, Mull, Iona and of course Staffa. We have also sailed on seven different vessels.

One thing is clear in our minds. The trip has been so enjoyable and successful that we feel this is just the start of our Island Hopping. Next year we are going again – but where?

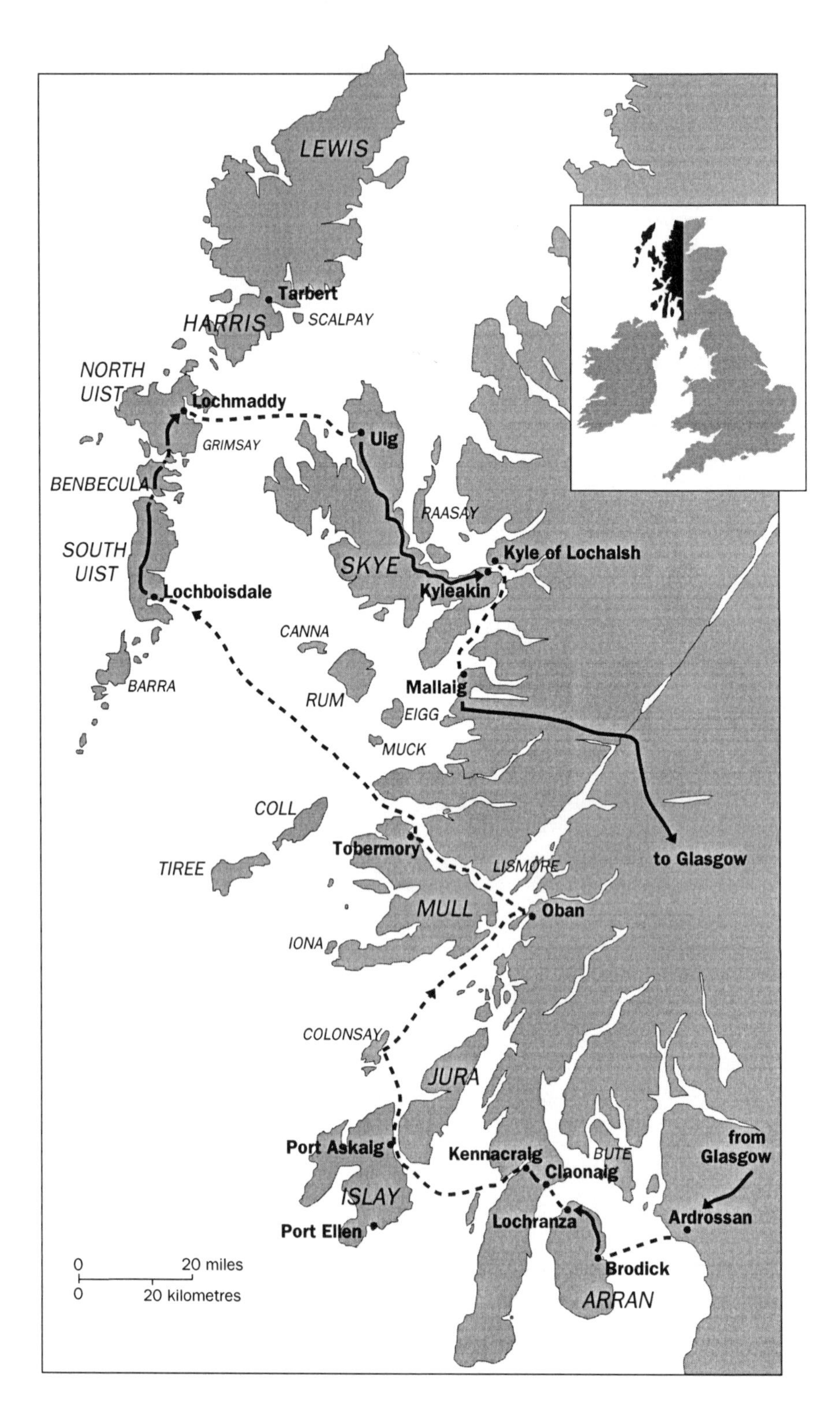
LEWIS
Tarbert
HARRIS
SCALPAY
NORTH
UIST
Lochmaddy
GRIMSAY
BENBECULA
SOUTH
UIST
Lochboisdale
BARRA
Uig
RAASAY
SKYE
Kyle of Lochalsh
Kyleakin
CANNA
RUM
EIGG
MUCK
Mallaig
to Glasgow
COLL
TIREE
Tobermory
LISMORE
MULL
Oban
IONA
COLONSAY
JURA
Port Askaig
ISLAY
Port Ellen
Kennacraig
BUTE
Claonaig
Lochranza
from
Glasgow
Ardrossan
Brodick
ARRAN
0
20 miles
0
20 kilometres

1990 A Western Isles Circle

The Plan

Following last year's success it was inevitable that another, similar trip would follow. The seeds of Island Hopping have been sown and by the time May 1990 comes around the plans for Hop Number Two are all arranged.

Some cardinal rules to Island Hopping are already beginning to emerge. The idea is not necessarily to get to as many islands as possible, or on as many ships and ferries as possible. Of greater interest is the picking of a challenging route, that can be completed in three or four days, and have a theme. The theme may involve trying to get onto particular ships or islands. It may involve a route based on the geography of a particular area or fulfil the need to visit waters previously unvisited by us.

For Hop 1990 the idea was to follow a circular route over to the Outer Isles and back home via Skye. Again, we wanted to avoid using a car if at all possible. This could be feasible by sailing out of Oban and returning to the railhead at Mallaig via Skye and Kyle of Lochalsh.

When the success of the 1989 Hop reached the ears of one of Gibbie's long-time friends, Ian McLaren, he agreed that Island Hopping was the best way to spend the third week in May.

Ian and Gibbie have known each other for aeons, well at least since the days of apprenticeships when they both served their time at Stephen's Shipyard in Linthouse. Ian moved away from Glasgow many years ago but retained an interest in ships and the Clyde. Although he now lives in Godalming in Surrey, the idea of coming up to his old home territory for a trip around the Western Isles greatly appealed to him. Thus two Island Hoppers became three.

From this year onwards the planning of the trips fell into a distinct pattern. Gibbie reckoned that he was the strategist – he let us know what kind of targets we should be aiming for. I was the tactician – I worked out how we were going to do it. Ian had the power of the veto and would come up with useful suggestions and changes to the plans, although for this first trip he was just glad to be coming along.

The route chosen for 1990 was, of course, going to be different from last year. First of all we wanted to get further afield – none of us had ever been on the Uists. Secondly the new *Lord of the Isles* was now serving the Western Isles in place of the *Claymore* which had been sent down to take over the Islay service. This fine new ship was a worthwhile target.

The main plan involved sailing out to South Uist on *Lord of the Isles*, taking the bus to Lochmaddy on North Uist and sailing on *Hebridean Isle* to Skye. We could then head down through Skye and cross to Kyle of Lochalsh where we would pick up the *Lochmor* for the cruise to Mallaig and hence the train home. No more chances would be taken with the accommodation and rooms were booked at Lochboisdale (South Uist) and Uig (Skye).

A final addition was made, mainly for Ian's benefit. Gibbie and Ian wanted to add the first day of the 1989 trip to the beginning of this one, adding another day and a half as well as the islands of Arran, Islay and Colonsay. This would give Ian a taste of what he had missed last year and allow Gibbie to live the experience all over again. Accordingly, a further night's accommodation was booked on Islay for them. I decided not to join them on this repeat of last year but would meet up with them on the Wednesday afternoon at Oban pier when their ship arrived from Islay and Colonsay. There would be a two hour gap between their arrival from Islay and our departure on the *Lord of the Isles* to South Uist. It should all work out perfectly but the best laid plans never do.

Day One – *1989 Reprise*

It is in pouring rain that Ian and Gibbie reach Ardrossan on the morning of Tuesday 15 May 1990. The connections go as planned but as they get totally soaked on their way from Brodick pier to the bus fifty yards away Ian admits that he is beginning to wonder. 'What have I done....it was dry in Surrey!'

The north circular bus connects with the ferry sailings, just as it did last year, and calls at Corrie and Sannox on the fifteen-mile journey to Lochranza.

Once the call of famous Clyde ships such as the *Duchess of Hamilton* on her way to Campbeltown, the north Arran pier is now derelict and the only vessel calling at the slipway is the 'Loch class' *Loch Ranza*. She makes nine or ten return trips a day in the summer months to Claonaig on the Kintyre peninsula.

The same problem as last year is encountered in that there is no bus at the Claonaig side and if foot passengers want to reach the Islay ferry terminal at Kennacraig, five miles away, or Tarbert, the nearest town twelve miles away, they have to personally organise a minibus or taxi to meet them at Claonaig. Gibbie and Ian choose the latter and the same driver takes them across Kintyre for the same three pound fee as last year. Gibbie exercises his considerable generosity and gives him four.

This year the vessel to Islay is the *Claymore* which has replaced the usual vessel *Iona* on this service. The *Claymore* has a faster turnaround time than the *Glen Sannox* and reaches Port Askaig without delay. Their overnight accommodation is at a hotel a few miles inland.

While the two travellers are tucking into their *a la carte* dinner I am, unknown to them, setting out on a little adventure of my own. Instead of meeting up with the others at Oban on the Wednesday I have discovered that I can work a full day on the Tuesday and still catch the 1800 bus from Glasgow to Tarbert, Loch Fyne. I will then be able to join the *Calymore* at Kennacraig on the Wednesday morning on her way out to Port Askaig to pick up Gibbie and Ian. As the ship is due to leave Kennacraig at 0830 on the Wednesday morning it is essential that I make my journey to Tarbert (which is only six miles from Kennacraig) the previous evening. The fact that I am saving the cost of a train fare to Oban more than compensates for the price of a bed for the night in Tarbert. Ian and Gibbie, of course, will not be expecting to see me until the *Claymore* reaches Oban.

So, feeling like a sneaky little schemer, I take taxi and Underground to Buchanan Street Bus Station. I almost miss the bus because, since my last visit to the bus station, someone has built a concert hall across the top of Buchanan Street, which results in me losing my bearings for a minute or two. I eventually board the West Coast Services bus just a few moments before it departs at 1800.

By 2115 I am at Tarbert after an enjoyable journey and a twenty-minute stopover at Inveraray. Before I settle into my guest house for the night I arrange for a taxi to take me the short hop to the ferry terminal at Kennacraig the following morning. By now my two colleagues, one of whom I've never met, should be on Islay.

Day Two – *Two becomes Three*

On the Wednesday at 0800, as planned, I am at Kennacraig pier watching the *Claymore* swinging in. I buy my Rover ticket. This is an essential piece of paper for all Island Hoppers. Covering either eight or fifteen days it gives almost unlimited travel on the routes served by CalMac. Apart from being excellent value for money it saves having to buy tickets on every sailing. And on Island Hops like ours there are lots of sailings. The Rover ticket also includes unlimited travel for a bicycle, should one be required. However Gibbie would no sooner take a bike Island Hopping than a horse and cart.

I sit down to watch the ship load and notice with some amusement that it is the same lorry driver as last year who is manoeuvring the trucks and trailers onto the car deck of the ship. Just like last year they all have to be reversed on as the *Claymore* is not a true ro-ro ferry. Perhaps this is a good time to explain the term 'ro-ro'. 'Ro-ro' means 'roll on–roll off' – that is to say one can drive a car on and at the destination drive it back off without having to turn it around or reverse. The ship must have a bow door and a stern door. Vehicles can loaded by the bow and driven straight through to the stern – but not at the same time otherwise they would fall into the sea! The *Claymore* has a stern ramp and side ramps and so, strictly speaking, is not a true ro-ro. It does not make much difference to cars but ro-ro ferries do make life easier for lorries, coaches and other long vehicles.

The *Claymore* was built in 1978 by the same yard, Robb Caledon of Leith, that built the *Pioneer*. The similarity between the two vessels is obvious. Like her sister she does not have Caledonian MacBrayne emblazoned in large white letters on her hull – a fact which immediately improves her appearance. Built for the South Uist and Barra service from Oban she has now become the Islay ship (promotion or demotion?) since being displaced from the route by the new *Lord of the Isles*. To my eye she looks a bit top heavy up front – like a seagoing Samantha Fox – with a towering white superstructure at one end and an open car-deck at the other.

This is my first ever sailing on her and I am quite impressed. She has two lounges: a large upper one, forward on the main deck which houses the cafeteria and a lower one, directly below, which contains the bar. On the boat deck there is access forward to the all-important 'view-over-the-bow'. She has a reasonable area of open deck space for a car-ferry and is generally very comfortable.

In a light breeze she sails at 0832, only two minutes late, with her open car-deck almost full. I settle down with a mug of tea and ponder with keen anticipation the look on my companions' faces when they see me aboard their ship at Port Askaig. Looking at the faces around me at the moment I see a few bleary eyes, reflecting the early start. I am sure mine are just the same. I wonder if any of the other passengers are doing anything as mad as I am – spending the best part of a day sailing from West Loch Tarbert to Lochboisdale. I console myself that at least I *know* what I'm doing is mad. That must count for something on a psychiatric score.

As we approach Port Askaig I have my binoculars pressed against my face, searching for the plume of John Players that will give away Gibbie's presence. As for Ian I do not know what to look for as I have never met him before. I expect to see Gibbie crouched down with his camera, photographing our arrival, but as the pier comes into view from around the wooded headland there is no sign of him.

Claymore awaits the departure of Western Ferries *Sound of Gigha* from her slipway to Jura before docking at the pier. As she ties up and discharges her load of passengers and vehicles, Gibbie and, presumably Ian, are conspicuous by their absence. I look out over the tiny village from my vantage point on the ship's upper deck but can see no sign of them. What will I do? In ten minutes the *Claymore* will set off again, for Colonsay and Oban and I am alone.

I know it now, my surprise plan has back-fired. Something has obviously gone wrong and they have missed the boat to Islay the previous day. I get off the ship and strut up and down the pier looking for them. Perhaps they will be up at Oban, wondering why I have not got off the train from Glasgow. I will have to sail on up to Oban without them and hope that the rest of our plans will come together from then on. My smugness of earlier in the day has now evaporated and been replaced by near despair. I might end up doing the Island Hop on my own !

Five minutes to go and just as my concern is reaching a crescendo a small coach comes racing down the steep hill and pulls up just short of the pier. Out steps Gibbie and a silver-haired, white-bearded chap that I know just has to be Ian. I step out from behind my concealment like Eamon Andrews on *This Is Your Life* and observe the look of bewilderment on Gibbie's face.

'How the hell did you get here?'

It turns out that Gibbie is not all that surprised by my sudden appearance but he could not work out how I could get down to Kennacraig for 0800 in the morning from Glasgow. He had not figured on me getting the bus the night before. The reason for their late arrival this morning can be blamed on their antics last night. They sampled a few of the local malts – claiming that the barmaid had led them astray (a likely event) – and decided on an extra hour in their beds rather than getting the early bus.

Ian and I are introduced and for the first time these three intrepid Island-Hoppers get on a ferry together. Our adventures are just beginning.

The ship sails a few moments later with a three-quarter full car-deck towards the island of Colonsay. The light drizzle has stopped now and we are not to see rain again during the rest of our trip.

As we sail past Bunnahabhain distillery, just as last year, Gibbie questions the presence of the wrecked hulk of a ship lying on the shore. It is the *Wyre Majestic* which ran aground on the shore at Bunnahabhain on 18 October 1974. Apparently she had landed her catch at Oban and as there was no berth for her had set off in search of one. She obviously found a pretty secure one at Bunnahabhain.

As the wind today is coming from the north-east we do not experience the slow swell on clearing the northern tip of Islay that accompanied our sail here last year. Gibbie and I notice something that has not changed from last year's sail on this route - the elderly English couple with their little white poodle are again sitting out on deck.

Claymore arrives on time at Scalasaig on Colonsay and we all jump ashore, during the brief fifteen-minute visit, for a photocall. Off we sail again at 1230. This time we pass west of the Garvellachs and East of Insh Island on route to Oban but increasingly dull weather results in poor visibility and we cannot see much of the islands. We are keen to point out the various landmarks to our newcomer Ian. He remarks on how large Mull seems. Today, on two different ships, we will be taking a few hours to sail around two-thirds of it.

In the Sound of Kerrera, a green buoy guards our passage. Gibbie predicts that we will pass to the left of it. We do and Ian asks him which side we would pass to if coming from the opposite direction, but all we get is a puzzled look.

'I'll need to look that one up!'

At Oban Ian and Gibbie take up camera positions on the pier while I climb up my favourite hill to photograph the *Claymore* at the linkspan. From my position I will be ideally placed to record the *Isle of Mull* swinging into the Bay. However, to my surprise it is the *Lord of the Isles* that rounds the northern end of Kerrera first, some forty minutes early on her return from Coll and Tiree. She ties up ahead of the *Claymore* and discharges her foot passengers.

Ten minutes pass and inevitably the *Isle of Mull* also comes swinging into Oban Bay. She reduces speed and sits out in the middle. All three vessels remain in their respective positions for a further ten minutes as the Islay vessel awaits the arrival of a late train. Meanwhile we three watch all of this from our respective positions.

Eventually the *Claymore* departs, heading back to Colonsay, Islay and Kennacraig. The *Isle of Mull* then docks at the linkspan. Her turnaround is very quick and she is soon on her way back to the island after which she is named. *Lord of the Isles*, our next ship, then tip-toes forward onto the linkspan to discharge her vehicles and load up for the Outer Isles. As she does this, the final arrival of the afternoon, the 'Island class' *EIGG*, scurries across from Lismore to tie up. It has been a fairly busy pier. With all our business in Oban complete we board *Lord of the Isles* for the five hour sail out to South Uist – a new island aboard a new ship. This all sounds a bit like train-spotting but I make no excuse for it. Seeing three major CalMac ships in Oban Bay would arouse interest in anyone. Wouldn't it?

Despite lacking deck space and not having a view forward this is a very comfortable ship. We immediately take a liking to this newest acquisition to the CalMac fleet which has been in service less than a year. From the front she looks very similar to the *Isle of Mull* but differs in having two 'funnels' – one either side – and in having an open stern. She is a fast ship, faster by one knot over the *Claymore* and thus taking five hours on a direct sailing to Lochboisdale where the *Claymore* took six. She has a nice name as well, recalling the two famous paddle-steamers of last century.

We sail up through the Sound of Mull, between Mull and the mainland of Morven, sitting out on deck. Ian is still remarking on how large the island is. 'Is that still Mull?' 'No, Hawaii actually.'

We are now passing the eastern, sheltered side of Mull and will be for the first two hours of the journey. Three other CalMac vessels pass us: the *Isle of Mull* returning to Oban, the *Isle of Cumbrae* crossing between Fishnish on Mull and Lochaline on Morven and the *Coll* returning to Ardnamurchan.

Once clear of the Sound and beyond the rocky tip of Ardnamurchan Point we are officially upon the Sea of the Hebrides. I never knew such a romantic sounding waterworld existed. It is the name given to the open waters bounded by Skye to the north, Tiree and Coll in the south and the Outer Hebrides, or Western Isles, away to the west. Various isles and islets float around on it. Out on deck I scan the Sea of the Hebrides. It is difficult to tell which island is which as all the distant lumps of land around us are reducing to a sepia haze as the sun drops. Away out to the west an indistinct low line of land is just discernible. It represents Barra and South Uist. The ship's bow is pointed in that direction. She pitches expeditiously through the water leaving a lingering broad wake behind her which only gradually blends back into the deep grey sea. I have never been in such open waters before and I find that looking out over the rail of the ship into the gathering gloom is quite a humbling experience. It must be time for a meal and a drink.

After the meal and a 'couple' of drinks in the bar we eventually feel the ship slowing and we go back outside to see where we are. The light is fading into a grey pink glow but we can still make out the dark shapes of land between which the ship is slowly picking her path. A large grey lump of a hill looms above us to our starboard side and the sheltered loch leading up to Lochboisdale seems almost too narrow for the ship. The sodium lights at the pier guide us and the ship gently noses in towards the linkspan. We can see our hotel sitting above the pier. Thankfully we will not have far to walk, which is maybe just as well, for apart from a few minutes ashore at the various ports of call I have been at sea since eight-thirty in the morning and it is now ten at night. I have sailed from Kennacraig to South Uist. As we step off *Lord of the Isles* I feel a sense of great achievement. Our Island Hop is falling into place very nicely. Our two long sea journeys have been very enjoyable but it is also good to put our feet onto dry land. Up in the hotel any elation is fast dissipating as we watch Egypt beating Scotland 3-1 in a friendly football match.

Day Three – *The Trans-Uist Highway*

The following morning and sunshine is streaming gloriously through the dining room windows as we all three tuck into Hebridean kippers of Moby Dick proportions. The *Lord of the Isles* had departed at 0700 but none of us had felt particularly inclined to get up and photograph her, despite the parlance to the contrary the night before. In fact the bravado about getting up early was pretty hollow, for Gibbie and I had actually taken photographs of the ship lying at the pier illuminated by the harbour lights before retiring. Gibbie reckoned on a time exposure of four seconds. I opted for two. This speaks volumes for our photographic prowess – neither picture turned out particularly well.

I gather my belongings from my room and take one last look at the jocular note attached to the shower cabinet:

> *The taps in the shower are the wrong way round. turn to* HOT *to get cold and turn to* COLD *to get hot. Please bare with this discrepancy.*
> P.S. *the wash hand basin is the same.*

Now I know why I had almost poached myself in the shower this morning.

Speaking of poaching, the hotel is such a magnet for fishermen that the Reception is offering emergency repair kits for fishing lines. This is of no use at all to Gibbie who is more in need of emergency rations of non-tipped cigarettes and is now contemplating a long bus ride to Benbecula, the next link in our journey, without them. The bus leaves at 0950 and the journey promises to be an 'experience'. It might be a particularly acute one for Gibbie.

We are heading along the 'Trans-Uist Highway' to Lochmaddy on North Uist, from where we are due to sail at 1610 over to Skye. We have to traverse four islands on the way, none of which require a boat or ferry of any kind. The islands of South Uist, Benbecula, Grimsay and North Uist are all separated by shallow waters and are thus linked by road causeways, a series of which hold the islands together like a string threading through a mosaic of green gems. Our first stop will be at Benbecula – twenty-five miles away – where we will change buses – hopefully – for the final land link to Lochmaddy.

The bus sets off on its bumpy ride along the length of the island. The road may be flat and straight in a north/south dimension but as far as up and down are concerned we have to hold onto our bags and our stomachs. We muse over how long a set of tyres and a suspension last on a road such as this.

The flat landscape of South Uist takes us by surprise. The high land lies away to the east where the hills form the backbone of the island. The flat landscape to the west, over which we are travelling, is dotted with hundreds of crofts and farms evenly spread across the land and contrasts with the narrow bumpy road which could have done with a bit of an even spread of tarmac. However we are making good progress and, provided the bus does not blow a tyre or the suspension doesn't collapse or we don't fall off the road into a ditch, we are confident that we will reach Benbecula and finally North Uist in time for our ferry connection.

Our bounding comes to abrupt halts at various points along the way. Workmen are resurfacing the road (good idea) and one party in particular has abandoned their bulldozer in the middle of the white line and are sitting in the warm sunshine eating their mid-morning sandwiches. With a nonchalance bordering on reluctance they eventually stir and move the digger over to the side of the road to let the bus past. Further on, at a small community called Stoneybridge, a broad-spoken, tousley-haired character gets on the bus and throws himself down into a seat a couple of rows ahead of us. Even from that distance the smell of whisky from him is pungent. He sits and chats in his native tongue to two female passengers who obviously know him well. We cannot understand a word of what he is saying but judging from the reaction of his audience it is obviously hilarious.

Yet again the bus pulls up at a depot, a ramshackle dump of a place which looks as though it has been hastily erected in the middle of nowhere. Numerous buses, bits of buses, and bits that look as though they might have belonged to buses, in varying states of corrosion, are strewn about the yard and the roadside. We sit here for ten minutes while our driver converses with a colleague. I get out for a stroll around the bus, to see if any bits have fallen off, checking my watch nervously as the minutes to our next connection tick away. The driver reappears and off we go again. We have only gone forty yards when our merry friend from Stoneybridge gets up and announces to the driver, 'This is my stop!'

We eventually arrive at Balivanich, the capital of Benbecula, at noon. Capital is kind of a euphemism. It is a mish-mash of a place. There seem to be more buildings here than in Lochboisdale and there is an airport but it still has an empty look about it. Several featureless modern houses which somehow don't seem to blend into the landscape are congregated at the side of the road. To me the name Benbecula has always had a romantic ring to it. Now that I am actually here for the first time I am slightly disappointed by what I see. It looks somewhat higglety-pigglety, but then I am not stopping long enough to take in the beautiful beaches that make up the west coast of the island or climb the highest hill, Rueval, to view the mosaic of freshwater lochans.

What is obvious on this briefest of visits is the dominating presence of the army base, established here in 1958. The army personnel boost the native population of the island which is a consonant mix of Catholic and Protestant.

The southern islands of the Outer Isles archipelago, mainly South Uist and Barra, are predominately Catholic whereas the northern isles of Lewis, Harris and North Uist are Protestant. The graduation from one persuasion to the other coalesces ecumenically at Benbecula. Equal measure of Rangers and Celtic scarves here, I presume.

The bus stops at the airport and we arrive just in time to see a Hawker-Sidley 748 land and taxi to within thirty yards of us. I don't know that it is a Hawker-Sidley 748. Gibbie and Ian tell me, which just goes to show that they are plane-spotters as well as ship-spotters. We move inside to the smallest and cosiest departure lounge I have ever seen. It is busy with intending passengers waiting for their flight to Glasgow. What a strange thought that having travelled so far in the preceding thirty-six hours I could be back in Glasgow aboard this plane in forty minutes. I resist the temptation.

Back outside to await the arrival of our bus to Lochmaddy. I discover that my bag, which I left outside in the car park next to the perimeter fence, is causing consternation to the security officer who is eyeing it warily from the inside of the fence.

'Is that yours?' he demands.

There is a look of relief when I nod and pick it up. As we watch the plane refuelling an adult peregrine falcon floats by, only ten feet off the ground. Soon the Hawker-Sidley is following suit.

Benbecula does not seem like a true island as we reached it by causeway and will be leaving it in a similar manner. Perhaps if we had sailed over we would have had a different impression of it.

The substantial military presence, including the missile range, has resulted in a new village of concrete and rough-cast covered buildings splaying across the flat fields and marshes. To the west, however, we can get a glimpse of the beautiful sands which give way to the Atlantic Ocean.

Our bus to our next island pulls up at the airport and to the comfort of the security officer we are on our way again – perhaps to blow up a causeway or two.

The 'bus' is a Post Office Ford Transit and the next island is North Uist, but not before we cross the in-between island of Grimsay. An island in its own right, joined to Benbecula in the south and North Uist in the north, Grimsay is the smallest of the islands so-linked, the causeways being completed in 1960. It is only a true island at high tide and still inhabited. Being only a mile or two across we are on it and off it before Gibbie can say: 'Island number six!'

The 'post-bus' is a very handy way of getting around rural areas where there is a limited bus service. For a small fee we are conveyed to our next destination with a bit of chat and humour thrown in at no extra cost by our driver.

The landscape of North Uist looks totally different from its southerly counterpart. Not necessarily an improvement, just different. The green fields and crofts have given way to mile after mile of wet bog with very little cultivation. The road is just as bumpy. The sea and innumerable freshwater ponds coalesce into a plexus of waterways that make North Uist seem composed more of water than land, just like Finland. At least, that is how it looks on the map.

At 1330 we arrive at Lochmaddy, the largest community on North Uist. We have more than two hours before the *Hebridean Isles* arrives. Aboard her we will sail over the Little Minch to Skye. We head for the hotel and lunch. When we return outside we find the sun is now shining and warm, having won its thermal contest with the continual cool Atlantic breeze.

We inspect the pier, an absolutely mandatory ritual on an Island Hop. In any case we don't see much else worth inspecting in Lochmaddy. Optimum positions are then taken to watch and photograph the ship's arrival. Ian and I sit on the grass adjacent to the pier for almost an hour while Gibbie goes forward onto the rocks. This will be no ordinary ship – none of us have ever sailed on the *Hebridean Isles* before and none of us have any photographs of her. We will soon put that to rights.

The *Hebridean Isles* takes a different route through the network of small isles on the approach to the pier than we have anticipated and we are almost caught out. I manage to take some good shots of her making her way past the rocks to the pier, Gibbie's head appearing in every one of them.

The *Hebridean Isles* sails from the small port of Uig in Skye out to the islands of Harris and North Uist in a pattern of sailings that has become known as the 'Uig Triangle'. This is an important link to the Outer Isles which is much favoured by commercial traffic as it involves more driving, across Skye, and less time on the expensive ferry, as the sea route is shorter than the other Outer Isles routes out of Oban and Ullapool. We are sailing out on the southern-most leg of the triangle today on a crossing that will take less than two hours.

Sheltering from the north-easterly wind on the stern deck of the ship, forsaking the 'view-over-the-bow' for fear of being blown away, we are soon basking in glory; sitting in shelter from the wind, enjoying a beer and congratulating ourselves on having successfully negotiated the Uists and on reaching this stage.

Out to sea the view over to the hazy, smoke-grey mountains of distant Harris and the acute cliffs of Vaternish on Skye add depth and texture to a panorama of blue sea and white wake.

We decide to have a toast to 'Island Hop 1990'. Cameras are set up on tripods and the three of us sit like bold-spirited, smug wayfarers, with our glasses raised to the lenses, as if we had just crossed the Pacific instead of the Little Minch. It's not even 'real' full blown Minch, just the Little Minch. Our fellow passengers look on in bemusement, probably wondering where we have come from and where we are going. We hardly know the answer to that ourselves. On all future Island Hops the 'Toast' is to become an integral part, taking place at a moment such as this when we are feeling well pleased with ourselves and there are not too many people around to laugh.

Uig arrives too soon and we wander forward to watch the ship berth at one of the longest piers in Scotland, which is built out into a beautiful, round bay to reach as deep water as possible. We are the last to disembark and make our way along the shore towards our guest-house.

Our accommodation proves to be excellent. Ian and Gibbie are sharing a room but I have a room to myself. It is the tiniest but neatest and cosiest room I have ever seen, containing a wash-hand basin and wardrobe of Lilliputian proportions. After a rest Ian and I steer Gibbie, reluctantly, half a mile uphill to the local inn for some food.

Ian has his fifth fish of the trip – cod – to add to the mackerel, herring, haddock and kippers that he has already ingested. He then swims his way into the crowded bar, with the rest of us, to watch the FA Cup Final replay live on the telly. Manchester United are beating Crystal Palace and the total population of Uig seems to be in the bar watching the game, giving the place a football ground atmosphere of its own. A fair percentage of the population of Australia is also in the bar in the rounded form of a bunch of Aussie girls. From the noise they are making it would seem that it is a long time since they saw anything as exciting as an FA Cup Final. At full time, Gibbie seems to be the happiest of all – the way back to our digs is all downhill.

Day Four – *Completing the Circle*

Wake to dazzling sunshine, yet again, streaming into my tiny little bedroom. Dreamt that I was playing a part in 'Alice in Wonderland' last night. Must have been the beer. Ian and I are down to breakfast first where we are joined at the single large round table by the only other guest. She is a rather nervous nurse, from the south of England, whom we quickly realise is capable of out-talking even Gibbie, who has yet to appear. She rambles on in a desultory fashion with Ian and I trying hard to follow. We dare not catch each other's derisory eye for fear of giggling, so confine ourselves to intelligent head-nodding, wishing that the bacon and eggs would arrive. It is Gibbie who arrives, however, and he blindly launches into his usual cheerful discourse with the poor girl. Within a couple of minutes of the recounting of the story of her life Gibbie has fallen silent and his face is graced with a look of bewilderment that, for me, is one of the highlights of the trip: an expression that I will never forget. The nurse is anxious about purchasing her ticket for the impending sail by *Hebridean Isles* back out to the Outer Isles but despite her desperation she is taking a long time to get out of the door. We each note silently and individually and with considerable relief, that she will not, therefore, be heading in the same direction as ourselves. She finally bids farewell, after asking for the fifth time where the CalMac ticket office is.

'Phew!' exclaims Gibbie. 'She can certainly talk.'

We settle down to finish our breakfast. Ian is moaning that he has drawn the short straw by sharing a room with Gibbie on account of his snoring, when the door bursts open and in comes our nurse again.

'I'll think I'll have another cup of tea before I go.' She continues: 'You know, when I saw you chaps arriving last night I was wondering which one of you would be put in the room with me. I have a spare bed in my room you see.'

We drain our cups quickly and race out to see if the *Hebridean Isles* is any nearer the pier.

The ship is in at the pier. We have been so busy chatting that we miss a good photo opportunity. We do not hang around but set off to secure our next line of advance. This comes in the shape of the bus to Portree. We are heading for Kyleakin and the ferry crossing back to the mainland, in the south of the island but reckon that we will have time to stop off at Portree, the largest town on Skye, on the way.

At 0940 the bus roars its way up the hill out of Uig for the fifteen mile ride to the capital of Skye.

Portree has a cosy setting below the mountains. It sits in a snug bay sheltered by headlands and the island of Raasay out to the east. It is very touristy. Many visitors to the islands head for, and go no further than Skye and Portree is by far the biggest town on the island. After the empty moors of the Uists, the busy streets of Portree, thronging with multi-coloured tourists, seem like a culture shock. The shock makes its mark on us, too, for the first place we head for is the tourist office. If you can't beat them join them!

We have taken a bit of a chance. Having left our bus to carry on its journey without us in order to see something of Portree, we are now anxious to find out when we can get another bus, that will allow us to complete our journey to Kyleakin, in time for our crossing to the mainland. We have to be at Kyle of Lochalsh by 1530 in order to make our final sailing to Mallaig.

After a brief fright we eventually discover that the only connecting bus leaves the Square at 1140. So we have an hour. Time for a coffee, a check on the pier and a bit of shopping. Skye is rubbing off on us.

The weather is now improving by the minute and on our bus journey south through Skye to Kyleakin we obtain superb views of the famous Cuillin Mountains. There are two kinds of Cuillin. The dark, jagged and foreboding 'Black Cuillins' in the south of the island and the rusty, scree-covered, volcano-shaped 'Red Cuillins' in the south-east. Our route is among and around the latter. They rise up from the shores of the island like giant slag heaps formed from some fantastical, Herculean excavation. The road is fast and curves along the shores of the sea lochs that push their way inland and around the base of some of these great red peaks.

We reach Kyleakin, some fifty miles from Uig (Skye is big) in plenty of time for our next sailing. There are two ferries operating on the crossing over the Sound of Sleat to the mainland: the *Lochalsh* and the *Kyleakin*. Both look like floating garages. We join the former for the very short crossing back to the mainland. When Gibbie discovers that there is no charge for foot passengers he wants a refund on his Rover ticket.

As we cross we spot our next ship, *Lochmor*, making her way up the Sound of Sleat towards Kyle of Lochalsh. She normally serves the 'Small Isles' of Muck, Rum, Eigg and Canna out of Mallaig but today she is sailing up to Kyle and, as I thought, performing a cruise to Loch Duich before the return journey back to Mallaig. My two companions are all geared up for the cruise, so when we are informed that the ship will be staging a boat drill instead

(I had mis-read the timetable) they turn their wrath onto me. Compensation comes in the form of lunch at the Kyle of Lochalsh Hotel where we sit outside watching small fishing boats and the two Skye ferries scuttling back and forth. This is one of the busiest ferry routes in Scotland and the two boats are hard pressed conveying locals and visitors across the narrow strait. Ian is still on the fish haddock this time. As we now have more time than anticipated, and as my intrepid friends are moaning about missing out on a cruise to Loch Duich, I decide to abandon them and add another vessel to my list. In any case the only toilet I can see is the one over on Skye. So I re-cross to Kyleakin, this time on the ferry *Kyleakin*.

On board I ask of a crewman why this vessel has one mast while the *Lochalsh* has two. He tells me that one of the ships is longer than the other and regulations dictate that she must have two masts. I am not sure that I believe him as they both look the same size to me.

I briefly disembark onto Skye, as does a fire-engine which promptly drives around the toilet block and back onto the same ferry again. It must be the day for drills. I head for the same toilet but instead of going around it I go in.

To give retribution to my two denouncers I let the *Kyleakin* sail without me so that they might fear that I have missed the boat. As I find out it has no effect on them. Had I not made the *Lochmor* sailing in time they were going to sail without me.

I am soon back at Kyle of Lochalsh via the *Lochalsh* and we join the *Lochmor* with twenty-one other passengers for the two-hour cruise to Mallaig down the winding Sound of Sleat.

The wee *Lochmor* is a small passenger ship which none of us have been aboard before. She is a neat, if slow, little ship with two saloons below and with several small areas of open deck at varying heights in order to allow embarkation at differing states of tide. Her stern is open and from it sprouts a small crane for the loading of goods and machinery. Several times a week, in addition to her 'Small Isles' duties, she provides a connection between the railheads of Mallaig and Kyle of Lochalsh. She also cruises to Loch Duich – but, of course, not today!

We sit out on deck enjoying the late afternoon sunshine. The atmosphere is now tainted, however, with a rather subdued air. This is our last sailing of the trip. Soon we will be on the train back to Glasgow and we have that 'going home' feeling that one gets on the last day of a good holiday. We pass Kylerhea, on Skye, where, until recently, an independent operator ran a tiny ferry over to the mainland. At this point the hills of the giant island are at their closest to the mainland, closer even than at Kyleakin. Further on to the east we sail past the entrance to Loch Hourn, a sea loch which winds twelve miles into the hills and mountains of the Western Highlands. South of the loch lies the huge empty land of Knoydart, with its one village but no roads. Over at the other side of the little ship at Armadale, the most southerly ferry-point on Skye, we spot the CalMac ship *Iona* berthing at the pier. She serves Skye from Mallaig but we have no time to sail on her today.

By 1740 we are arriving at Mallaig. Behind us two fishing boats race abreast for the best berth at the harbour. We reluctantly disembark and trot off solemnly, like schoolboys returning from a school outing, to find our train.

The train is due to depart at 1822 but is late in getting underway. The journey time to Glasgow will take five and a half hours and has no catering facilities of any kind on board – even though the timetable indicates a buffet car. When we bring this to the attention of the ticket collector he sighs with an air of resignation, 'Yes, I know . . . .'

The final insult is the cost of the single ticket.

'That will be £19.10 – *each*.'

I explain that we don't want to buy the seats – just sit on them until we get to Glasgow. We have obviously been spoiled on the ships. The only moment of light relief on the journey, apart from the stunning west coast scenery, is when someone goes to the toilet and pulls the communication cord instead of the flushing lever. As the train screeches to an abrupt halt the conductor passes by us on his way to investigate.

'Not again!' he mutters.

We are muttering the same thing as the train pulls up for its fourth unscheduled stop just beyond Helensburgh station. This time the train reverses for half a mile back up the line. Gibbie rouses us from our slumbers and transfers us into a state of near terror by announcing that the driver is not supposed to do that without permission and that the Fort William train is only ten minutes behind us and that we are still running late!

We arrive safely without further incident at Queen Street Station just five minutes before midnight and a taxi soon has us wearily back home.

The trip has been an outstanding success. The seeds of the Island Hop adventure are not merely sown – they are sprouting. The addition of Ian to the party has added a new dimension and personality. The talk on the journey back to Glasgow was not just about the experiences we had lived through these past four days, it was about the ones that were still to happen – in future Island Hops. The ideas for our 1991 Hop are committed to the trusty notebook, and the third week in May 1991 is scored off.

Over the years the ships and island tally will mount up and different circuits and routes will evolve. Looking back, the circular excursion chosen in 1990 was an ideal one for mixing new islands and new ships. On the 1990 trip we had, between us, sailed on eight ferries, most of them new to us and reached eight islands. The challenge now was to find just as exciting routes that could be done in three or four days from one year to the next.

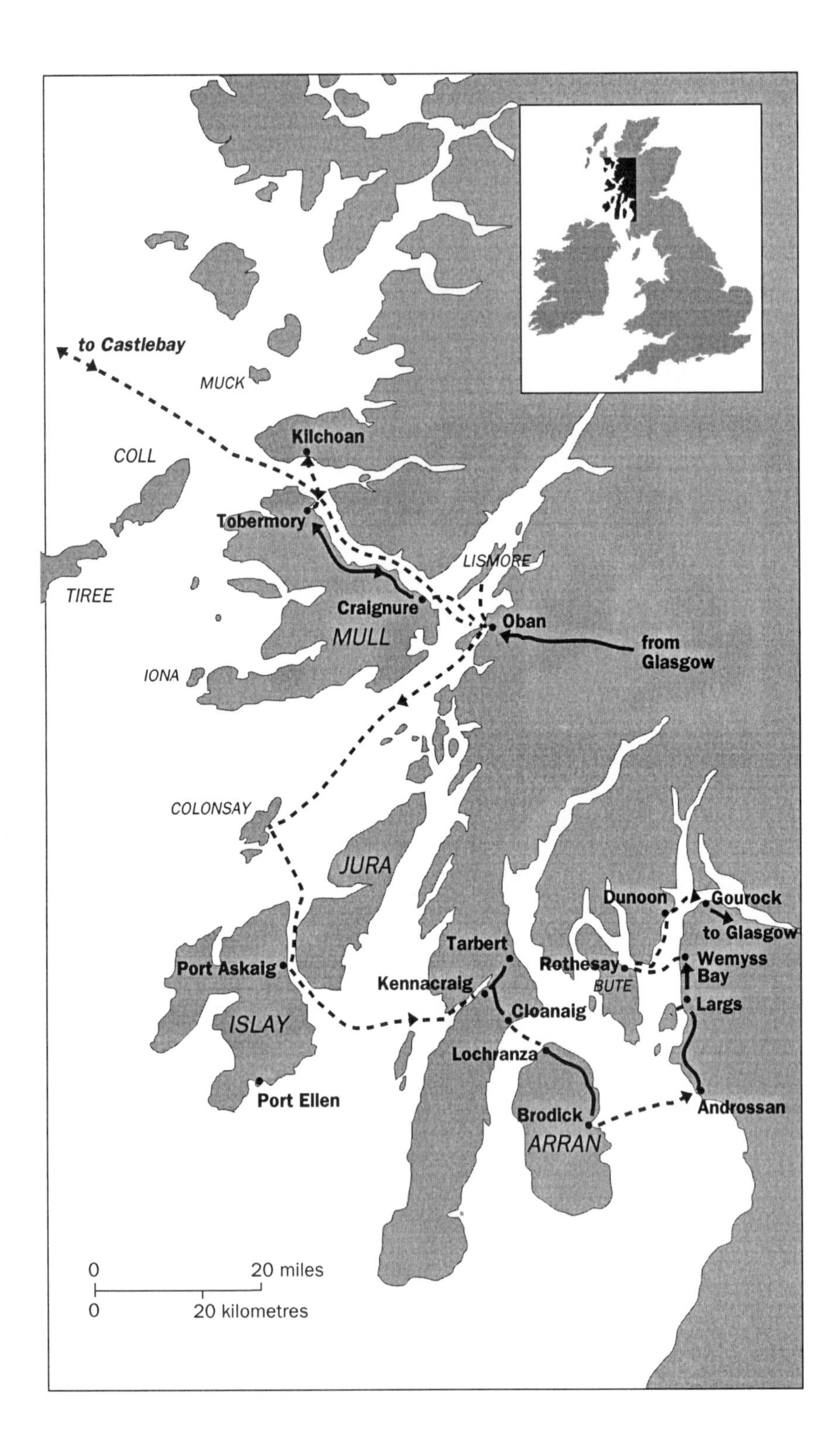
to Castlebay
MUCK
Kilchoan
COLL
Tobermory
LISMORE
TIREE
Craignure
Oban
MULL
from
Glasgow
IONA
COLONSAY
JURA
Dunoon
Gourock
to Glasgow
Tarbert
Rothesay
Wemyss
Bay
Port Askaig
Kennacraig
BUTE
Cloanaig
Largs
ISLAY
Lochranza
Port Ellen
Brodick
Androssan
ARRAN
0
20 miles
0
20 kilometres

1991 Outward Bound from Oban

The Plan

In February 1991 the final plans for Island Hop Three were drawn up, after consultation with my two colleagues and numerous timetables. Ian had enjoyed the 1990 trip so much that he had no hesitation in assuring us that he would be back this year – if we wanted him, which of course we did.

Various options were considered, trying to pick new ground but the plan that won through in the end was one which involved four different trips out of Oban, the last of which would link up with the Clyde. Our trip would then culminate in a spot of hectic Clyde cruising. Yet again, no car was to be used and yet again Ian and Gibbie took an extra day over me, at the beginning, to partake in the first of these four Oban excursions, namely a sail out to the island of Barra, at the southern tip of the Western Isles.

Day One – *Kerrera excluded*

It is Monday 20 May 1991 and Island Hop Number Three gets underway when Ian and Gibbie catch the 0812 train from Glasgow's Queen Street Station to Oban. Gibbie is lucky to be on the trip at all. The previous day the toilet in his home ceased to function and, much to his family's annoyance, he did not have time to repair it before embarking on his trip.

They arrive at Oban in pouring rain. Another wet start! No extra-curricular sailings are available in the time before their departure to Barra so much of the time is spent in a local hostelry sheltering from the rain, at least that's what they tell me. They have considered taking the small ferry to the island of Kerrera, which sits out in Oban Bay, but as it leaves from a somewhat bleak spot two miles out of Oban they decide that the rain is the winner and forget that idea.

Lord of the Isles leaves on time at 1640 with the two of them aboard. It is a dull, grey crossing with not much visible on either side of the ship due to the rain and low cloud. A fairly heavy swell causes considerable pitching and they are glad to see Castlebay on Barra eventually appear out of the mist just before ten at night. Due to my ambiguous instructions they almost check into the wrong hotel but are soon on the telephone to me announcing that part one of the trip has been satisfactorily completed. They are also checking that I am still at home and not planning any more surprises, as last year. The scope for such wayward plans does not, unfortunately, exist this year.

Day Two – *Mull revisited*

Ian and Gibbie leave fifteen minutes late the following morning on the same ship, having seen very little of Castlebay, let alone Barra. The low cloud and drizzle persist but the sea is calmer. A party of school teachers are sailing with them. They had been due to fly out but the high winds meant that no flights to or from the island were possible.

Barra is the southern-most inhabited island making up the long chain of the Western Isles. It has one village, Castlebay. A more erudite description of it can wait for another visit in another year.

At the same time that Ian and Gibbie are sailing back across the Sea of the Hebrides I am departing on the same train that they had caught yesterday to Oban. Yet again they are a step ahead of me and I admit slight envy. From now on, I vow, I will ignore the pressures of work and we will all commence our Island Hop together.

The first sight I get of a ferry is the new Skye vessel being assembled at Ferguson's yard at Port Glasgow, across the Clyde from my train as it speeds towards Helensburgh. The vessel is later to be christened *Loch Fyne*. Further on, I spot the *Pioneer* berthed at the James Watt dock in Greenock as spare ship. Both will hopefully be sailed upon on future Island Hops.

I plan to greet my two friends on Oban pier when their ship arrives. I reach Oban more than two hours before the *Lord of the Isles* is due. What can I do for two hours?

Visit Kerrera? (Great minds think alike) but I dismiss the idea on account of the weather. Sit for two hours in the pub? Not likely – I might not make the the rest of the trip.

A two-hour shopping trip? You've got to be joking. No – my stomach as usual wins the day, hunger pangs make the decision of how to spend my time easy – I purchase my eight day Rover ticket and board the *Isle of Mull* for the 1200 return sailing to Craignure on Mull and an early lunch at sea.

As I sail away from Craignure pier on the return leg an hour later, the clouds begin to part and the sun comes out. Just like last year the weather has waited for my arrival into the scheme of things before improving; a point not missed by Ian. Upon the raised after-deck of the ship I scan the Sound of Mull behind us for the incoming *Lord of the Isles* which should be a half hour behind the Mull vessel. Sure enough, there she is, passing Lochaline.

Back at Oban I run up Pulpit Hill yet again, I don't know why I don't just walk, in order to obtain the best view of the *Lord* and my two fellow travellers. With binoculars I can make them out on the deck. I watch them carefully in case they play a trick on me – like hiding behind a funnel and pretending they're not onboard. I know how their minds work.

As the *Lord of the Isles* approaches the pier the *Isle of Mull* departs and the little *Eigg* scuttles across to the slipway – she is the Lismore ferry and will be our next vessel. I scuttle down to the pier and join a windswept Ian and Gibbie. They can hardly believe the change in the weather. I remind them that I am the cause!

We swap tales of our respective journeys. Gibbie had found the hotel on Barra the lap of luxury and consequently his first words are typically perfunctory: '. . . It was good to have a flushing toilet.' Ian makes me promise that in view of the improving weather we will all leave together on the first day of all future Island Hops. And from now on we do.

The 'Island class' ferry *Eigg* is waiting on the slipway adjacent to the pier, ready to depart to the island of Lismore. The *Eigg* is one of eight similarly designed small ferries that carry up to eight cars and can reach islands which have no piers. Their loading ramps can be run up onto concrete slips or, if all else fails, even the beach. Their names are inconsequential for they all look exactly the same. Gibbie and I had previously sailed on one of them, the *Morven*, on our 1989 trip to Iona. The *Eigg* is usually to be found on the service between Oban and Lismore.

The long, ribbon-shaped island of Lismore has a privileged position within the shelter of Loch Linnhe, but is one of the least visited islands on the tourist trail. Skye and Arran draw the tourists like a magnet but how many of them have heard of Lismore? Well we have. It is a green, fertile island, sitting slap-bang in the middle of Loch Linnhe, like a long skinny skelf of land, measuring nine miles by one or two. Being stuck up Loch Linnhe one could argue that it is not a Western Isle at all. The population is over one hundred, the people mostly involved with farming. Indeed, Lismore in Gaelic means 'great garden'. None of us have ever visited it before but our visit today is to be a very brief ten minutes. At least we will be able to say that we have been there! This is just simple island bagging.

The fifty-minute crossing is very pleasant with a small swell giving us the desired feeling of 'being on a boat'. Gibbie is even assuaging his prejudice that these small ferries '. . . are not real boats as they do not possess a proper bow and stern'.

We sit out in the sun on the small upper deck of the ferry. There are no cars aboard but about fifteen other passengers. The crew resemble those aboard Para Handy's puffer, the *Vital Spark*, of Neil Munro and television fame. When Para Handy himself shuffles round to collect the tickets he stares in bafflement at our Rover tickets as if he has never seen the like before. Although the tickets are not actually valid on this route he gives a bewildered nod and moves on: 'That's chust fine, bhoys.' He then gives us heart failure by trying to collect the tickets from us.

'No you can't have them, we need them for all the other sailings.' More baffled looks.

We arrive at Lismore on schedule and have ten minutes in which to take the usual photographs. I have my picture taken standing next to a rusting hulk of an old ferry which is lying on its side high up on the beach. Despite its advanced state of decay Ian reckons it is the relief vessel. Then it is back on board and back to Oban. Para Handy gives us a cursory nod this time.

As we sail into Oban Bay we are joined by an interesting looking ship named the *Fingal* which has appeared from the Sound of Mull and is coming into the Bay just astern of us. Gibbie is able to tell us its function with his customary sagacity: 'It's a lighthouse-maintenance, pilot, buoy-tendering, depot ship.'

It ties up at the life-boat jetty and we pull up onto the slipway and dis-embark via the ramp.

We have time for a quick snack in McTavish's Kitchen – where you get self-service with a smile – before returning to the pier to witness the arrival of our next ship the *Isle of Mull*.

At 1800 we are sailing across to Mull, for the second time today as far as I am concerned, on the third of our four sails out of Oban. This time I stretch out in the observation lounge and watch as the elusive island of Kerrera slips past on the port side. Sailing aboard the *Isle of Mull* is already becoming a regular event for us, linking Oban with the island of Mull. The observation lounge on her upper deck with its large picture windows is our second favourite haunt, next to the cafeteria, where you can stretch out half asleep on the very comfortable upholstered seating and watch the passing scenery with one eye. You can, of course, use both eyes.

Soon the southern tip of the island that we have just left – Lismore – is passing to starboard as we swing up the stretch of water that separates Mull from the mainland mass of Morven and is known as the Sound of Mull.

We arrive at Craignure, which looks exactly as it did six hours previously. This time we need a bus to get us the twenty-one miles to Tobermory on this last part of today's journey.

Our hotel is on the waterfront of Tobermory. A water-colour paintbox of a town, the buildings on the shore road are picked out in primary colours, which contrast against the deep green hues of the wooded hills around. Our hotel is a bright pink with baskets of colourful flowers hanging above the front windows. The shops and restaurants in the town reflect the dominance of the affluent yachting fraternity amongst the many tourists who come here. You can purchase anything from a windlass to a sheepshank. A flotilla of yachts are spread across the famous Bay, in the depths of which the hidden treasures of *Almirante de Florencia*, the doomed Spanish galleon which finally came to rest here in 1588 following the Armada rout, are believed still to lie. Many attempts have been made to dive down and find the gold but no one has struck lucky yet; or if they have they are not telling. There are other ships of interest in the Bay when we arrive, the former CalMac ship *Columba*, now luxury cruiser *Hebridean Princess* is anchored well out from the shore with the training sailing ship *Malcolm Miller* nearby. Both are having an evening stop-over before continuing their busy schedules – just like us. The *Columba* plied these waters to Coll, Tiree and Colonsay until 1989 before being superseded by the larger and more accommodating Isle of Mull. Instead of being scrapped, the *Columba* was bought over and converted for her new role as luxury cruise ship, with luxury prices to match.

The difference in employment could not contrast more. Cocktails are now sipped from crystal glasses, where polystyrene beakers of cafeteria tea were once the order of the day.

The *Malcolm Miller*, on the other hand is used to train young people in the arts of seamanship and sailing and is a frequent sight in the waters of the Hebrides. Indeed we met her on our 1989 trip.

Dinner is in a neat little restaurant on the front aptly called 'The Gannet'. There we have an excellent meal washed down with a bottle of Muscadet. Ian's choice is influenced by the fact that none of us are sharing a room tonight – so he has the bean hotpot.

In the latter part of the evening there is only one place that any self-respecting traveller on Mull should be seen in and that is the Mishnish Bar. This local hostelry is well known among sea-faring people, like ourselves of course, and we find this most excellent pub to be full of crew from the *Malcolm Miller*. There are no obvious crew or passengers from the *Hebridean Princess*, however. They will be all tucked up in their beds by now, digesting their paté-de-fois-gras and Black Sea caviar. These young sailors are sitting around the bar in anticipation of more than one kind of pint for at 11pm the barman announces in a loud voice:

'If there is anyone here from the *Malcolm Miller* then please collect your milk as it has just arrived.' A few dozen cartons of milk stand by the doorway and the Mishnish almost empties as the *Malcolm Miller* mariners shuffle out, clutching a few cartons each, and head off to their dinghies like a bunch of modern day pirates carrying off their booty. We manage a couple of pints ourselves before retiring for the night. We also choose a different whisky with each round. The barman has to open a new bottle three times.

'Are you guys doing this deliberately?'

Day Three – *Gannets and Kilowatts*

The following morning, while my two companions doze, I am up at 0745 just in time to see the *Hebridean Princess*, sailing off down the Sound of Mull towards Oban. At the pier the *Lord of the Isles* is tied up on her outward visit, en route to Coll and Tiree. I stroll up to watch her load a couple of vehicles by her side ramp and reverse out into the bay to continue her journey.

The *Coll*, another 'Island' class ferry and the next vessel in our journey, takes her place at the pier and I retrace my steps, looking forward to a hearty breakfast. This turns out to be a culinary experience. Ian asks our German host if she can make porridge. She replies in the affirmative but the Tutonic variant of porridge obviously differs from the Scots version for Ian's breakfast looks like a mix of sand and glue. He eats it anyway.

We check out and make our way to the pier for the 1000 sailing on the *Coll*, to Kilchoan on the Ardnamurchan peninsula. We have a good look at her to see if we can spot any differences between her and the *Eigg*. Gibbie, never one to miss fine detail in ship design, is convinced that the yellow painted lines on the *Eigg's* turntable do not match those painted along the rest of the car deck. On the *Coll* they do match, he claims. We are not in a position to argue.

This morning we are taking a little cruise over to Ardnamurchan and back, on a little side diversion, simply because the ferry is there – and we have the time. It will add another vessel, although not another island (Ardnamurchan is part of the mainland), to our list.

This route has operated as a seasonal service (summer only) for many years using such vessels as the *Lochnell, Aoolecross* and now the *Coll.* It makes a handy link for the intrepid tourist between Mull and that most western of peninsulas Ardnamurchan.

The thirty-five minute crossing is very calm and, as usual, our visit to the other side is going to be very brief. This is probably just as well as there is nothing much at the other side except the ferry slipway and the ruins, nearby, of Mingary Castle, home to the MacLeans of Ardnamurchan for nearly four hundred years. I'm surprised they stuck it out for so long. The usual photocall giving proof of our visit lasts a little bit shorter than that and we are soon back on board again. We are getting used to the funny looks we get from ship's crews by now. This is the first week of the first season that cars are being carried on this service and quite a few are waiting for the ferry on our arrival back at Tobermory.

By now the sun is rising high and the temperature is reaching a very pleasant degree. We are now heading back south down through Mull to catch the ship back to Oban. We will then be sailing south, ultimately heading for the Clyde. The bus is waiting, ready for the journey back to Craignure, and we leave Tobermory with a fair degree of regret. But we have more adventures ahead and Tobermory is bound to figure again in a future trip. For Gibbie the regret is so great that he quickly books accommodation for the following weekend so that he can return with his wife, Janette.

The road from Tobermory to Craignure is single track for the first ten miles – as far as Salen – and is a badly surfaced and badly aligned affair which demands considerable agility at the wheel from the bus driver. As it climbs higher through the hills the panoramic sea-scape of the southern reaches of the Sound of Mull comes into view and is quite bedazzling, almost unreal. Yachts heel over, their spinnakers entrapping what wind is available, as they glide towards their haven at Tobermory, looking like toy boats on an artificial blue sea. It makes us more anxious to get back on the waves ourselves. Half an hour later we are – on board the *Isle of Mull,* yet again, for the sailing to Oban. As we sail off, our nutritional adviser, Ian, gives us the nod and we head off to the restaurant for lunch. We sail past the *Hebridean Princess* anchored off Duart Castle and ponder on what kind of lunch her clientele is enjoying. Not CalMac soup or bacon butties, we reckon. To be fair to our hosts, however, the standard of food aboard the various big ships is very good indeed and our nutritional adviser seems well pleased. We continue towards Oban, while the *Hebridean Princess* sails up Loch Linnhe.

At Oban we have an hour before embarking on the fourth and last of our sails out of the Bay. This time we will not be taking a return journey but will be sailing southwards, to Kennacraig in West Loch Tarbert, as a link between our cruising out of Oban and our cruising on the Clyde. We split up for the hour and I telephone Tarbert (Loch Fyne) to organise a taxi to meet us on our arrival at Kennacraig at 2200. In a cafe on the North Pier I sip tea and wait for our next ship, the *Claymore*, to arrive. She almost takes me by surprise, arriving a few minutes early, and I have to sip quickly.

We have been looking forward to basking in the sun on the decks of the ship for the duration of the six and a half hour cruise to Kennacraig but to our disappointment her departure at 1515 coincides with the sun vanishing behind the clouds and a cooler air enveloping us.

We sail out of Oban for the fourth time in two days, down the Sound of Kerrera in reverse direction to the last two Island Hops. On clearing the southern tip of Kerrera, that island that we never quite reached, heading out towards the island of Colonsay, we again seek the opinion of our 'nutritional adviser' and, after twisting his arm, make for the bar, for a heat.

By now a southerly swell has built up and the *Claymore* begins to pitch into the oncoming seas. It is a curious feeling, sitting in a room without windows to the outside world, with the floor rising and falling by several feet. Gibbie starts on his 'I like the *Claymore*' bit (this is his favourite ship) while Ian and I try to pick holes in his arguments. My criticism is that due to a lack of reclining seats, the seating in the bar and lounge are strewn with comatose bodies as passengers collapse in their efforts to pass the time on what is a relatively long journey. Not us, of course. The long journeys are the reason that we are here and to pass the time sleeping would be a total waste of time.

After a quick snooze I am up on the top deck to see where we are. We try to put names to the numerous islands that the ship is passing in what is becoming an annual guessing game. Luing, Seil, Lunga, Easdale and Scarba – but not necessarily in that order. Although we passed them on the last two years' trips it is no easier working out which is which this time – especially as we are now sailing past them in the opposite direction.

Colonsay nears, the pitching slackens and the comatose figures in the bar, including Gibbie, begin to show signs of life. The *Claymore* approaches the north side of the linkspan and reverses around the front of it to dock stern in. The stern rope is thrown prematurely and the ropeman on the pier, who looks eighty if he is a day, huffs and puffs and glares malevolently at the ship's crew as he struggles to haul in sixty feet of wet hawser. Just as it looks as though he isn't going to survive the effort he manages to loop the end of the hawser around a concrete bollard and flops into a heap on the pier.

We debate whether we will bother stepping ashore. When I announce that I am not going to run around the bay for a photograph as I have one already.

Gibbie replies, 'Well, can you run around and take one for me, then?' I oblige.

At around 1800 we depart for Islay and I glance at Ian. He takes the hint. 'Cup of tea just now and dinner when we leave Port Askaig.' There is no arguing with the man.

The sail down the Sound of Islay between Islay and Jura is always magnificent and produces some good bird-watching. There is a black-throated diver and a dozen great-northern divers in a huddle just off the Jura shore.Unfortunately my two colleagues are ornithologically ignorant. Gibbie has great difficulty in distinguishing an eider from a gannet (the thought of an eider diving head first into the sea from forty feet is quite entertaining) and Ian can only recognise a bird if it's sitting on his dinner plate covered in a sauce.

As we stand on the forward deck looking over the bow we are joined by a couple of teenage girls who also have binoculars. After watching me point out a few birds to Ian and Gibbie, one of the girls approaches me and politely asks:

'Excuse me, can you please tell me what those floating black and white birds are over there?'

'Certainly,' I reply, taking on the demeanour of a ship-loving Tony Soper. 'They're black guillemots.'

'Thank you,' she says, and then turning to her friend, she proclaims in a confident voice: 'He says they're black *kilowatts*!'

We reach Port Askaig a little ahead of schedule, which is surprising as the current in the narrows has been against us. As we disembark for the brief stop-over the *Sound of Gigha* pulls away from the slipway. If we had been quicker, and bolder, we could have joined her and ticked off another island, Jura. Instead we watch her struggle sideways across the turbulent waters between the islands – always a source of amazement to me.

The *Claymore* skipper, whom Ian refers to as 'The Old Man', which is a complete misnomer as he is the youngest looking skipper we have seen on our travels, is standing chatting next to us on the pier. He seems completely indifferent to the unloading and loading of his ship. I ask him when we will be departing Port Askaig. He responds by taking my CalMac timetable from my hand.

'Well, let's see what it says in here. 1945 – well that's when we'll go!' I am left with the feeling that I have asked a silly question.

We watch several large trailers being loaded for the last leg of the journey to the mainland and then we join them onboard. By the time we sail, the *Sound of Gigha* has returned from Jura. Oh well, another opportunity missed.

We almost sail without 'The Old Man' who seems reluctant to finish his conversation with one of the pier staff. With the ship ready to sail he glances up, gives a nonchalant swagger and with his hands in his pockets skips up the gangway with a: 'Let go fore and aft!'

We sail away from Islay on the last two-hour leg of our journey – hoping that our pre-booked taxi will be waiting for us.

Dinner time! Gibbie is most disappointed that shark steaks are off the menu. None have been caught that day.

The sky is now overcast but the darkening sea is calm. The last stretch up the beautiful waters of West Loch Tarbert is enlivened by more bird-watching. Ducks, seals, more great-northern divers and several more black kilowatts.

In fading light, at 2140, we dock at Kennacraig and scan the pier for our truant taxi. We look and look. For the first time something in our itinerary appears to be going wrong. We peer in vain into the gloom, searching the road for something resembling a taxi and contemplating a six-mile walk to our guest-house in Tarbert. Evidently we are not the only ones, a middle-aged Canadian couple, who have also come off the *Claymore* and whom Gibbie had overheard asking about accommodation on Colonsay, can be seen striding out in the direction of Tarbert. They seem totally disorientated. Perhaps they are surprised that Colonsay has such a well-surfaced road !

Meanwhile the *Claymore* and the CalMac office are shutting up for the night. I hurriedly call our taxi company and am assured that a car will soon be on its way. An employee of CalMac kindly offers to give us a lift into Tarbert. Another five minutes passes and we are literally climbing into this chap's car when our taxi appears. A game of 'musical cars' ensues and we are on our way, at last, to Tarbert.

We want to negotiate, with the cab-driver, the price of an early morning taxi ride to Tayinloan, for a return trip to Gigha, prior to the rest of tomorrow's cruising. We will have to telephone first thing in the morning, we are told. Nothing for it but to retire to a Tarbert hostelry to discuss our options and ideas for the following day.

The problem is this: we have to catch the 1140 sailing to Arran from Claonaig in order for tomorrow's hectic schedule to work. Until 1140 we are free and we plan to ask the taxi driver (who would be taking us the twelve miles to Claonaig anyway) to take us firstly down to Tayinloan and wait for us while we sail over to Gigha and back. Obviously this is going to cost and we have to decide on a limit to which we are prepared to pay. Gibbie is persuaded that 50p each is not realistic enough and we settle democratically on £8 each – a total of £24.

Tomorrow promises to be an exciting day, with or without Gigha. Ian still has one or two reservations about the itinerary – but then he doesn't share my eternal optimism.

'What if one of our connections is late?'

I assure him that everything will work out perfectly, with my tongue firmly welded to my cheek and my fingers tightly crossed behind my back. In fact it is going to be a more frantic schedule that we could have anticipated.

Day Four – *Clyde Cruising*

The following morning we are up sharp and I call the taxi office and put our idea to our driver. His price is £27.50. Oh dear, too dear! We therefore decide to leave Gigha for another year and instruct the driver to pick us up at 1100 to take us to Claonaig in time for our sailing to Arran. We now have some time on our hands and head off to the shops – a very unusual way to spend time on an Island Hop. The main retail attraction for us are the bookshops with which Tarbert is well furnished. At least we can have a decent look at Tarbert rather than simply racing through it as is usually the case at one of our overnight stopping points.

Tarbert lies half way down the Kintyre peninsula, that long strip of land which separates the Clyde from the innermost of the Hebrides, and is one of the more interesting villages in this part of Scotland. It straddles a strip of land a mere two miles wide ('tarbert' refers to a narrow isthmus, which is why there are a few Tarberts in Scotland i.e. Loch Lomond [Tarbet] and Harris). The town faces eastwards onto Loch Fyne, which is part of the Clyde estuary, but across the isthmus to the west is the shallow West Loch Tarbert, which we sailed up last night and which is unquestionably a West Highland loch. This narrow isthmus was the scene of an interesting piece of pantomime (apart from our own) way back at the start of the twelfth century. King Magnus of Norway made a pact with Scotland's obsequious King Edgar enabling him to take the islands of the west for the Norwegians provided he could pass a ship between the islands and the mainland. The rapacious but inventive King Magnus then dragged his ship from East Loch Tarbert across the narrow strip of land to West Loch Tarbert and thus claimed the whole of Kintyre to the south as an island. Kintyre came under Norwegian rule until King Alexander lll wrestled it and the Western Isles back in the mid-thirteenth century.

The town of Tarbert is popular with tourists on their way up and down the Kintyre peninsula and with yachtsmen and women. Due to the nearby ferry links it also acts as a crossing point between the islands of Arran and Islay. Similar to Tobermory, many of the shops and hotels have a nautical feel to them. In fact the town is bracing itself for the arrival that evening of the annual yacht race from Gourock to Tobermory. Strange that we should also be travelling between the same two ports – only in the opposite direction.

At 1100 we are assembled at the pre-arranged roadside spot waiting for our taxi. I am also looking out for the Canadian couple who should be reaching the town by about now.

We are soon on our way to Claonaig for a 'tenner'. On the way the driver Stan recounts his favourite 'Belgian-tourist' story. He had picked up this chap in Tarbert a few years ago who had jumped into the car and given the instruction: '*Sheep!*' As this has been the weekend of the Skipness sheep-dog trials Stan had set out across Kintyre on the same road as we are taking this morning. The Belgian seemed well pleased at this but kept demanding in his limited English vocabulary, '*Sheep.*'

'Yes, yes, I know, I know,' Stan reassured him. As Stan drove past Claonaig the Belgian tourist suddenly became more agitated as he watched his goal slip past:

'There! There! *Sheep Sheep!*' he exclaimed, pointing at the Claonaig–Lochranza ferry.

We are dropped at the Claonaig slipway just as our 'sheep', the *Loch Ranza* is approaching. This vessel, it is rumoured, will become the new Gigha ferry next year and a new larger vessel will take over and hopefully cope better with the ever increasing traffic demands on this back-door route to Arran. This is the first of six 'sheeps' that we will be sailing on today.

The half-hour crossing is pleasant and uneventful, with Gibbie insisting that from mid-channel we will see the towering carbuncle of Inverkip Power Station, now well moth-balled. We are firmly of the opinion that the manic depressive who designed and built it, in the midst of one of the most beautiful estuaries in Europe should be made to climb it each day as penitence.

In any case Gibbie is only half correct. Today we cannot see it. It is so misty that we can hardly make out the nearer land – Bute – our next island but one.

We have lunch on Arran at the strategically placed Lochranza Tearoom. The xenophobic waitress is serving some Dutch customers with flair and good Scottish hospitality. 'Get your Ordnance Survey maps off the table, this is a restaurant not a waiting room. If you're not going to order something to eat you'll have to get out!'

We quickly order our lunch and push our maps and timetables deeper into our bags. She is soon on the war-path again.

'If you've finished your lunch, hurry up and get out!'

We hurry out also but only because our bus to Brodick is due at any minute. In fact it arrives ten minutes late which causes one or two heart flutters as it is essential that we reach Brodick in time for the 1350 sailing to Ardrossan. As it happens we make it in plenty of time and settle down on the forward deck of the *Isle of Arran* to enjoy the returning sunshine on a crossing that will take fifty minutes.

I am experiencing that feel-good sensation as the ship departs island number six on time. I know I should not count my chickens; all we need is for a squall to blow up and for the ship to be diverted mid-passage to Gourock and all our plans will be snookered. I have not warned Ian about that possibility, partly on account of his nervous disposition regarding schedules and partly on being totally confident about the settled weather conditions which usually prevail on the Clyde in the month of May.

The sun is still shining as we reach the Ayrshire port of Ardrossan but another potential impediment looms. We have just seventeen minutes in which to march Gibbie, who is not exactly the Roger Bannister of Island Hoppers, from the harbour to the town to catch the bus to Largs. All seems well when the ship arrives on time but it takes eight minutes to get the first passengers off the ship, due to a languorous gangway crew. Our safety margin is cut to a minimum. The thought of carrying Gibbie briefly crosses my mind but I spot the solution pulling up in front of us: a taxi. We look at each other, nod and jump inside. When the driver learns that we are actually heading for Largs he offers to take us there for £9, thus skipping the idea of the Ardrossan town centre and the bus. Anything that avoids Ardrossan town centre seems like a good idea and off we go.

When we get to Largs, the plan is to catch the 1600 connecting bus to Wemyss Bay (for the Rothesay ferry). But we are now ahead of schedule, thanks to our speedy taxi and another piece of opportunism springs to mind. If we can reach Largs by 1515 we might be able to take a return crossing on the ferry to Cumbrae and still be back in time for our bus connection. This will give us the unexpected bonus of another island and another vessel and might compensate for missing out on Gigha. The suggestion is put to our driver, who responds by putting his foot down. Ian, sitting in the back, clutching bus and ferry timetables, shakes his head in confusion. Island Hopping at its most hectic, or should I say frantic.

As we speed down Charles Street towards Largs pier, we have only two minutes to spare. We draw up next to the slipway, thrust £9 into the driver's hand and we are on board the *Loch Striven* on our way to the Island of Great Cumbrae with seconds to spare. It will be my briefest ever visit to the island.

There is time for the customary photocall at the slipway on Cumbrae before jumping back on board. As we sail back across on the ten minute crossing to the mainland the small cruise ship and former Largs–Millport ferry *Keppel* is pulling up at the pier to join the *Loch Linnhe* which is already tied up there as relief ferry. We are due to meet up with *Keppel* two hours later at Rothesay and, with the weather deteriorating and the rain starting to fall, I look anxiously at her decks, searching for passengers. It would not be the first time that a *Keppel* cruise is cancelled due to bad weather and a low turn out. Ian is looking forward very much to his cruise on this, the oldest CalMac vessel and, although her decks look sparsely populated, she pulls away from Largs pier on schedule, heading out across the firth towards Rothesay. We head up the Main Street towards the bus station quietly confident that the rest of the itinerary will now go according to plan.

Our bus connection to Wemyss Bay leaves at 1605. Although the railheads of Wemyss Bay in the north and Largs in the south are separated by only six miles the respective original railway companies, Caledonian Railway at Wemyss Bay and the Glasgow and South-western at Largs, never closed the loop. How inconsiderate of them. So a bus it has to be. Yet another mode of transport. Island Hopping is not all about ships.

So we are on the move again and arrive with twenty minutes to spare before our ferry sailing to Bute. The ship will be any one of the three 'streakers' *Saturn, Juno* or *Jupiter*. Their nickname is on account of their pace and speed of turn-around at piers and nothing to do with the state of dress of their skippers.

The sisters *Jupiter* and *Juno* arrived on the Clyde ferry scene in 1973–74 and were put into service on the Gourock–Dunoon route. They were joined by their planetary cousin *Saturn* in 1978. She became the Wemyss Bay–Rothesay vessel. Their arrival heralded the end of Clyde service for previous car-ferries such as the *Arran, Bute, Cowal* and *Maid of Cumbrae*.

These utilitarian ships may look like floating garages but finding a better design for an estuarial car-ferry would be difficult. What they lack in grace they make up for in manoeuvrability. The three ships have served the two main upper Clyde ferry routes extremely successfully for almost twenty years on a rotational basis. The 'rotation' can also be taken literally; their Voth-Schneider propulsion units enable them to spin in their own length and they are thus very manoeuvrable at piers. I have many times eagerly watched them spin around on arrival at a pier or slip sideways at three knots when departing. My reaction to seeing them for the first time was less sanguine: Rothesay 1974 and as I disembarked from the cosy wee *Bute* I spotted this floating car-park named the *Jupiter* coming round from Toward and wondered if I really was seeing the future. Over the years I suppose I've come to accept them for what they are. Spinning around on one of them at Gourock pier is actually quite good fun. This is our first Island Hop sail on one of these ships.

Back to today – a haze has now settled over the water but with binoculars I can make out that our approaching 'streaker' is the *Saturn*. The lack of a high flying bridge distinguishes this ship from the others, even at distance. Her presence on the Rothesay route today is good news as only this 'streaker' has a 'view over the bow' from the small forward deck below the bridge. This makes her immediately endearing to Gibbie, although he is reluctant to admit it.

To Ian's amazement, the *Saturn* speeds head on towards Wemyss Bay pier without reducing speed and not even flinching. Just as it looks as though we should be running for our lives she swings suddenly to port and pirouettes to dock stern in at the linkspan. She discharges a car-deck full of vehicles and loads a full complement of forty cars (leaving two behind) in twelve minutes. She then sails on time at 1645 with us aboard. Ian is impressed. Gibbie and I have seen it all before.

In the cafeteria, sheltering from the rain, Ian approves a half pint and a scone – it is all that is on offer. As we pass Craigmore on Bute we finally brave the elements to take in the 'view over the bow'. The view, from a nautical point, is the *Keppel* and the puffer *Old Vic 32* tied up ahead of us at Rothesay pier. The *Saturn* is soon tied up beside them.

Bute is one of my favourite islands. Many family holidays have been spent there – individually by all three of us – but as there are only twenty minutes to go before the *Keppel* sails, reminiscing will have to wait for another time.

Despite the deteriorating weather, CalMac's last cruise ship does not look as though she is going to abandon her cruise. On we get for a sail to Dunoon. It has been years since Ian last cruised on the Clyde and this is the bit that he has been really looking forward to. In the recent years of renewal of much of the Clyde and Western Isles fleet and the loss of the great cruise ships like *Queen Mary, Duchess of Hamilton* and *King George V* it is perhaps surprising that the wee *Keppel* is still here, purring around the Clyde resorts at a steady nine knots. Indeed since 1986, when CalMac scrapped the direct route from Largs to Millport in favour of a direct car-ferry crossing to the Cumbrae slipway, she has taken on a new lease of life as summer cruise ship.

My personal memories of her started in 1967 when I sailed home from Millport pier on her at the end of a Sunday School trip, having sailed out on *Maid of Ashton*. I remember being puzzled by her strange narrow funnel, which is really a disguised diesel exhaust.

We are away from Rothesay pier on the *Keppel* at 1740 with the sum total of fourteen passengers. As the rain slackens off we are able to sit out on the surprisingly spacious deck. A chat with the skipper reveals that the little ship has taken on sixty-four passengers today. Yesterday she had over three hundred. This, the penultimate sail of the trip, is definitely one of the highlights of Island Hop 1991. As we circle round to head away from the pier the *Saturn* gives us a splendid view of how to move off a pier sideways – at three knots.

We all agree that it is now time for the celebratory drink – The Annual Toast. Gibbie descends to the saloon bar to see what he can muster. He comes back with three beers and a look of shock on his face. The steward had called him 'pet'. From then on we only descend downstairs in twos.

The sky is clearing dramatically as we sail northwards up the Cowal shore, past Innellan and its decaying pier, towards Dunoon. The cameras are set to self-timing and we pose without embarrassment, clutching our glasses, to the amusement of our eleven fellow passengers.

The *Keppel* arrives at Dunoon slightly ahead of schedule and although she is continuing over to Gourock we decide to get off here and take the ferry to the mainland port, purely for the sake of adding another ship to the list.

We hang around for twenty minutes on Dunoon pier awaiting the arrival of that last vessel, the *Jupiter* As we set off, the yacht race can be seen departing Gourock. More than one hundred and seventy white sails are curling around Cloch Point on their way to Tarbert and ultimately Tobermory. Their trip is beginning just as ours is ending. Their sheer number creates a bit of a problem for the skipper of the *Jupiter*. He has to reduce speed and alter course on several occasions as yachts threaten to sail in front of him.

As we approach Gourock pier the *Juno* is sitting out from the linkspan awaiting the unloading of the *Jupiter* before she moves in to take the last sailing of the day to Dunoon. We watch from the upper deck as the *Jupiter* pivots round to berth stern-in. On the pier we then watch as the two sister ships swap over, passing within a very few feet of each other. Our train is waiting so we do not linger. It pulls away from Gourock just after 2000 and we settle down amidst the litter for the journey to Glasgow Central. There it is, a change of trains and we are back in Shawlands just after 2100.

Yet again the trip has been very successful, with every ship except the *Coll* sailing on time. We have, between us, landed on eight different islands and sailed on eleven different vessels, visiting nineteen ports. 'New' islands are Lismore and Barra, although we have missed out on Kerrera, Jura and Gigha. Looking back, the highlight for me was that last day of dashing around the Clyde, on six different vessels, jumping from one ship to another with literally only seconds to spare in some cases. Will we do it all again? It is a question that we do not really have to ask ourselves.

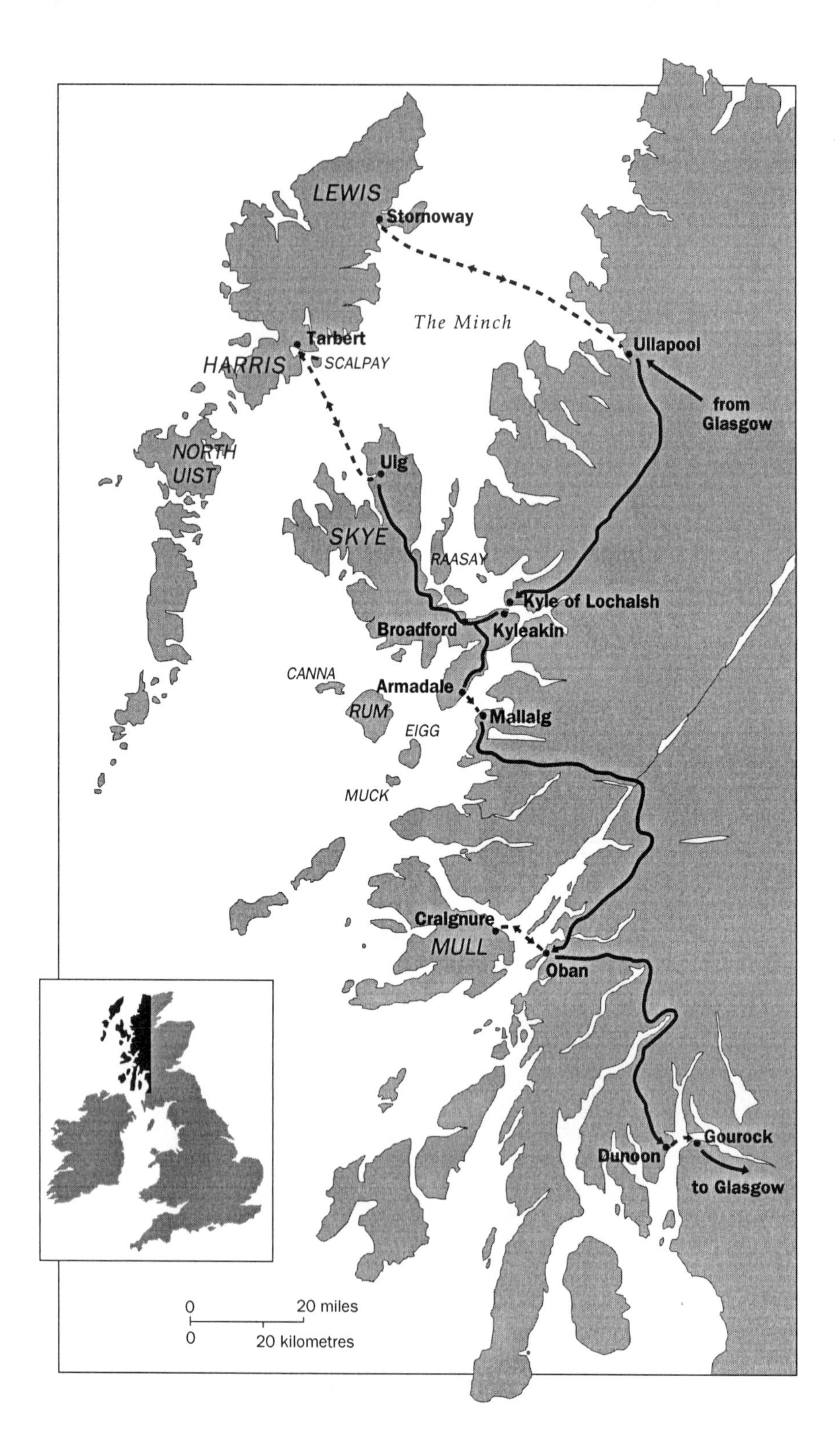
LEWIS
Stornoway
The Minch
Ullapool
from Glasgow
Tarbert
HARRIS
SCALPAY
NORTH UIST
Uig
SKYE
RAASAY
Kyle of Lochalsh
Broadford
Kyleakin
CANNA
Armadale
Mallaig
RUM
EIGG
MUCK
Craignure
MULL
Oban
Gourock
Dunoon
to Glasgow
0
20 miles
0
20 kilometres

1992 Minch Machinations

The Plan

After three Island Hops visiting fifteen islands and sailing on nineteen vessels there remained two unfulfilled ambitions.

The first was obvious: to sail to yet more 'new' islands, but the second and more important target was to sail on the two large CalMac Western Isles ships as yet untried on Island Hops: the *Iona* and the *Suilven*.

I had only ever sailed once before on the *Suilven*, from Oban to Craignure in 1989, on the only occasion that she had strayed from her Ullapool to Stornoway route. I had been aboard the *Iona* several times including a trip from Ardrossan to Brodick earlier this year when she was performing her usual roster of winter relief sailings. Neither Ian nor Gibbie had sailed on these ships. The inclination was, therefore, that the trip this year should involve both ships.

Incorporating Ullapool to Stornoway on an Island Hop using only public transport is not easy, as the timetables and the tightness of our schedule was to prove. In fact our normal three-day stint would have to stretch to about five days with some interminably long bus journeys at unsociable hours. So we decided early on at the planning phase to break with tradition and take a car. This might seem to break with the traditional aim of our trips but the increased flexibility of having our own means of getting from terminal to terminal more than compensated for the misgivings at having slackened our Island Hopping morals.

One drawback of using a car is that we would have to return to it. Either that or leave it up in the Western Isles until next year ! Our route this year would, therefore, not be a circular one but more a series of daytrips with the car taking us from one starting point to the other. The first starting point was to be the home of the *Suilven*, Ullapool. The following morning we would wake up on Skye and sail to Harris and Scalpay. On the third day we would return to the mainland on the other target ship – *Iona* – and then sail out to the 'Small Isles' on the *Lochmor*. This interesting route would satisfy both ambitions, the aforementioned ships and the new islands (notably Lewis, Harris and Scalpay). There was doubt, however, on whether we could actually set foot on any of the 'Small Isles' of Canna, Rum or Eigg, but we would try, as long as we didn't have to swim. Ian volunteered the use of his car – a Citroen XM – for the journey but we agreed to share the driving. We needed to book the car on one sailing only: the 0915 Armadale – Mallaig.

The plans were thus laid out for my colleagues' approval. But the best laid plans . . .

Day One – *134 degrees*

The day of our departure, Sunday 17 May 1992, is a scorcher. I leave a thermometer on the dashboard of my car, in the full heat of the sun's rays, and return to find it recording a temperature of 134 Fahrenheit.

In Ian's somewhat cooler car we leave Glasgow at 1520, with me driving. Over the Erskine Bridge, up Loch Lomondside towards Fort William we speed on quiet roads and under a cloudless sky. For once the summit of Ben Nevis is clear of haze and we pause to record the unusual sight of its visible summit on film. It doesn't have the initial demeanour of the highest mountain in Scotland or, for that matter, Britain. I can think of other mountains that give the impression of being higher. Goat Fell overlooking Brodick Bay looks huge. The shape of Ben Nevis is also a bit disappointing, sort of round-shouldered, like an old-aged pensioner of a mountain. But at 4406 feet it is indeed our highest mountain, whether we like it or not. It is good just to see the top for once.

On again towards Loch Ness and Fort Augustus (where Gibbie has also never been) for a quick snack in a small cafe which is no more than a Fish and Chip shop with tables.

I never seem to be able to escape them. Across from me on trains, beside me on buses, last week on Glasgow's Underground and now even here in the Scottish Highlands. I'm referring to drunks ! They pop up everywhere with the same hang-dog demeanour and lugubrious expression. This one wants to sit beside Ian despite the wealth of empty seats around the cafe. Ian smartly despatches him to another table where he labours over fish and fags, lifting his head every now and then to ask: 'Whit time is it? Whit day is it?'

Off we go again – continuing up the side of Loch Ness. No sign of the monster, Gibbie doesn't believe in it anyway but I'm not so sure. I recalled passing here many years ago in the family car with my parents and sister Anne, searching the waters of the loch for 'Nessie' as we drove past. A huge man, his head enshrouded by tously red hair and a shaggy, over-sized red beard and sporting an undersized kilt was emerging from his parked car as we slowly passed. 'Look !' screamed Anne pointing at him. 'The Monster!' Everyone in the lay-by instantly span round to face the loch.

We pass through Beauly and then north-westwards across the north of Scotland towards Loch Broom, into which the town of Ullapool juts.

As we approach Ullapool we catch our first sight of a ship, sailing up the Loch, which Ian immediately identifies as the *Hebridean Princess*. Another encounter with her, only this time in a halcyon setting. We stop the car and get out to witness a truly beautiful sight. The old CalMac ferry, now plush cruiser, is silhouetted by the setting sun upon the silver and gold shimmering waters of Loch Broom. There is not a sound to be heard except the quiet mutter of her diesel engines as she passes. Yet even this does not spoil the serenity of this quiescent scene. She is heading well up the loch with her complement of forty-odd passengers to anchor for the night in completely silent surroundings. Well – if you have paid £3,000 for a week long cruise then you would expect a good night's sleep.

At 2120 we are at Ullapool and, after checking into the hotel, we take a stroll out to the end of the promontory upon which Ullapool is built. The windless evening is interrupted only by the disyllabic call of a cuckoo echoing across from the other side of the loch. We sit there for what seems like ages, enjoying the warmth of this incredibly beautiful evening. It is the midges which eventually force us to move on. What spoilsports they are.

Up to the pier and two Peterhead registered fishing boats are preparing for another week's work. Nowadays the fishermen arrive in style, from a posh looking coach, with their bags, provisions and crates of beer. Fishing is thirsty work.

At the head of the pier there is a refrigeration plant. It produces the ice which will keep the fish fresh, when it is landed in the forthcoming days, as it is conveyed by truck to various parts of the country. The generator bellows loudly – reverberating off the hills opposite. As I lie in bed that night, a hundred yards from the plant, with the constant drone blocking out the silence, I realise why the *Hebridean Princess* has sailed so far up the loch to find a peaceful anchorage.

Day Two – *Mediterranean Minch*

Breakfast is at 0800 and very nice it is too. The *Suilven* is due in at 0900 and we are checked out by 0845. The sky is cloudless, and will remain so for the next two days. Already the temperature is above 70 F.

Gibbie has had a bad start to the day. He has shared a room with Ian and to his embarrassment had pulled a pair of black tights from his bag instead of socks. He is now trying to convince his suspicious colleagues that some kind of mistake has been made and that Janette had been the last person to use the bag – but we have our doubts about him. Steamer matters take over and we head up the promontory to photograph the arrival of the *Suilven*. We are too late as she comes speeding round the point before we can get our cameras set up.

The Ullapool-Stornoway route was inaugurated in 1973 by the *Iona* when it was decided to serve Lewis from Ullapool instead of the more traditional ports of Mallaig and Kyle of Lochalsh. The *Clansman* took over for a while until the larger, Norwegian-built *Suilven* entered service on 28 August 1974. The *Suilven*, re-named as such after a local mountain, has served Lewis well for almost twenty years now. This will be our first sail on her.

The *Suilven* sails on time at 0930 and her position at the pier is taken up immediately by the *Hebridean Princess* which has emerged from her slumbers. The three of us sit out on the upper deck and hardly budge for the duration of the three and a half hour crossing.

Suilven is an impressive ship with a huge, cavernous car-deck capable of holding one hundred and twenty cars (we have left our car at Ullapool). There are long decks on either side with a raised deck astern. Internally there is a cafeteria forward, with part of it divided into a seating area. Aft of this there is the ticket office and toilets and further astern from this the bar. This is also split, into an area with tables and chairs on the starboard side and a lounge on the port side.

We are sailing through the various isles and islets littering the entrance to

Loch Broom where several Russian factory ships, sporting their 'new' national flag of red, white and blue horizontal stripes, instead of the 'hammer and sickle', clutter the entrance to the loch. Their dirty hulls are dappled and speckled with corrosion and their decks appear devoid of human life. The 'Klondyke' days of the early eighties when Loch Broom was littered with these fish processing ships seems to be coming to an end.

It is a full hour before we are into the open waters of the North Minch where the real drama of the morning suddenly unfolds. An air-sea rescue helicopter, by the name of Loch Fyne, suddenly appears above the ship. After a few moments it repositions itself right above the stern of the *Suilven*. It is hovering only twenty feet above the heads of the gathering crowd and the noise is deafening. A figure appears on its starboard side and is winched down towards us. He reaches for the stern rail of the ship and at the third attempt manages to grab it and pull himself aboard. All around fingers are in ears and cameras are clicking. An officer from the ship joins the figure who is still attached by rope to the helicopter. Something is shouted into a hand-held radio and then this messenger from above is hauled back skywards. What is wrong? Is someone ill? Are we on fire? Has Gibbie left his tights in Ullapool?

Again this huge wasp is over our heads and I am amazed, if not apprehensive, at how close the rotors seem to be to the ship's funnel. Another figure appears at the starboard door, this one clad in an orange survival suit, and is also lowered onto the deck. A middle-aged lady passenger rushes to greet him and after a brief chat he is hoisted back up again. The helicopter then retreats a few yards, banks steeply to starboard and roars over our heads and away westwards towards Stornoway. We stand shaking our heads in amazement at all these comings and goings.

An English cyclist, who apparently uses this route regularly, leans over to us and remarks: 'This happens every time I am on this ship'. I bet Ian that the pampered passengers of the *Hebridean Princess* do not get this level of cabaret excitement. It transpires that the middle-aged lady is a friend of the second winchman. She is from Kendal and is coming over to stay with his family in Stornoway. He has literally dropped in to make sure that she is on the ship. Seems a bit of an extravagance – could he not just have used a radio-telephone like everyone else?

On we sail. The sea looks flat calm but there is the gentlest of swells which rock the ship very slightly from side to side. How would she perform in a real howler, we wonder. Around us puffins flutter across the surface of the water in groups of two and three and as we approach Chicken Head on the Eye peninsula of Lewis a dark phase arctic skua chases a gull, trying to rob it of its last meal.

We arrive on time at Stornoway, our first ever visit here, the largest town in the Western Isles. It is bustling with children as it is the school lunch break. The biggest drawback from our whirlwind visit to the islands is that we do not have much time to look around these new places that we find ourselves in. Today we have only thirty minutes in which to discover Stornoway. Ian reckons it is thirty minutes too long in any case. We split up and in my thirty minutes I phone home, photograph the local fishing fleet (including the smallest traditional-shaped fishing boat that I have ever seen) and have a quick jaunt around the town centre. I nip into the Tourist Office to enquire about taxis on Harris (for tomorrow's trip) and am told that a much older man has been in just five minutes earlier enquiring about the same thing. This description suggests that Gibbie must also be 'securing his line of advance' (his favourite phrase apart from 'Is my brow turning red yet?' and 'Just a splash of water in it, please.') I am the last passenger back on board and off we go again, with a new assortment of passengers.

The weather is now glorious, making our seven hour sail on the *Suilven* the hottest of any Island Hop to date. Combined with the hazy sunshine the Minch has a Mediterranean feel to it. We could be cruising to Corfu. When Gibbie starts to complain about his reddening brow we know we are having a grand day. Much of the return crossing is spent lounging on the top deck. Then it is into the restaurant for a meal followed by, for me, a snooze on one of the reclining chairs. As I lie back with my eyes shut I am privy to an interesting conversation between an American couple who, judging from their accents, are from the deep south. They are observing a young couple nearby who have a toddler in a pushchair. They call prams 'carriages' and pushchairs 'strollers'.

'What a cute stroller, Martha, why didn't we have one of these for our children?' 'Because we didn't walk anywhere, honey, we drove.'

We disembark at Ullapool at 1700 and, after a brief pause to allow Gibbie to photograph the rear (blunt) end of the *Suilven* re-unite ourselves with the car and set off on the eighty-six miles to Kyle of Lochalsh. Ian drives. The roads are uncluttered and the scenery beautiful. For once we are in no rush – the ferry to Skye, our next island, runs twenty-four hours a day.

At Kyle the new ferries are in operation – or at least the *Loch Fyne* is. Her sister the *Loch Dunvegan* is redundant at the pier. We decide to cross over to Skye, a stone's throw away, immediately. This is the first time we have taken a car onto a ferry on any Hop to date but it hardly feels like a momentous event.

The new ships seem to be giving Skye a much better service – but there are mutterings about the introduction of an even better service – a bridge! Plans are afoot to build a permanent concrete link across the narrow Sound of Sleat. Will this mean the end of the ferries?

Across on Skye we push on towards Portree, the island capital, some thirty miles away. This time I drive. In the Royal Hotel we have a meal washed down with a little wine. This brings the subject of weekly alcohol consumption to the fore. We all seem within the recommended levels, apart from when Island Hopping and provided Gibbie doesn't include wine.

Day Three – *the Scalpay Mini-marathon*

The weather on the following morning is boringly predictable again – I wish I'd brought my Factor 24. We are motoring up to Uig in the north of Skye in harmony with Beethoven's 'Eroica'. This morning we are heading for the Western Isles again, this time Harris. As we circle round the top end of Uig Bay our ship *Hebridean Isles* can be seen way below approaching the pier and lends herself to an ideal photo opportunity.

The car is deposited in the car-park and we are soon crossing the Minch again on a trip into the unknown.

Harris is the last of the big Western Isles that we have still to reach. The guide books tell us that it is a land of mountains and golden beaches. We have to take their word for it as we won't have much time to see them. The ship will berth at the main village of Tarbert (another one) after crossing on one of the legs of the 'Uig Triangle'. We have several options when we get there and so retire to the cafeteria to discuss them.

When we get to Tarbert at 1125 we want to cross the six miles to Kyles Scalpay in order to catch the 1215 ferry to the island of Scalpay. We should have time to see a bit of this 'new' island before getting back to Tarbert for the 1610 sailing back to Skye. The difficulty is the six miles between Tarbert and Kyles Scalpay. We have no transport lined up and our schedule is sufficiently tight that a connecting bus is considered unlikely. I am assigned the task of materialising such land transport during the twenty-five minutes that the *Hebridean Isles* lies at Tarbert pier. If I am unsuccessful then we will get back on board the ship for a triangular trip to Lochmaddy (North Uist) and Uig but as the weather is glorious we are very keen to make Scalpay. I await our landing at Tarbert impatiently.

By now I have noticed on our Island Hopping trips that whenever there is any running-around, chasing-after, or pleading-with-the-locals to be done it is always me who is volunteered to do it. Gibbie says it's because I've got more energy than the others but I don't fully believe him. Needlesss to say, when the ship ties up at Tarbert pier I am the first off. Spying an assembly of buses parked nearby I approach the group of drivers who are standing in a circle chatting.

'Are any of you going to Kyles Scalpay?'

Their collective answer is a blank look and a shake of the head. I make for the Tourist Office, that little oasis of knowledge found in all corners of the Isles where all travel problems are solved. Here I am treated more sympathetically by a well-rounded, smiling lady with a delightful Hebridean brogue. I enquire about a taxi to Kyles Scalpay and ask why there are none on the pier awaiting the arrival of the ferry.

She tries two numbers without reply. 'Och, it's such a nice day they'll be away out.' I grimace and look over at the waiting ship at the pier. She tries a third number and after a few words in her native tongue, the tone of which implies to me that she has been successful, she hangs up and smiles broadly. 'Wilmonald (William Donald) is on his way, He'll be here in five minutes.'

'Will he meet us here?' I ask.

'Oh yes.'

'What kind of car are we looking for?'

'It's a red one!'

By now Gibbie and Ian have found me, with ten minutes before the ship is due to sail. Gibbie has but one thing in mind:

'Is there anywhere on Scalpay where we can get a cup of tea? I mean, it's not like Staffa, is it?'

The lady hesitates. 'Yes, Mrs McTavish will see you right.'

Back outside we only wait another minute before a red car zooms up. We jump inside and are soon off, delighted to be on the move again.

Wilmonald is very chatty. I remark on the lunar-like landscape all around us. It is as rocky a landscape as I have ever seen. Bare, grey rock pushes through the bracken and the brown heather. It all looks so different from the other Western Isles we have been to. Some workmen are digging at the side of the road, trying to even out the tortuous bends in the road. 'There does not seem to be much top-soil,' I remark.

'You're right,' says Wilmonald, 'we have an awful job burying our dead on Harris.' I am unsure if he is serious or not, until he breaks into a laugh.

He chats continuously, as if we are his first passengers this year, while throwing the car around every sinuous bend, on the road to Kyles Scalpay.

It transpires that a bus will connect with our return ferry crossing from Scalpay at 1400. This will get us back to Tarbert in plenty of time. We have no need to book Wilmonald's services for later in the day and so bid him farewell. His final question is: 'Why do you want to go to Scalpay ?'

'Well it's there, isn't it?'

'It certainly is,' he grins. We pay him the £5 he asks for and away he spins back to Tarbert. We still do not know what kind of car he has.

Kyles Scalpay is nothing more than a concrete slipway. Our next island, Scalpay, lies a few hundred yards across the rocky shore. It is a small island, three miles by one mile, with the surprisingly large population of three hundred – mostly crofters. My Ordnance Survey map shows no mention of a hotel or pub and my main concern is how far the 'village' is from the slipway. And where will we find this Mrs McTavish? The lady who will 'see us right'.

We sit on the slipway at Kyles Scalpay, basking in the sun and watching, somewhat enviously, the local constabulary eat his lunch. With a splutter the ferry scurries across the narrow sound to get us. It is the *Canna,* another of the 'Island class' vessels. This one is new to us however. We have never seen her before, let alone sail on her. We get on and are immediately joined by the chattering contents of the school bus who come running gleefully down the slipway onto the little ship. Gibbie ignores them, he is searching the car-deck for yellow lines to see if they match up with those on the turntable. To his disappointment there are none on this ship.

On the five-minute crossing I engage the deck crewman in conversation. 'Is there anywhere to get a cup of tea on Scalpay?'

He hesitates. 'Yes, there's Mrs McTavish.'

'Where will we find her?' I ask.

'Just ask in the village, you'll find her,' he says confidently.

'How far is the village?' I ask apprehensively.

'Oh, it's just about a mile.'

Gibbie's face falls. I explain to him that this is an adventure. He is not impressed.

We set foot for the first time on Scalpay and stride out for the village and the elusive Mrs McTavish. A minibus has arrived to collect the school children but as it crawls past us the driver chooses not to notice Gibbie's pained, foot-sore expression. I picture him sitting in it surrounded by fifteen children, but it is not to be.

There is a homely, secure, comfortable feel about the island that makes me immediately like it. The houses and public buildings are neat and well maintained – giving it a smaller, more affluent appearance than some of the islands we have visited. It is home to an attractive array of double-glazed cottages and re-roofed bungalows. Each one seems to be set at a different angle from its neighbour. We peer at each dwelling, searching for the name – McTavish. No joy. We walk on.

The one spoiling feature of the island is the amount of metallic litter lying around haphazardly – at the side of the road, in gardens, on the rocky shores. The remains of a ship's superstructure lies in an attractive little inlet, the rusty boiler lying beside it.

The road twists and turns around the various dwellings. The overall scene is a very attractive one.

Stop at the village shop. The magnanimous owner seems sympathetic to our quest to find Mrs McTavish. He kindly offers us a cup of tea and even tries to organise a lift for us to her house. We settle for being pointed in the right direction. Just another five minutes, he assures. He bellows after us, 'I'll phone and tell her to put the kettle on. What kind of sandwiches do you want?' In the heat of the midday sun Gibbie is past caring.

We happen upon the McTavish dwelling. An attractive cottage, double-glazed and re-roofed with a neat privet hedge enclosing the front, lawned garden. There is a *B n' B* sign hanging outside and beneath it is written *Teas.* Mrs McTavish is also well-rounded and smiling. She welcomes us warmly, and shows us into her front room.'I thought there were three of you?'

I gesticulate to the road outside where Gibbie, who has been lagging a few hundred yards behind us, turns up the path and then appears at the door, panting and mopping his brow with a handkerchief.

'This wasn't one of your better ideas, Stuart,' he growls.

Mrs McTavish seems sympathetic. 'Would you like the fire on?'

Gibbie collapses into an armchair in incredulity. Our hostess hurries off at Hebridean speed to muster up some lightly peppered tomato sandwiches and some tea.

We are left to look at the surroundings which we have toiled so hard to reach. It looks like anyone's granny's best room. Immaculately clean with display cabinets full of china and assorted crystal glasses. Framed photographs, the older ones hand-coloured, show the McTavish family in various stages of development; in nappies, at the altar, clutching university diplomas. It is very homely but I can't help feeling that we are intruding.

The lightly peppered tomato sandwiches and tea are delicious, as we knew they would be. It is a strange feeling, having travelled all the way from Glasgow, to be sitting in this elderly lady's front room, sipping tea. We could easily sit here all day but we now only have forty minutes in which to get back to the ferry for the 1400 sailing. We bid farewell to Mrs McTavish. Little does she know how hard we have tried to seek her out. Even Gibbie is by now agreeing that the effort was worth it.

On the way we pass the shop where the chap rushes out to ask us how we had fared at Mrs. McTavish's. 'Was everything OK? Were the sandwiches nice?'

At the slipway we prepare to leave Scalpay with the impression that the people here try hard to look after their visitors, no matter how brief their visit.

A line of cars are waiting to board the *Canna*. At the head of the queue is the mobile Bank of Scotland van. For once our ship is late in departing, but only because Gibbie decides to cash a cheque just as it is about to drive on to the ferry. The drivers of the cars behind it are looking out of their windows.

Gibbie has chosen this moment to perform an important ritual of Island Hopping. Normally I have to pay for just about everything – tickets, accommodation, fares, lunches etc. I have to keep a tally of who owes me what. Then the moment of reconciliation finally arrives, usually after a bit of prompting followed by the necessary coercion and I am reimbursed by my two colleagues. So although Gibbie has picked a bad moment to replenish his wallet, I am loathe to intervene as he can now replenish mine. While all this is going on, Ian is securing our next line of advance. This comes in the shape of an elderly woman from Campbeltown who has just driven onto the ferry. We seem to be having quite a rapport with elderly ladies. She has also experienced tea at Mrs McTavish's and having found common ground with us is willing to offer us a lift back to Tarbert. This will save us a half hour wait for the bus and she does not have to offer twice. In return for her kindness we pay her ferry fare as we are now flush since Gibbie's visit to the bank. Her car waits at Kyles Scalpay. In we pile, three total strangers amidst the wilds of Harris but she doesn't seem to mind. With Gibbie in the front seat we race off at a speed that has me grabbing to engage the seat-belt. The little lady (we forget to ask her name) is a bit of an Island-hopper herself. She explains her travels to us in a continuous monologue which only stops when we are on an elevated stretch of road above a little lochan. She pulls up sharply, on a bend.

'Do you mind if I just get out to take a photograph of this lovely loch?'

'That's OK.'

'I'd better remember to put the handbrake on.' She gets out of her seat and the car lurches forwards nearer the edge as she forgets to put the gears into neutral.

Once she is out on the road Gibbie turns round to Ian and me huddled in the back seat: 'We were a bit close to the edge a few times there, lads,' he says reassuringly. And we still have three miles to go.

Back at Tarbert, which we eventually reach in one piece, we have more time than usual for a decent look around. It is a mish-mash of fairly substantial buildings assembled along the eastern shores of East Loch Tarbert. There are a few shops and a hotel, which is at the far end of the village. I tempt Gibbie and we stride off for it, with more than tea in our minds. The hotel is situated on a narrow isthmus of land which separates West and East Lochs (yes, King Magnus was here as well).

The Presbyterian image that one associates with Harris and its neighbour Lewis seems to be in evidence. Several men we have seen today have been formally attired in black suits with white shirts and black ties. The townsmen certainly dress smartly here. The manager of the hotel looks the same. He is similarly dressed with a weather-beaten, tanned face. His expression is solemn and yet welcoming. As we sip a beer in the hotel garden he barks instructions in Gaelic to his gardener whose face is even more tanned and weather-beaten. 'My, how smartly and formally dressed these Harris people are.' I comment to Ian. It is only when we get back to the pier later that I discover that the townsfolk have been to a funeral this morning.

We move around the bay for a photo-call of the incoming *Hebridean Isles*. It is then a quick jaunt round to reach the ship before she departs. It really has been an energetic day. The ship sails on time at 1610.

The *Hebridean Isles* is fast becoming my favourite ship. Comfortable accommodation in various lounges and a view over the bow. But Ian has some problems with her. He recently impressed a group of friends by telling them about his travels around the numerous islands of the west coast of Scotland aboard her. He was surprised at the degree to which their envious curiosity extended, until he discovered that he had been referring to her as the *Hebridean Princess*! In fact Gibbie and I are of the opinion that Ian is in need of some ship identification lessons. At a recent seminar promoting the concept of 'Total Quality in Business' the lecturer showed a slide of one of CalMac's newest ships and commented on the poor standard of lettering on her side. Ian spoke up and commented that the real problem was one of quantity as she couldn't carry the loads for which she was specified due to a design fault and had subsequently to be lengthened at the expense of her builders. This, he explained, was the reason for the poor spacing of her lettering. The lecturer was very impressed and would offer this explanation at future seminars. It was only when he returned home that Ian realised that the photograph on the screen was of the *Lord of the Isles* and not the lengthened *Isle of Mull*.

We arrive back at Uig at 1800 and watch the ship leave, heading for Tarbert again. Gibbie tries yet again to capture a rear-end on film. A lady with a very large one is just strolling past but it is the ship's rear-end that he is interested in. Ian meanwhile obligingly brings the car up the pier to save Gibbie the long march down what is one of the longest piers in the Hebrides. He has, after all, had a very active day.

We take full advantage of having a car and of being in no particular rush, by driving through the bizarre Quiraing rock formations of Trotternish, at the north of Skye instead of taking the more direct route to our hotel for the night, which is at Broadford. As we drive eastwards across Trotternish the land quite suddenly falls away below us creating the awe-inspiring and fabulous chasm of the Quiraing. Phallic, rocky pinnacles with such quixotic and fanciful names as the Prison, the Needle and the Table rise up from a valley floor which is hundreds of feet lower on the eastern side of Trotternish than it is on the west. This has to be one of the most amazing views in Scotland.

Suitably impressed, we carry on towards Broadford on the south-eastern coast of Skye. Here, our hotel puts me in mind of *Fawlty Towers,* although I don't quite see the funny side of it. I head for the pay-phone, only to find it missing and its wires dangling from the wall. My shower can only run cold and the floor of Gibbie's room rises alarmingly towards the window. Ian has a kettle and tea-making facilities but no teaspoon. Gibbie has a kettle and teaspoon but no place to plug it in. We dump our bags and head off for another hotel, a mile along the road, for a bar meal, and a cup of tea.

When we return to our woodchip dormitory for the night the private car-park is empty save for another Citroen XM. Ian parks his XM right alongside, despite having half an acre of car-park to choose from. An hour later, as I lie in bed, there is much giggling from the car-park as the XM's occupants return – at least I presume that the car confusion is the cause of such merriment.

Day Three – *A Hash of a Dash*

Breakfast – in the 'Breakfast Room'. Where else. This exhibits another dangerous-looking slope to its floor which almost has my scrambled eggs falling off my plate. Down to settle our bill and the girl who served us breakfast is lying back with her feet up on a nearby table drawing heavily on a cigarette and watching TV from a set on the other side of the room which is blaring out at full volume. Our empty glasses from last night's 'night-cap' lie untouched on the table where we had sat.

'I thought you were staying two nights,' she exclaims. Heaven forbid.

It is a gloomy, misty morning as we drive southwards towards Armadale, at the southern end of the island. The car has been booked on the 0915 sailing out of Mallaig on the *Iona*. Although this is one of CalMac's oldest vessels I am surprised to discover that Gibbie and Ian have never sailed on her. When they see her close up they can understand why. She is not exactly the Helen of Troy of the West Coast shipping scene.

It is now decision time – and we manage to take the wrong one. Due to the disappointingly overcast weather coupled with the news that we will not actually be able to set foot on any of the Small Isles, except Canna, we decide to abandon our cruise on the *Lochmor* out of Mallaig. Instead, after crossing to Mallaig on the *Iona* we will make a hasty run for Oban, catch the noon sailing to Craignure, take a bus to Tobermory and sail back to Oban on the *Lord of the Isles*. Standing as we are on Armadale pier this seems an excellent alternative idea but we will require a speedy crossing to the mainland and an even speedier drive down the notoriously 'slow' road to Fort William.

The first part is going well, *Iona* cuts a swift passage to Mallaig and as Ian drives us off we are pleased to be one of the first cars disembarked. We now have two hours and ten minutes to get the one hundred miles to Oban in time for our noon sailing and we speed off with optimistic enthusiasm.

Half an hour down the tortuous, narrow road towards Fort William the optimism has evaporated and the enthusiasm for the excellent idea hatched on Armadale pier is somewhat less appealing. We have never seriously interfered with our Island Hop agenda before while on the road and with good reason. The plans are carefully prepared in advance, investigating all possibilities, calculating journey times, to ensure that all sailing times can be reached, attained, achieved. Unfortunately I have forgotten that this change of plan was considered at the planning stage and dismissed at that time as being impractical.

Ian is making a valiant attempt but the condition of the road and the need to pull over to allow oncoming traffic to pass us is hindering our progress. Still, Ian pushes us onwards unflinchingly.

Past Fort William the road improves and we pick up speed in an effort to make up time. When I look at my watch for the umpteenth time since leaving Mallaig I remember why I dismissed this idea at the planning stage.

We near Oban but the chances of making our ship are looking slimmer by the minute. No other sailing will do, our plans will only work if we make the noon sailing. Ironically the mist that made us change our plans in the first place is lifting and the sun is starting to shine through. As one gloom lifts, inside the car another is settling.

We arrive in Oban ten minutes too late, the *Isle of Mull* is turning around the northern end of Kerrera on her outward journey and we are feeling deflated and just a little silly for trying this madcap dash.

What now. Lunch is the first thing on the agenda. We buy sandwiches and set off with new plans for reaching a new island. We will go to Kerrera. We gave it a body swerve in 1991 but today we will make amends and finally get there. This will assuage our disappointment at not attaining the 'Small Isles'.

The ferry point to this non-CalMac island is two miles south of Oban. At the crossing point, however, there is no sign of the ferry or the ferryman. We sit around for a while watching the water lap up onto an empty slipway and stare across at this very green-looking island, so tantalisingly within our reach but still half a mile away across the sound. Eventually we decide that as well as not going to Canna, we are not going to Kerrera either.

Before heading back to Oban we can see the *Claymore* sailing northwards on her crossing from Colonsay. What if we sail back to Kennacraig on her via Colonsay and Islay? We toy with this idea. It seems an attractive way to end Island Hop 1992, although the arrival back at the Kintyre base at Kennacraig will be late and will entail a hundred-mile drive home afterwards. When I ask at the CalMac office about the possibilities of taking the car from Oban to Kennacraig, the chap behind the desk looks at me in puzzlement.

'Kennacraig is also on the mainland – you can drive there in two hours!'

He has obviously never been Island Hopping.

'It will also cost £64 for the car!' This has a deterrent effect.

The 1400 sailing by *Isle of Mull* to Craignure has to suffice until we can think of anything better to do. Planning the last day of an Island Hop while actually on the Island Hop is not easy to do objectively.

We climb onto the rear deck of the *Isle of Mull* as she sails out into the Bay past Kerrera, the island that 'might have been'. From out in the Bay we get excellent views of the *Claymore,* the ship that 'might have been'.

The *Isle of Mull* is sparsely populated and the restaurant empty but for three lost souls hunched over their soups and reflecting over a day that should have been better.

We don't bother to get off at Craignure and, on our return to Oban, head back down to the Kerrera ferry to have another go. This time the ferry, a small exposed motor boat, is at the slipway. We ask the ferryman if he could ignore his published timetable and take us over to Kerrera and straight back again – just to claim another island. But even the £6 fare does not tempt him and so Kerrera becomes a bogey island, never to be included in an Island Hop itinerary again. Gibbie wants to go further – we've never to mention the name of the place again.

We decide to head for home but our sailing is not over yet. If we drive down through Inveraray we can turn off for Dunoon and cross over to Gourock. As there is plenty of time for all this we do the only sensible thing and adjourn to Auley's Bar to view the famed collection of steamer photographs on its walls.

Inside I count one hundred and twenty-four pictures reputedly depicting every steamer that has ever called at Oban over the decades. There is no sign of the Kerrera ferry among them.

The seventy-odd miles to Dunoon are driven by Gibbie. It is an uneventful drive apart from giving me my first ever view of the Holy Loch on the Clyde without the American presence that has dominated the scene since the 1960s. All submarines, supply vessels and the Mother ship from the much environmentally vilified and ultimately, much economically appreciated, naval base departed some weeks ago. Row upon row of empty semi-detached houses stand as a legacy to the American domination of the area that seemed permanent and synonymous with the Holy Loch. At Dunoon the long column of star-spangled taxis is also gone. The end of the Cold War has had its drawbacks for the Cowal peninsula.

There is time for a quick coffee in an equally empty Italian cafe before joining the *Saturn* for the 1835 sailing to Gourock. Just like last year our journey ends with the unglamorous car-ferry from Dunoon to Gourock. The carousel manoeuvring at Gourock pier is, however, still of interest.

On the way home a visit to James Watt dock in Greenock reveals the *Pioneer* hiding there, languishing in her sedentary role as spare vessel. Like us she is well travelled but our paths have yet to cross. Perhaps we'll get a chance to sail on her on a future Island Hop.

We had now seen every one of CalMac's major ships during the course of our journey, with the exception of the *Isle of Arran*.

On reflection many bits of this Hop were great fun. The long sails on the *Suilven* and the glorious weather made it memorable. The car had given us welcome flexibility – perhaps too much. Now that the *Iona* and the *Suilven* have been conquered we might return to our more traditional circular route for next year. But no Kerrera. Oops, did I mention it?

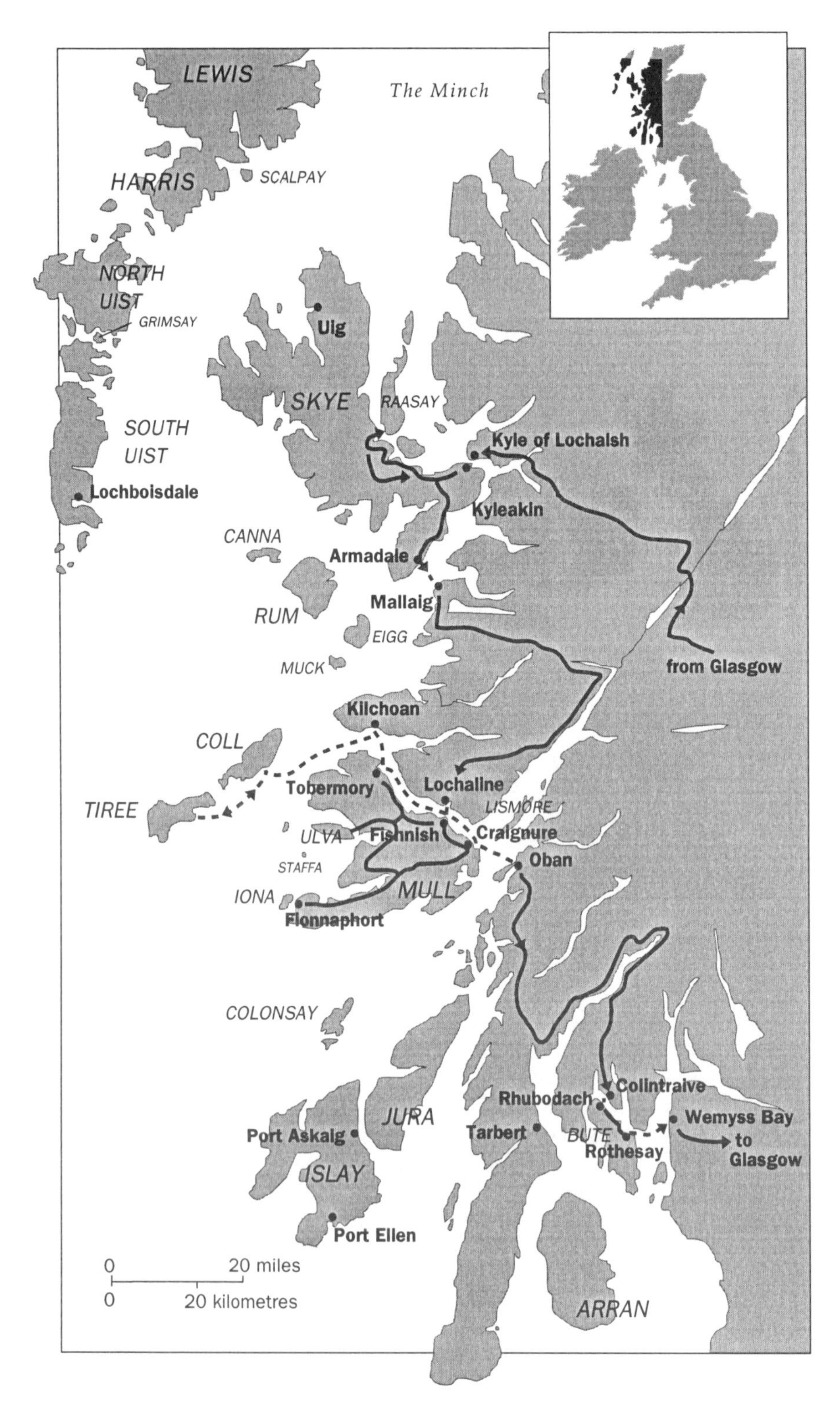
LEWIS
The Minch
HARRIS
SCALPAY
NORTH
UIST
GRIMSAY
Uig
SKYE
RAASAY
SOUTH
UIST
Lochboisdale
Kyle of Lochalsh
Kyleakin
CANNA
Armadale
Mallaig
RUM
EIGG
MUCK
from Glasgow
Kilchoan
COLL
Tobermory
Lochaline
TIREE
LISMORE
ULVA
Fishnish
Craignure
STAFFA
Oban
IONA
MULL
Fionnaphort
COLONSAY
Colintraive
Rhubodach
JURA
Wemyss Bay
Port Askaig
Tarbert
BUTE
Rothesay
to
Glasgow
ISLAY
Port Ellen
0
20 miles
0
20 kilometres
ARRAN

1993 Mull Meanderings

The Plan

The original plan, this year, was to leave the car at home and follow a circular route on the basis of our 1990 trip to Arran, Islay and the Outer Isles. With the new *Caledonian Isles* coming on to the Arran route and the *Isle of Arran* being moved to the Islay station there would be opportunities for sailing on and photographing new ships in new ports.

We learnt, however, that the new ship would not come into service until late Summer 1993 and therefore our plans were shelved.

The revised aim of the 1993 trip, then, was to try to reach the 'new' islands of Raasay, Coll and Tiree and, for Ian, Staffa and Iona. The difficulty in attaining these, however, without using a car to connect between the various mainland ports proved insurmountable and the car became an essential part of our trip.

Although the original ideal of 'Island Hopping' was to travel purely by public transport, it was becoming obvious that there are places that would be impossible to reach without our own vehicle in the three days that we allow ourselves. The alternative was to take a month for the trip but then our careers and marriages would both be in jeopardy.

This year we used the car to very good effect, travelling out to Skye and then working our way back south on a trip that was essentially Mull based. Overnight stops this year were at Sligachan on Skye and, unusually, two nights at the same place – Tobermory on Mull. The car was Ian's new Audi 80 and the dates of our trip were Sunday 16 May to Wednesdsay 19 May 1993 inclusive.

Of added interest this year was the fact that we recorded our trip on video for the first time. This was then edited into a travelogue film – of the Alan Whicker genre, only we had to make do with me presenting it. The filming of this trip and the other trips to follow, would add a new dimension to Island Hopping. It turned me into Michael Palin for four days and Ian and Gibbie into nervous wrecks whenever the camera or notebook were produced.

Day One – *Kiwi Pakora and trout*

I met up with Gibbie at lunch-time on the Sunday to check that Ian had arrived in Glasgow and to decide on a departure time. Ian had indeed arrived, the night before, and departure time was set at 1415 that day.

'By the way,' I asked, 'what colour is Ian's new car?'

'Dark bluish,' Gibbie replied. At 14.10 Gibbie phones. 'Are you ready? Good, we're just leaving. Oh, by the way, Ian's car is grey.'

At 14.20 they arrive at my front door. Ian's car is green. Within five minutes we are on our way, with me at the wheel on the start of Island Hop 1993 – number five – and at the beginning of one hundred and seventy-eight miles to Kyle of Lochalsh.

Our route takes us over the Erskine Bridge, up the west side of Loch Lomond to Crianlarich, through Glen Coe, past Fort William and turning west in the Great Glen at Invergarry. Crianlarich, Ian and Gibbie inform me, is the birthplace of Pontius Pilate. I am somewhat dubious about this as they are always coming out with these esoteric facts which they know I cannot argue with. Where do they get them from?

On past Lochs Garry, Cluanie and Duich and down into Kyle of Lochalsh. Our estimated time of arrival is . . . *stop*! I'm beginning to sound like an airline pilot.

By the time we reach Fort William we are keen to stop for a cup of coffee and a break from Gibbie's Cajun music which is driving Ian and me mad, especially as he is trying to sing along to it. After all, this is the Scottish Highlands *not* the Everglades.

We try the same cafe as last year. Just like last year it is closing. A brief pause to decide whether or not to purchase a new cap, it might look good on the Video, (I decide not to) and we are on our way again. At Invergarry, where we turn off the main road through the Great Glen towards Inverness, we encounter a small tea-room at the side of the road and I pull over. Out comes the video-camera for the first of the day's 'shoots'. I want to film my colleagues entering the tea-room. Gibbie is full of the right kind of advice for Ian: 'walk slowly, act normally.' As he says this he trips over the threshold.

Despite the time of year (mid May) the mountains and hills still show a considerable dusting of snow – more than I can recall seeing before on an Island Hop trip. As we climb above the still waters of Loch Garry another stop is imperative to film the view that greets us. The yellow-tinted mountains of the southern shores are bathed in sunshine and resemble a row of huge rock buns sprinkled with icing sugar. Peculiarly, or perhaps fancifully, the loch is shaped like a map of Scotland itself, and the beauty around it is reflected in its waters. A large gull flies over and drops a plop of excrement onto the giant map. 'That's just where Kilmarnock is,' comments Gibbie. Kilmarnock is where Gibbie works and it has a special place in his heart.

On to Kyle, still in sparkling sunshine. Will it ever rain again on an Island Hop? (Unfortunately the answer to this is *yes*, as we are about to find out.) We arrive at 1900 and instead of dashing onto the awaiting ferry over to Skye we decide that there is much to see on this side of the Sound of Sleat.

That luxury cruise ship which follows us around wherever we go, the *Hebridean Princess,* is berthed at the pier on another of her 'quiet' overnight stops. Nearby CalMac's *Loch Dunvegan* is tied up, redundant. At the small railway station a Class 37 diesel locomotive with the name *Oor Wullie* heads a small rake of green and white tourist coaches.

We stroll up the pier to examine the *Hebridean Princess* at close range. This is our closest yet view of her – so we take full advantage and have a good ogle.

It looks every bit the Hebridean haven of high-class hedonism. Tuxedo-clad, middle-aged gentlemen stroll on deck, clutching glasses of their favourite malt, totally oblivious to our stares. Their cruise is the ultimate in style and expense but somehow I rather like the way we do it.

Looking north of Kyle a couple of large cranes signal the commencement of work on the already infamous Skye Bridge. Due to be opened in 1995, its concrete span will soon bisect this beautiful view as it leap-frogs across the small islets to the Island of Skye itself. When it is completed the old verse over the Sea to Skye may not quite have the same romance to it.

The *Locy Fyne* is approaching and it is time to drive the car on to her and cross over to our first island. I was hoping it would be the *Loch Dunvegan* in service as we could then have added another new vessel to our Island Hop grand total. The five-minute crossing is a delight in the warm evening sunshine. This is likely to be our last ever crossing from Kyle of Lochalsh on a ferry.

Soon we are driving speedily northwards through Skye towards Sligachan to the music of Schubert's 'Trout'. The scenery around the Sligachan Hotel is so compelling to the camera that we spend twenty minutes filming and photographing the surrounding mountains before checking in.

The pyramidal, dusty Red Cuillins, and the jagged, Black Cuillins, come together at Sligachan and this is a popular assembly point for hill-walkers, mountaineers and campers.

The hotel has a purpose-built bar/diner, serving food up to eleven o'clock at night – enabling any lost hill-walker or Island Hopper who stumbles back to civilisation later than planned the chance of a good meal. We sample some Sligachan Real Ale, actually brewed by Belhaven, and vote it so excellent that we have to have another. Ian enjoys it so much that he won't allow me to tell how many he has. After being on the road for six hours it is particularly refreshing.

A mouth-watering menu, neatly displayed on a blackboard, becomes the subject of our perusal. Gibbie adjusts his modern Hank Marvin spectacles and announces that he fancies the Kiwi Pakora. Marvelling at the prospect of a unique blend of antipodean and Indian cuisine I turn to check the blackboard again.

'Kiwi Pavlova, Gibbie ! Put your old specs on.'

For me the subliminal effect of Schubert's music influences my choice.

Day Two – *Rain, Showers & Drizzle*

We wake to mist, drizzle and the call of a cuckoo echoing from a group of trees across the river from the hotel. After yesterday's beautiful weather we are struggling to conceal our disappointment.

Kippers for breakfast. This year it is me who is on the piscine diet. We have the usual calculation and confusion about who paid what towards our accommodation, subtracting whichever deposit from whomsoever's account, dividing it by three and adding on the number we first thought of. All this in front of an ever-smiling hostess. You would think we could have come up with a better formula by now. Then, we are in the car for the short drive to Sconser where we should catch the ferry to our next island, Raasay.

The 'Island class' ferry serving Raasay is named after the island it serves. We have sailed on the *Morven, Coll, Canna* and *Eigg*. The *Bruernish, Rhum* and the *Raasay* are unconquered, as yet. Noisy and ugly, the *Raasay* may be but she is ideally suited to serving the smaller islands where she can simply run up on to a concrete ramp, or beach. The light drizzle is persistent as we leave the car at Sconser and walk on board for the fifteen-minute crossing to an island that is new to us.

We had originally intended spending a couple of hours on Raasay but discovered that the hotel was a mile from the ferry slip. I had divulged this some weeks ago to Gibbie and received a look that I hadn't seen since our trek to Mrs McTavish's cottage on Scalpay last year. I had decided to discreetly change our sailing times and forget the idea of lunch at the Raasay Hotel. This turns out to be a fortuitous change of plan as the rain is now streaming down over the island ahead of us. Not the kind of weather for trekking – unlike our visit to Scalpay last year. By paying only the briefest of visits to Raasay we can open up further sailing opportunities later in the day.

The most interesting features that we can see on Raasay, as we approach the slipway, is a collection of small ruined, stone buildings situated just above the substantial pier. These turn out to be the ruins of an iron ore mine which was still in production in the 1920's. A crewman aboard the ferry produces a guide book which describes the history of the mine in considerable detail. It was worked by German prisoners of war during the last years of the First World War and the years immediately following.

Thirty of them succumbed to the influenza epidemic which reached the island in 1919. Their remains are buried on Raasay. The iron ore mine is the first of a trilogy of mining activities that we are to encounter during our travels today.

After the most fleeting of visits to Raasay we make our way back to its larger sister, Skye. Raasay is our furthest point from Glasgow at exactly two hundred miles. From now on we will be working our way back – with a few sideways diversions on the way.

We reach the shores of Skye at 1010 and set off through the lush 'garden' of Skye towards Armadale in plenty of time for the noon sailing back to the mainland.

Armadale is the scene of Gibbie's favourite craft shop. He volunteers this little ditty to us in a manner which gives more than a hint of a suggestion that he is being facetious, but he takes a bit of coaxing to explain why it secures such a firm place in his memory. He first visited it a few years back with Janette and admits, with a rueful sigh of resignation, that he once paid £300 for a cup of coffee. The coffee was only 60p but the ensuing purchases of woollen garments made a hole in his Visa account.

There is much activity at Armadale pier. Work has begun on building a linkspan for the ferry connection with Mallaig. This is the last CalMac route served by a major unit of the fleet which still uses a hoist to load the vehicles

– but not for much longer. A large mechanical digger, precariously perched upon a floating pontoon, is dredging up the sea bed fifty yards offshore and emptying the contents of its huge bucket onto an attending barge. With forty minutes before the ferry arrives and with the rain still torrential we choose not to hang around the pier and retreat to a nearby cafe.

Originally booked on the 1500 sailing from Armadale we have advanced our crossing time by three hours (as we had not lingered on Raasay) and over a coffee we plan our next moves. Once on the mainland at Mallaig we can either drive sixty miles to Kilchoan on the Ardnamurchan Peninsula and sail over directly to Tobermory on Mull, or we can drive seventy miles to Lochaline and cross to Fishnish on Mull. Whichever ferry route we choose we will have time to do an excursion return sailing on the other ferry later in the afternoon. We consider that if we cross from Kilchoan the prospect of a drive down to Fishnish and crossing over and back on the ferry there will seem less appealing. So, it is unanimously decided to drive the longer route to Lochaline and on eventually reaching Tobermory we can have a trip on the Kilchoan vessel, if we still feel like it. Overall it means less driving on Mull.

We make our way back to the pier just as our next ship the *Iona* is berthing. Ian loads the car while Gibbie and I watch from the deck as the hoist painstakingly unloads and reloads a dozen or so vehicles. It reminds me of the scenes on Rothesay pier back in the sixties when the car-ferries *Bute* and *Cowal* were in operation. They used to load their vehicles in this manner and it seemed to take an eternity. The only enjoyable bit was when the crewman spun the car around on the turntable.

CalMac's oldest ship is looking fairly spruce. Her galley is reputed to serve the best food of the fleet and as we pull away from Armadale pier we repair to the restaurant to see if this is true. We don't see any Egon Ronay signs but the tomato soup is freshly made and not the homogeneous orange tinned variety. *Iona* crosses the Sound of Sleat in just over eighteen minutes, on what is timetabled as a half- hour crossing. With me driving, we were soon on our way down the tortuous road towards Fort William. Unlike last year, time is now on our side as we have no particular ferry time to meet. It is just as well, for yet again we encounter a large truck ahead of us and become trapped behind it. Ian swears it is the same one as last year.

We turn off the A830 Mallaig to Fort William road at Lochailort on to the A861, across Moidart, along twisting single-track roads and through the villages of Acharacle and Salen. All but nine miles of the seventy mile journey is on single-track roads, but the traffic is light.

On the northern shores of Loch Sunart, a long sea loch that separates the peninsulas of Ardnamurchan and Morven, we happen upon the village of Strontian. This is where the element strontium 89 (not the radioactive isotope) was discovered last century; a soft, silvery-white element, similar to the alkaline earth metals, whose radioactive isotope 90 is used in nuclear power sources. Enough of the chemistry lesson. We stop the car at the Information Bureau and go in to see if we can find a sample.

The ample lady in attendance is sympathetic but clean-out of strontium today. She seems very interested in our journey and the filming of it.

'When you complete the film will you sell it ?' she politely enquires. If only I could. She seems so interested in our journey that Ian wants to take her along with us. Outside we film Gibbie holding a grey pebble from the car park at arm's length. Well – nobody would ever know.

On again. Another twenty miles of single track road across the higher plateau of Morven and we arrive safely at the small settlement at Lochaline. We are in plenty of time to catch the 1515 sailing to Mull.

This is our first time at the 'back-door' sea-route to Mull. Despite the long drive the sailing will only take fifteen minutes.

At the pier is a small coaster carrying silica sand, which is mined locally (our third mineral today). But what really catches our eye is the red and white canvas awning of 'Jean's Tea Bar'. Gibbie has read in the *Glasgow Herald* of the delights of Jean's cuisine and warmly recommends it. In fact he is almost beside himself with joy at having come across it and rushes off to tell Jean herself just how famous she is. He is very disappointed to find that the lady serving is not actually Jean but she soon has our order sizzling away on the hot-plate in any case. I opt for a 'Barge Special' – a cocktail of black pudding, bacon and sliced tomato in a bun. Health food the Lochaline way. It is made all the more delicious for eating it under canvas, looking out at the rain bouncing off the ground a mere two feet away.

We are still munching away when the ferry *Isle of Cumbrae* arrives. This open-ended craft, a new Island Hop vessel for us, and a precursor of the 'Loch class' of small ferries is used to serve Largs and Cumbrae. It was built in 1977 and its name was the winning entry of a competition held amongst the school-children of Cumbrae to christen the new ferry. I hope their teachers gave them ten out of ten for originality! Like any ferry given a geographical name it all sounds out of place when the vessel moves on to serve a different island. With foresight they could have called her the *Isle of Somewhere up the West Coast*. She now plies this increasingly popular route to Mull which is particularly useful in stormy weather when it can be the only means of getting to and from the island when the Oban ship is stormbound, as happened quite frequently last winter.

We drive on board and seek shelter in the small saloon from the incessant rain. Why on earth did we ever wonder if we'd ever see rain again?

Gibbie gets chatting to one of the crew – like he does – who is holding a bright yellow object resembling a flash-gun. Apparently he counts the number of passengers boarding, enters it on the instrument and points at a similar device situated on a pole beside the concrete slipway. This electronically logs the number of people on board – thus leaving a record on shore of the number of victims to search for, should the ship sink. There is obviously nothing to be gained in the captain knowing how many passengers and crew he has if he goes down with the ship. This device saves having an extra crewman ashore. I suggest that the crew should merely leave word with Jean at her Tea Bar.

We leave the murky mainland behind and eighteen minutes later we are crossing the misty moors of Mull on our way to Tobermory.

The island capital is a familiar destination. We were here in 1991 and this time have elected to stay in the same hotel – the Harbour House. Uniquely, we will be booking in for two nights and it is decided by ballot that I should share with Gibbie, which is to say that I lost the ballot. Before checking-in, however, we have yet another sailing to catch – our fourth today. We are in nice time to take the 1630 crossing aboard the *Coll* to Kilchoan, returning immediately. The *Bruernish* is spare vessel at the moment and is moored amongst the yachts in the Bay, minus a name on her bow. She has recently been superseded on her Gigha route by the larger *Loch Ranza*.

We park the car at the water front in Tobermory and before joining the others on board the *Coll,* I telephone home. All is well. My youngest daughter Fiona has had her booster injection today. 'It was nothing,' she says, 'just a wee spot.' I hurry aboard to reassure the others.

We have sailed on the *Coll* before but this time we are accompanied by a dozen nylon-clad German cyclists. They fill the small saloon on the ship so I choose to shelter from the rain and surf underneath the overhanging ramp. When it becomes too cold I, too, seek warmer cover. It is a grey crossing but still enjoyable if only for the occasional bounce as the little ship is hit by a large wave. In the corner of the cabin a weather-beaten, gnarled-faced crewman is sitting reading the *Business Herald.*

We disembark our cycle companions at Kilchoan thirty-five minutes later. I cannot help feeling a little sorry for them as they peddle off in silence onto a sodden Ardnamurchan peninsula, which we ourselves had driven across a mere two and a half hours ago. Such is the complexity of Island Hop routes. Gibbie doesn't feel sorry for them at all.

We have more space in the saloon on the return crossing. Out to the north-west the sky is brightening and the *Lord of the Isles* can be seen silhouetted against a buff tinted sky on her way out towards Lochboisdale on South Uist. To her left we can see the low hillocks of the Island of Coll, our target island for Wednesday.

Back to our own *Coll*, we chat to Simon – the youngest crewhand aboard. He is from Tobermory and spends most of his shifts on this vessel. He enjoys the occasional trip to the Clyde but admits the busy summer season is the best: 'There's more talent!'

I offer to buy him a drink tonight in the Mishnish Bar in exchange for him letting me film our conversation. He accepts. We are ashore, and in the aforementioned Mishnish, just to shelter from the rain you understand, which seems to be getting worse, by 1800. Twenty minutes and one Glendronach later we are checking into the hotel where I am shown to the same room that I occupied on our 1991 trip. The hotel has recently been refurbished and our hosts James and Shona are very welcoming. In fact it is to be an excellent base.

Dinner is in 'The Gannet' restaurant. Gibbie insists on scallops despite my stern reminder that he is sharing a room with me. Washed down with a bottle of Chianti. I am never one to choose the colour of the wine to match the colour of the meal. I produce the camera to film the bottle on the table and Ian shoos it away. 'Don't film this,' he says anxiously. 'My wife thinks we slum-it.'

After dinner I climb the hill above the cramped main street of the town and take some shots of the bay. By now the weather has changed. The rain has stopped, the sun is shining but, more ominously, the cruisers and yachts anchored in the bay are now dancing up and down like marionettes jangled by an unseen hand. The trees around me are shaking and whispering as the strengthening wind whistles across the bay. The whole scene is one of motion and noise and I realise then that if the gathering wind does not subside by tomorrow our planned trip to Staffa, which is very weather dependent, will be in jeopardy.

Back down the hill to the Mishnish where my two companions are chatting about their respective experiences with kidney stones. Their graphic accounts of the 'passing' of their calculi makes me wince. Is this an affliction that all Island Hoppers will eventually suffer from? The next time I go to the toilet it is with considerable trepidation. I believe the best form of prevention is to drink plenty of fluid regularly. We're in the right place.

Before we retire for the night we have to tick our choices for breakfast on small menus laid out in the hall of our hotel. By the time I have filled my menu out Ian has retired for the night. I mischievously change his selection from scrambled eggs to kippers.

Day Three - *Stormy Crossings*

Woken at 0415 with a loud bang outside. Had it been inside I would have blamed Gibbie and his scallops. I sit up. A flash in the sky is followed by a second bang a split second later. Maroons (rocket flares) are being set off to summon the volunteer crew of the lifeboat. Outside, the wind is still howling like a banshee. I feel sympathy for anyone in trouble out there.

Breakfast is large. James serves it to us clad in his painter/decorator apron. The colours on his front match the colours of the seafront of Tobermory. A splash of egg yolk and a dash of tomato sauce complete the colour palette. Ian tucks into his breakfast: 'Mmmm, I glad I picked the kippers, they're smashing.'

Over breakfast I suggest another alteration to our plans – this is turning out to be a 'make it up as we go along' Island Hop. We have to be at Fionnaphort by noon for the sail to Staffa but will have time to tick yet another island on the way if we set off fairly sharply. By driving to Fionnaphort via the west side of Mull we might just manage a return trip to the island of Ulva.

Ulva lies a quarter of a mile off Mull's western shores and is easily reached by a small launch which sails on request. We agree that it should be worth the effort and are on the road by 0900. I note that the lifeboat has returned. (We learn later that it went to the aid of a small coaster off the west coast of Mull – no casualties, thankfully). Ian drives us to Ulva Ferry – more single-track roads – past some spectacular coastal scenery. The wind is still high and the Atlantic waves are dappled with white crests. Staffa, visible in the distance, seems untenably remote.

Neither Ian nor Gibble have ever visited Ulva but I made a trip over last summer with my family to visit friends, Karen and Steven Bell. Steven works at a local fish farm and is a patient of mine. Two weeks after our visit to Ulva he fractured a tooth and had to make the journey down to Glasgow to see me. Today, as we stroll down to the slipway and the awaiting ferry, Steven is propping up a shed door, sheltering from the wind with a cup of coffee clutched in his hand. He looks at me, recognition dawning, 'Oh no, I'm going to get toothache now!'

The 'ferry' was the smallest craft we've ever sailed on in any of our trips. Barely 10 feet long it is a galvanised motor-boat with a tiny sheltered bow. The boatman, Donald, needs all the skill he can muster to keep the boat against the side of the concrete slip as the wind is trying hard to batter the metal hull against the wall. We look at each other apprehensively. Should we really be doing this? Is it worth risking our lives just to trainspot another island? Obviously it is, for we willingly climb aboard and off we bounce across the narrow sound to island number four. Gibbie sits beside Donald to keep the boat balanced while Ian and I crouch in the first class accommodation at the bow. The wreckage from last night's gale is evident around us. A small motor boat lies bobbing, barely afloat, with a foot of water in it. Donald admits to having risen at 4am to drag his boat further up the slipway. The five-minute crossing is rough but exciting. Some care is required to land at the other side.

Ulva is no more than an extension of the volcanic 'trap' landscape of Mull. Its name means 'wolf island' and it measures about five miles by two miles lying east to west. Apart from a lush wooded eastern end, it is a barren lump of volcanic rock. A few families live on the island, mostly involved with fish farming. Various tracks reach out westwards across the island towards its smaller neighbour Gometra. The two islands are linked by a short bridge. Not that we are going to see it today – the walk over Ulva is six rough miles.

Above the jetty is the Boathouse which serves as a cafe downstairs and a museum upstairs. We have about thirty minutes in which to enjoy both aspects.

Donald acts not only as ferryman but as tour guide to the island and as chef in the cafe. He skilfully splits his time between conveying people across from Mull and brewing coffee.

The next boatload after us produces four walkers from Ayrshire. They are dressed for the winter on top and for the summer below – well, the weather can be very changeable! They have tweed caps and green waxed jackets which almost totally hide their shorts in a way that makes them look as though they are wandering about with no trousers on. We have considerable difficulty in determining the gender of one of them. Another of them turns out to be the brother of Gibbie's boss! They're about to head off to find the Gometra bridge.

We have a discussion amongst ourselves in the museum. A change of plan, Staffa doesn't look hopeful and we could, therefore, take the car over to Oban earlier than planned. This would allow us some time in Oban and free up more time to travel home via Bute tomorrow.

Back downstairs in the cafe we signal to Donald that we would like to cross back over to Mull. He is in the middle of brewing coffee but quickly hands the coffee pot to one of the four walkers. 'Eh . . . help yourself, here's the coffee pot.'

Off we bounce again back to Mull across the three hundred yard gap with Gibbie and I clutching our *Ulva potpourri* – presents for our wives. Gibbie sees a sense of the ridiculous in this and can hardly stop laughing all the way back over to Mull.

Back on the big island we have an hour and twenty minutes to drive the single track road to Fionnaphort some forty miles away. Our intention is to reach Fionnaphort by noon – the sailing to Staffa normally leaves at 1215.

Fionnaphort lies at the western tip of a twenty-mile long arm of Mull known as the Ross. From spring to autumn it bustles with tourists of all nationalities planning on crossing to the 'Sacred Isle' of Iona.

When we reach Fionnaphort the news is worse than expected. The mile wide channel between the two islands is being whipped into a frenzy by the near gale force wind. No sailings to Staffa today and possibly no sailings to Iona either. We enquire at the ticket office. The ferry to Iona has not sailed all day but at this moment, the skipper is trying a practice run to see if landing on the Iona side is possible.

Six coaches stand nearby. Their contents – in the form of a couple of hundred middle-aged day trippers – stand around in bewilderment as if they have just landed on Mars.

As we stand in the office the radio crackles into life. It is the skipper of the ferry – the *Loch Buie*. 'Hello – we're at the other side, I think we can make landings okay so long as they don't mind getting their feet wet.'

My imagination immediately produces an image of two hundred silver-haired day trippers standing on the slipway holding their shoes, socks and tights in their hands. Exciting stuff. We skip down to the slipway to film the *Loch Buie* rolling and pitching her way back to get us. She is bobbing about like a plastic duck in a bath of water. The shore staff warn us: 'If any of you are not good sailors, I suggest you stay here.'

White faces around us turn glum, ours beam with delight. This is the stuff that Island Hops are made of. All disappointment about not getting to Staffa is forgotten with the prospect of a really rough ride across to Iona. Mad, isn't it!

The *Loch Buie* is new and is a modification on the usual 'Loch class' ferry. Her car-carrying capacity has been reduced in order to accommodate more foot passengers in comfort. These are the usual cargo for Iona. The skipper pushes her ramp as far up the slipway as he dares and in between the waves that crash over it we are herded aboard in a thin line, with the two hundred and fifty other passengers for company, like the animals embarking on the ark.

In beautiful sunshine we roll in every conceivable direction for the ten minute crossing to Iona and jump back off at the other side, two by two. While 90% of our fellow travellers head for the shops and restaurant to calm their stomachs we seek the solitude of the hotel.

In the serene dining room, we sample bottled beer and mackerel for lunch. Sitting in tranquillity over our excellent meal, looking out at the white wave tops splashing in the sparkling, clear sunshine and watching the ferry pound its way back to Mull we feel like spending the rest of our journey right here.

What a transformation the ferry-loads of visitors must make to this tiny community. The quiescence of the traffic-free village, Baille Mor, can be suddenly overwhelmed by black and white-clad nuns and clergymen, cagoule-clad campers and inappropriately clad Americans clutching cameras and books on genealogy. Despite all this, Iona feels like a very special place.

It is just after 1300. We want to be back an Mull by 1400 in order to dash over to Craignure for the 1500 sailing to Oban. This will allow time on the mainland to deposit the car before taking the last 1800 sailing back to Craignure and the bus to Tobermory. Our sail back is equally exciting and boisterous. I admire the skipper's skilful handling of his vessel – especially once he reaches the slipway.

We hurry ashore, time is precious now but we will have a considerable advantage if we can make Craignure in time for the ferry sailing. Craignure is thirty-seven miles away – across single track roads – and we have less than an hour to do it in. I drive.

The 1500 sailing is the only way we can get the car over to Oban today. And, if we could achieve that, it means that on arriving at Oban off the *Lord of the Isles* tomorrow we can immediately get on our way south as we won't have to collect the car from Craignure. We will have time to cross to Bute instead of merely crossing from Dunoon. This will give us another island and a more attractive route home.

As we speed down the hill into Craignure, the *Isle of Mull* is within three minutes of leaving. It has loaded its passengers and vehicles but its ramp is still down. We race on - without pausing. We have made it – just. Although disappointed about not achieving Staffa, this change of plan has been inspirational and it wasn't even *my* idea!

The sea is calmer on this side of Mull. We amass on deck to film the *Lord of the Isles* as she passes on her way to Castlebay on Barra. She is due to pass us off the tip of Lismore. As we near Kerrera with no sign of 'Lottie' it suddenly occurs to me that she isn't just late in leaving Oban, she isn't there at all! I guess that she has been stormbound out in the Western Isles and as we turn into Oban Bay the absence of tomorrow's ship confirms my fears. If she isn't there she must be stormbound somewhere and what will that do to tomorrow's tight sailing schedule?

Today, though, due to our rescheduling, we are rewarded with an hour and twenty minutes in Oban before heading back over to Mull. Time to park, shop, find out what is happening with our absent ship and visit Aulie's Bar to 'study' the shipping prints on the wall.

We achieve all four of these goals. The good news about the *Lord of the Isles* is that, despite being stormbound at Lochboisdale on South Uist, her trip to Coll and Tiree (with us) tomorrow will go ahead as scheduled. She has cancelled a further Outer Isles sailing this afternoon and is due to arrive several hours late at Oban tonight. Everything seems to be going to our script now, although we have difficulty in understanding it ourselves. We split up in Oban and agree to rendezvous in Aulie's Bar at 1710.

Oban is bustling with people and traffic. It is a culture shock after the peace and tranquillity of Iona and Ulva. It seems like a metropolis. Aulie's Bar seems like a haven and the beer is refreshing, if not the atmosphere. It gives Gibbie an opportunity to clean the dried salt spray from his glasses. He hasn't realised how dirty they are – he just thought that it had been snowing in Oban.

At the pier again for the 1800 sailing back to Craignure, minus the car. Two elderly ladies from Yorkshire are strolling past arm in arm. 'Did you have an awful wind last night?' One asks the other. She must have had the scallops as well. Two policemen are escorting a handcuffed chap off the ferry and into an awaiting police van. Ian is amazed that they are treating him in a friendly manner and have even offered him a cigarette. He thinks that they should be showing him a bit less respect but I reassure him that a cigarette is usually proffered before the prisoner is shot.

We are securely on board the *Isle of Mull* and the ramp is up ready to sail when an Irishman in a state of near panic races up in his car and gesticulates that he wants to board. To his dismay a crewman ushers him away to buy a ticket – thus prolonging his agony. He eventually manages to get on.

An uneventful sail across in weather which is certainly moderating. This is our fourth sailing over to Mull in two days! Anyone would think we like the place. The bus is waiting for us at Craignure – we are the only passengers. Yet again (as in previous Hops) there are no passengers at Fishnish when the bus turns down to the slipway there.

On the ride north we gaze out over the Sound of Mull, looking for the *Lord of the Isles* sailing down to Oban. Roger Whittaker sings mournfully over the speakers about mountains, valleys and streams. Outside, our own geographical features slide quietly by. In the distance, over Morven, a huge black cloud is sweeping southwards, rain streaming beneath it.

Out on the Sound the elusive *Lord of the Isles* at last comes into view, herself sweeping southwards now six hours late on her return from South Uist. At least she can tie-up and have a rest tonight before meeting up with us again at Tobermory tomorrow. It is a tranquil, unhurried scene. Back in the bus Roger is chanting about rain splashing off Midlands motorways in the rush-hour.

In Tobermory, eleven hours and four forms of transport since leaving it, the *Hebridean Princess* has caught up with us and is anchored in the Bay.

At our hotel we chat to James. Ian is telling him about the arrested individual at Oban. 'That is my cousin!' he claims proudly. 'He's probably been arrested for poaching salmon and beating up his wife again.' He says this as if the two vices were somehow inextricably linked. 'He's just served six months for poaching. They'll lock him up again and he'll be out in time for the start of the salmon season.'

Another excellent meal, another bottle of Chianti and a stroll up to the pier, where Gibbie's scallops are being unloaded from a filthy, rusting fishing boat.

We have an early start tomorrow and so our customary visit to the Mishnish is briefer than usual. Tonight, the chat is about hangovers. Gibbie reckons it is the sleep that causes them: 'I always feel great before I go to bed!'

Two men sitting beside us cannot complete a single sentence without venting f . . . at least twice. Gibbie reckons they must be from Kilmarnock.

A phone call home before bed. The Danes have changed their minds and voted *yes* to the Maastricht Treaty. There is something on the News about CalMac being privatised and Tony, my four year old son, has pulled the tail off one of our canaries, again. We pay our bill tonight and arrange breakfast for 0700. Gibbie prepares himself for tomorrow's early start by shaving. It has to be done at night because: 'I'm too puffy in the morning.' We have never noticed any difference.

Day Three - *The Big Blue Hole In The Sky*

I am awake at 0640 – two minutes before the alarm clock sounds. This always happens to me. I don't know why I bother setting it – or indeed have an alarm clock in the first place.

The *Lord of the Isles* is due at Tobermory at 0740, having left Oban almost two hours previously, hopefully.

It is a calm, mild morning and around thirty-five passengers have assembled at the small pier which is dwarfed by the bulk of the *Lord* when she arrives. The *Hebridean Princess, Coll, Bruernish* and a host of yachts and cruisers are at rest in the bay, exhausted after spending all of yesterday bobbing up and down. I film the arrival of the ship at the pier and am attacked by a swarming multitude of biting midges. It is a bit of a shock to my already delicate system.

Our four walkers from Ayrshire are at the pier – still looking as though they have no trousers on.

Five minutes late we purr off, out into the Sound at the start of a seven hour journey and swing round to point our bow north-westwards towards the distant Isle of Coll. To our right the hills of the small isles of Muck, Rum and Eigg are clearly visible – it all sounds like a good breakfast.

Passing Rubha Nan Gall lighthouse to port and Ardnamurchan Point to starboard the low rocky shores of Coll seem close in the best visibility we have experienced so far on our journey. As the north tip of Mull recedes the Treshnish Islands, distant blobs on a hazy sea, pass slowly astern of us.

Rubha Nan Gall has happy memories for me. About half an hour's walk out of Tobermory along a cliff path, it was the scene of a four day camp for myself and three friends back in the scorching heat of summer 1976. Four glorious days spent sunning ourselves, cooking dreadful meals such as spam and boiled rice and watching otters dance in the surf at midnight. Each night we would sit up late in our tents to see who would be the last to fall asleep. We never found out. I remember one afternoon we climbed up onto the bracken-covered slopes above the automatic lighthouse and watched a ship called the *Iona* sailing up the Sound of Mull, unaware that almost two decades later I'd be chasing my tail around the west coast trying to sail on her.

A gentle swell is now apparent and the ship pitches in a quite pleasurable motion. I look at my watch. It is 0830 and I would normally be rushing the children off to school. Instead of the bustle and traffic and schedules to meet all I can hear is the deep purr of the engines and the swish of the sea thrown aside by the bow.

Coll is a new island for Ian and me. As a child I once wrote a story about it, describing it as a wooded plateau with a harbour and glen. Now I that I am about to step foot on it for the first time the contrast between my imagination and reality can hardly be greater; barren, rocky low mounds (too low to be called hills) with no sign of any habitation. The main settlement, Arinagour, and the pier and linkspan come into view – the only features to break the monotonous landscape. There must be more to Coll than this. Unfortunately we will not have time to find out. As the ship will be calling here again on her inward journey she is only stopping for five minutes to allow passengers to disembark. This is nearly Ian's undoing.

As the ship docks Gibbie remains on board while Ian and I disembark. While I go up to the head of the pier to film the ship, Ian strolls off. By the time I have taken a couple of photographs I realise that the gangway is being pulled off the ship. I race down the pier and jump aboard. And then I spot Ian still heading away from the ship oblivious to its immediate departure.

'You can't go yet, one of us is still ashore!' I yell at the crewman.

'Och, we'll get him on the way back.'

'No, you can't! He'll miss Tiree. Ian!' I bawl. At the last minute lan hears my shout and comes gasping up the gangway. The ferry leaves Coll five minutes late and Ian is denied (some might say spared) being the Laird of Coll for two hours.

On now towards Tiree which looks more habitable. Tiree is renowned as being the sunniest place in Britain – and the windiest. Atlantic winds breeze continuously across its flatness. There is an American CIA presence here and numerous crofts dotted across the island. These same Atlantic winds have made Tiree very popular, in recent years, with wind surfers. It is certainly living up to its sunny reputation today but the wind is very light. Gibbie enlightens us to the fact that 'Tiree' means 'blue hole in the sky'. We believe him but it must mean it in Cambodian or Senegalese or something like that as it certainly does not mean that in Gaelic.

We have slightly longer on Tiree – twenty minutes – and this time we tie Ian to a collar and lead. We all go ashore for photographs – taken in glorious sunshine – but the long pier means that we daren't go into the village, Scaranish, itself. If we miss this sailing we couldn't get back to Oban for two days.

What little we see of Tiree (another new island for Ian and me) reminds me of South Uist only with a gentler image. There is certainly quite a contrast between Tiree and Coll, reflected in that the former has around five times the population of the latter.

Off we sail again, now only seven minutes late, at 1042. The *Lord of the Isles* has a remarkable ability to make up lost time, a feature that is often called upon for she usually operates twenty-four hours a day.

Tiree, island number seven, recedes astern.

All good travel films have interviews with characters encountered en route. I insist that our film should be no different and who better to interview than the Captain of the *Lord of the Isles* himself, Colin Gilmour. I enquire of the Chief Steward if I can go up to the bridge. He telephones for me and permission is duly granted.

I am greeted by the First Officer and the Captain and am allowed to film. The huge, high flying bridge of the *Lord* gives a super panorama in every direction. I am shown the controls and equipment on the bridge: main engine controls, variable pitch propellers, Becker rudders, thrust units and retractable stabilisers. All very impressive – but what do they all mean? I'll have to ask my two ex-shipyard mates. The radar which highlights the approaching island of Coll in bright green is most intriguing. A small blip on our starboard side is pointed out as a yacht – two miles away – and heading north-east. A poignant addition is a camera view of the void between the bow visor and the inner doors of the car-deck. As the officer points out, 'If the outer door wasn't closed on this ship . . . we couldn't see where we were going!'

I stand out at the port end of the bridge, surrounded on three sides by glass and hovering almost forty feet above the surf. Looking aft I can see Gibbie and Ian leaning over the rail. Way behind them, Tiree, the big blue hole in the sky, is sinking lower into the horizon, as if someone had pulled a bung out of it. I turn to the skipper and ask him about the gales that forced his ship's idleness yesterday. There are no particular criteria that govern when the ship can or cannot sail in such a gale, just his experienced judgement.

'If I say she doesn't sail she doesn't sail. It doesn't always make me a popular man but that's just the way it is.'

I thank him for the opportunity of visiting the bridge, leave him and his two officers in their spacious, glass tower and descend to the decks where the ordinary passengers, like Ian and Gibbie, are accommodated.

At 1130 we are back at Coll. The gangway crew are giving Ian a dirty look that says 'Don't dare take one step off this ship.' We take back on board our four walkers. They have spent two and a half hours ashore – walking presumably. By now we are fairly certain that the ambiguous-looking one is also male. It is time for a snooze in the restful reclining-chaired lounge which is one of the most pleasing features of the *Lord*.

It is 1245 when I wake up and the weather has changed – drizzly rain is advancing upon us from the south-west and we seek shelter in the bar for a pre-lunch nip. The lubrication aids Gibbie as we put him through his paces pronouncing all the Gaelic place names (and some English ones) that he has been mis-pronouncing on all the previous Island Hops. Places like *Lochaline* and *Kilchoan* and his favourite of all, *Caol Ila*. This last one is the only Islay malt that Gibbie has never sampled, simply because he is too embarrassed about asking for it!

As we finish our drinks we are approaching Tobermory pier again and glad that we are staying on to Oban. The four walkers disembark, the rain running off their waxed jackets onto their bare legs. They are staying on Mull for the best part of a week. Each year they come away without their wives and pick a different part of the country each time to pursue their interests. They sound a bit like us – only we keep our trousers on.

As we bid fond farewells to Tobermory we make for the ship's restaurant and the traditional CalMac haddock and chips.

As we sail past Fishnish and southwards past Craignure the rain becomes heavier and forces us inside yet again. We pass the *Hebridean Princess*, yet again, anchored off Duart Castle. If her passengers had followed us they could have had the same cruise and saved themselves several thousands of pounds. The *Isle of Mull* approaches and sails past us to starboard. She passes the *Princess* – past Mull ferry meeting present Mull ferry.

I check the timetable – we are on time and due to reach Oban at 1450. I remember that this is Wednesday and that the *Claymore* should have left Oban at 1440 on her way south to Colonsay and Islay. If she is late we may see her. Indeed she is late. As we approach Oban pier both the *Claymore* and the *Eigg* pull away on their respective sailings and allow us good photo opportunities.

Back on the mainland, we find the car and, with Gibbie driving, are out of Oban at 1515. This is where we benefit from yesterday's sailings with the car. Our only schedule is that we have to be in Rothesay to catch the 1900 sailing to Wemyss Bay. No problem – we have three and a half hours.

On comes Gibbie's 'guess what' classical tape. An uppercrust game of 'Name That Tune' only without the prizes. Loads of Mozart, Beethoven, Vivaldi and Tchiakovsky – but no Mahler!

An uneventful journey of eighty-one miles via Inveraray and we arrive in good time and in markedly improving weather at Colintraive, Argyll, on the famous Kyles of Bute.

Our tenth vessel is the *Loch Riddon* – our fourth 'new' vessel this trip. Bute – our eighth island – is reached at 1715 and is also bathed in beautiful, still sunshine. Driving south we stop at Port Bannatyne to allow Ian to wallow in the nostalgic memory of past family holidays here.

Rothesay has been called the 'Madeira of the Clyde' – tonight, a beautifully warm, sunny evening, it must come close to living up to that description. Despite a few of the shops looking distinctly dilapidated, the town still retains its island charm and character. Like Ian I also spent many family holidays here as a child. I have a particular memory of my Dad's Ford Anglia breaking down on the turntable of the car-ferry *Cowal* and having to be towed off, leaving the ship running half an hour late for the rest of the day. Ian's memories are more sanguine; of peaceful holidays when the sun never failed to shine. Or so he tells us.

We park our car in the queue for the ferry and set off to a watering house to 'fortify the inner man', as Gibbie puts it.

Duly fortified, we sit out in the sun on Rothesay's new pier awaiting the arrival of our last vessel – the *Saturn*. In she speeds and off we sail at exactly 1900.

On her upper deck we toast Island Hop 1993 in our traditional manner. Our traditional manner is plonking ourselves down on a bench, watching Gibbie spend five minutes setting up the collapsible tripod that he's been lugging around on his shoulder for three days just for this moment, and explaining our madness to the puzzled passengers around us. We then raise our glasses of amber nectar and toast ourselves sycophantishly. Then we repeat the whole procedure for each of our cameras. The reader may think that by the time we finish all these shenanigans we're half-pickled. But this is not the case as we only pretend to drink the whisky. It all gets thrown away at the end. In previous years our traditional toasts have taken place aboard the *Hebridean Isles, Keppel* and *Suilven* but this year it is the turn of the *Saturn*.

Sitting out in the warm sunshine, with a dram in my hand, watching the beautiful scenery of the Clyde estuary slip past, the torrential rain of the first day of our journey seems a million miles away and I can not think of a better way to end an Island Hop day, or any other day for that matter.From above the bow we watch as the *Saturn* races towards Wemyss Bay pier, looking as though she is going to collide with the wooden structure, before swinging around purposefully to dock stern-in at the linkspan. A chap beside me shakes his head in disbelief. 'I can't be bothered with the sail, I just like the manoeuvring,' he says.

A final glance back at the Clyde and we are driving back towards Glasgow. There are five hundred and forty miles on the milometer.

On reflection this has been a trip with lots of variety – not least of all in the weather. We have finally attained Raasay, Coll and Tiree, difficult islands to reach on a three day trip. We've sailed on numerous small vessels and had our longest ever cruise – on the big *Lord of the Isles*.

To cap it all the pleasant trip to Bute has got us thinking about next year already. With a major change due in the ships used on several routes next year there are bound to be new experiences.

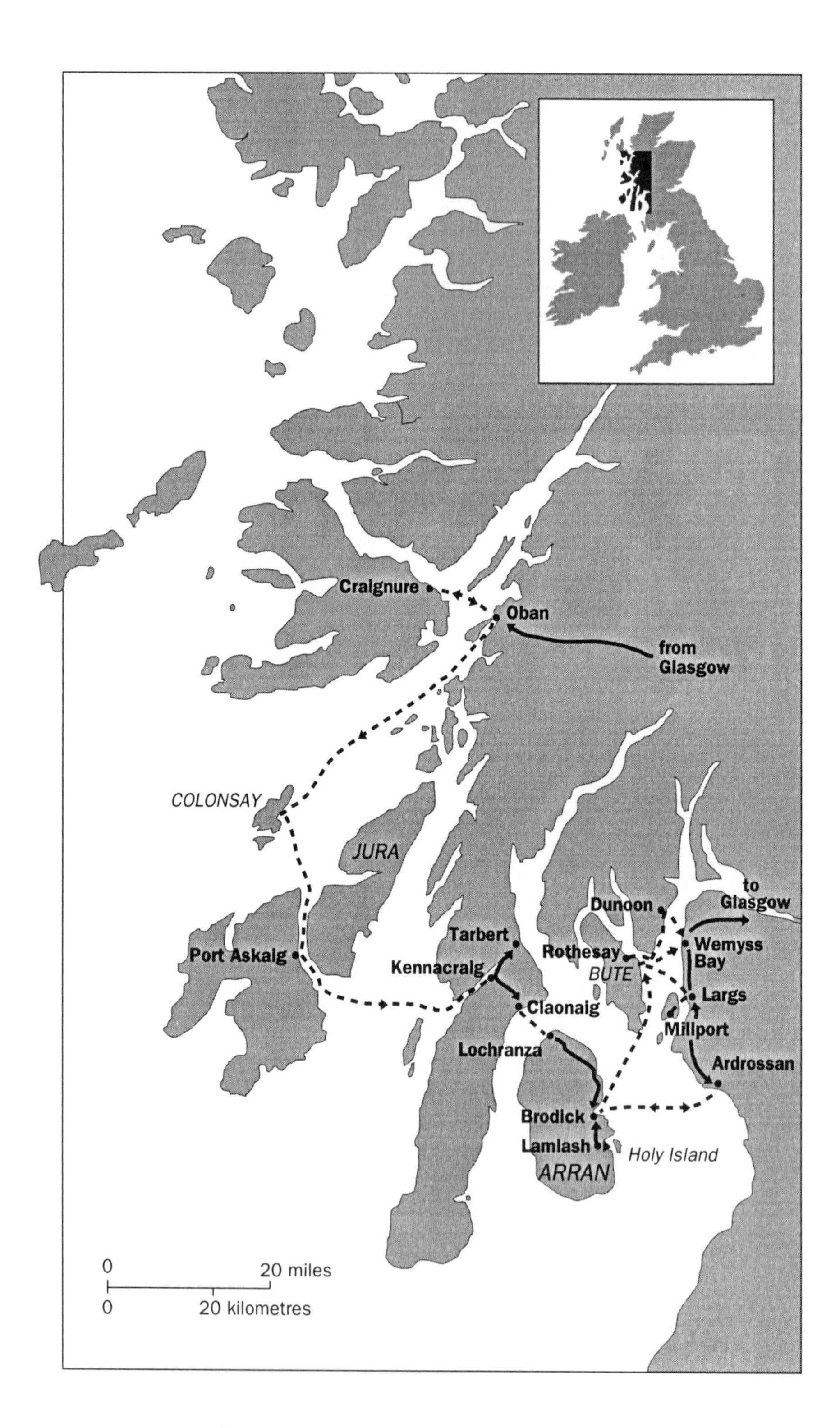
Craignure
Oban
from
Glasgow
COLONSAY
JURA
to
Glasgow
Dunoon
Tarbert
Wemyss
Bay
Rothesay
Port Askaig
Kennacraig
BUTE
Largs
Claonaig
Millport
Lochranza
Ardrossan
Brodick
Lamlash
Holy Island
ARRAN
0
20 miles
0
20 kilometres

1994 A Clyde Odyssey

The Plan

The strategy for the 1994 Island Hop, the sixth, was laid down during the last few hours of the 1993 trip.CalMac seemed to be showing a renewal of interest in Clyde cruising which appeared to have come to an end after the withdrawal of the *Keppel*. However in 1993 CalMac had introduced cut price cruises to Tighnabruiach which had proved to be a great success – over 33,000 passengers carried. The cost of a ticket, £5 from anywhere, provided proof that folks will turn out in numbers if the price is right.

We unanimously agreed that the 1994 trip should make full use of any cruising options on the Clyde. The arrival of the new *Caledonian Isles* into service on the Arran route was another opportunity that we felt obliged to take. When the new 1994 timetables appeared in January the cruising programme had been extended. The most interesting prospect, as far as a good route for our trip was concerned, was the opening of a new route from Rothesay to Brodick incorporating a cruise around Holy Isle. This gave us the opportunity of a circular route.

The replacement of the *Claymore* on the Islay roster by the *Isle of Arran* was another opportunity for a new experience. The *Claymore* had become spare vessel for 1994, releasing the *Pioneer* as cruise ship on the Clyde. This was to be our most extensive Clyde cruising since the hectic last day of the 1991 trip. Ian was particularly interested in a more home-based trip this year. Of particular interest to him was the prospect of visiting old piers and ferry-points still in use. In fact we were to call at eleven of them.

Another target was to sail on the three remaining CalMac ships which we had never used on an Island Hop, namely the new *Caledonian Isles*, the *Juno* and the *Pioneer*. The final attraction of the route chosen was that we did not need a car. This was to be a 'Back to Basics' Island Hop.

For some reason we decided on the fourth week in May instead of the usual third. Although we must have had good cause for this at the planning stage, by the time we assembled at Queen Street Station on the morning of 25 May none of us could remember why we had moved from our usual week.

Day One – *The Martyr to his Art*

A taxi takes us from Shawlands to Queen Street in plenty of time for the 0812 train to Oban. The weather has been beautiful for the last two weeks on the west coast of Scotland and a favourable forecast gives us an air of confidence that this is going to be a sunnier trip than last year. This should not be difficult as last year's trip was undoubtedly the wettest on record. We are not to be disappointed.

We stand around our bags and camera equipment in the concourse of the station, resembling a cut price BBC film crew, happy that today we are not any of the bustling commuters who scurry around affording us the occasional bemused glance.

I start the filming of our trip on the platform but have to stop almost immediately when an elderly man with a very artificial looking nasal prosthesis strolls in front of my lens. The viewer might think he is an actor whom we coerced into filming some kind of sick joke. Unfortunately he is for real.

Our sprinter train departs on time and we settle down to iron out the final details of our journey. As we reach Gareloch a buffet trolley advances along the aisle – aircraft style – serving drinks and various goodies. It doesn't advance itself – it is being pushed by a nice young lady in an attractive uniform. Her appearance is most welcome but we have prepared for the absence of catering facilities (*see* 1990 Hop) and have stocked up with sandwiches at the station. However a fresh cup of coffee is very welcoming.

The conversation drifts from the present Island Hop plans to highlights of past trips. Gibbie recalls the 1989 trip from Port Askaig to Colonsay on *Glen Sannox* as particularly memorable. Ian liked the Lochmaddy – Uig sailing of 1990 aboard *Hebridean Isles* and I mention the last day of the trip from 1991 when we dashed around the Clyde from Tarbert to Gourock in record time and on an assortment of vessels. More of the same this year will do nicely.

Meanwhile the sun shines over the waters of Loch Long as I seek permission to film from the driver's cab of the train. 'No more than five minutes,' the driver says.

Thirty seconds later I am back in my seat quite pleased with my quick take.

It is nice to sit back and relax and enjoy the scenery of this part of the West Highland line. With no car this year the pace of the trip seems to have stepped down a gear and the three hour journey to Oban is passing pleasantly slowly.

As we approach our terminus Gibbie announces that he does not want to join Ian and me on a return crossing to Mull. This sail has been slotted into the itinerary just to whet the appetite. While we are sailing the *Isle of Arran* is due to dock at Oban Pier and he decides that getting a head-on photograph of her is more important than a trip to Mull on the *Isle of Mull* (a 'sharp-ender' rather than a 'blunt-ender'). I suggest that he could join us and then photograph the *Arran* advancing onto the linkspan after the Mull vessel departs.

'I don't want a picture of her with her mouth open!' he replies. Referring, of course, to her bow visor being agape when moving into the berth. When I point out that he will be missing out on an island, he nods. 'Yes, but I'm a martyr to my art.'

We arrive in Oban just after 1100 and make our way to the pier. As I film on the pier a herring gull with its beak missing struts past me. My thoughts return to Queen Street station this morning, instead of 'Red Nose Day' this must be 'No Nose Day!'

Ian and I wave our farewells to the martyr on Oban pier and stretch out on the after-deck of the *Isle of Mull* to enjoy the glorious sunshine. Ian is visibly unwinding. A sail on this ship has been a feature of most Island Hops, for this particular crossing is always enjoyable.

To be completely honest we don't disembark at Craignure on Mull, which must play havoc with CalMac's counting system, but remain on deck. Returning into Oban Bay we lean over the starboard rail to film Gibbie filming the *Isle of Arran* at Oban pier.

To our surprise, the *Arran* is not at the pier but is still some way off down the Sound of Kerrera – fifty minutes behind schedule. Our eyes then focus on the 'martyr-to-his-art' on the pier. From where he stands he cannot yet see his subject. Poor Gibbie has missed out on an island and his ship and seems down-hearted. He had torn himself away from the pier briefly, however, in order to book us a taxi to meet us at Kennacraig later this evening.

I leave my two companions on the pier and climb Pulpit Hill to photograph the two *Isles* in Oban Bay. Gibbie eventually gets his shot of the *Isle of Arran*. She arrives late and sits out in the Bay for ten minutes until the *Isle of Mull* departs, at 1400.

Photographs completed, I rejoin Ian and Gibbie on the pier and we board the *Isle of Arran*, bound for Colonsay, Islay and, ultimately, Kennacraig. This is our first ever sail on her out of Oban. We have previously only sailed to Arran on her. She is due to leave at 1430 and Gibbie confidently predicts that she will be no more than seven minutes late, promising us a triple *Caol Ila* malt if he is wrong. At 1437 the ropes are thrown on board and the colour begins to return to his face. He hasn't had a very good start to his trip.

The ship has been loaded carefully as she carries vehicles for both Islay and Colonsay as well as a solitary car for Kennacraig. The occupant of the car, whom we are to encounter later on our travels, must have raised a few eyebrows at the Oban booking office. Who would want to sail for six hours from one mainland port to another when the distance can be driven in under a couple of hours? Nutters like us, I suppose!

The *Isle of Arran* points her bulbous bow down the sun drenched Sound of Kerrera and we watch from her forward deck as she weaves her way between the various buoys. In the distance the sea is as calm as I have ever seen in these waters and we retire to the open after-deck.

The Isle of Arran has been considerably refurbished since our last trip on her three years ago. The cafeteria looks freshly carpeted and smart bay seating has been put into the forward port lounge. The bar has also been re-seated. Downstairs, a reclining-seat lounge is on the port side and a shop has been created on the main deck assembly area. She is a much more comfortable ship now.

I enjoy a beer on the sunny upper deck. Gibbie produces his Arnold Palmer bunnet and almost loses it over the side in a brief gust of wind.

This is the fourth time we have sailed on this 'Wednesday' route from Oban to Islay; twice in each direction and now on our third ship, previously the *Glen Sannox* in 1989 and the *Claymore* in 1990 and 1991. We just cannot get bored with it. Today the sea is at its calmest and visibility is near perfect.

Colonsay nears and as we swing around to dock stern in at Scalasaig Ian decides that he is going to stay aboard during the twenty minute tie-up, claiming that CalMac have specifically instructed him to remain on board after he very nearly got left behind by *Lord of the Isles* at Coll last year.

I am among the first off and race around the bay to get a photograph. As the ship is running late I know that she will not hang around but will depart for Islay just as soon as she is loaded.

From the rear deck we watch an empty horse box being reversed up the linkspan and colliding with the side barrier. A seal pokes its head out of the still waters of the bay to see what all the fuss is about. It is no doubt happy that it lives in the sea.

Many more passengers join the ship here, probably day-trippers from Islay. Wednesday is the only day when a day trip to Colonsay is possible as the ship calls at Scalasaig on her outward passage to Oban. This allows visitors a few hours to explore the delights of Colonsay. And delights there certainly are. Since my last Island Hop visit I have spent a family holiday on Colonsay which allowed me to see a good bit more of it. It is a microcosm of the Hebrides. Rolling moorland hills, natural unspoilt woodland and two very wonderful features: the most beautiful beach of the Inner Hebrides at Kiloran and that special island remoteness – especially when the ship cannot get out to the island for a week at a time, something that happens not uncommonly during the winter. Then there is nothing for it but to sit back and wait until the sea moderates.

The ship leaves Colonsay some thirty minutes late and we head for the restaurant for our fish and chips. No long sail is complete without fish and chips for tea. By the time we finish and have returned to the deck we are approaching Port Askaig on Islay. A considerable tidal rush is sweeping us down the Sound of Islay and the skipper takes the ship past Port Askaig before swinging her round to starboard to creep forward onto the pier. The people on the pier must be thinking that she is going to sail right past!

Gibbie and I jump ashore to greet the usual mayhem that exists in Port Askaig whenever a ship calls. Lorries are roaring and spitting diesel fumes whilst passengers bustle off and onto our ship and the waiting Jura ferry the *Sound of Gigha*. We squeeze past the crowds to find the best spot to take the customary photographs. The Jura vessel reverses out of its berth to cross the stormy waters of the Sound. Buses and lorries strain their way up the steep hill out of Port Askaig.

Back on board the *Isle of Arran*. We chicken out of the quick return trip to Jura and content ourselves with filming the Jura ferry instead. She is soon struggling her way sideways back across to Islay against the swirling currents. In the middle of the Sound a lone yacht races southwards with the tide, travelling at a pacey rate of knots and yet her sails are empty of wind and are hanging limply.

A few minutes later we are following the yacht down the Sound, now twenty minutes behind schedule. The ship is quieter now and we make for the bar where we encamp beside a clutch of excitable school teachers who are gabbling and gesticulating to each other in a state of alcohol induced animation. Their red sweatshirts announce their respective schools. Gibbie's face now matches their colour due to a day spent exposed to the Hebridean sun.

Our conversation centres around Gibbie's glorifying trips to Germany over the past few years. This is probably where he has picked up all those esoteric and useless facts. The ones he continually regurgitates back at us. He has been to the Rhur to the scene of the Dambusters raid. He has been to Hamburg to see the city flattened by the RAF in 1943. He has been canal 'pharting' on the Rhine. The Germans cannot wait to welcome him back. He has even taken his long suffering wife Janette to see 'The Bridge at Remagen' on the Rhine.

'Where is the bridge?' Janette asked, not unnaturally.

'It fell down in 1945.'

By the time we reach Kennacraig on West Loch Tarbert most of us have spent eight hours on the sea. It has certainly been an excellent cruise and we peer out at the darkening ferry terminal to see if our taxi is waiting for us. Indeed it is. Our young lady driver has been waiting a while for our arrival but brushes this off as being 'part of the job'. She drops us off at our Tarbert hotel, relieves us of £5 and promises to return at 0815 the following morning. 'I'll come early, the traffic can be hectic in the morning.' *In Tarbert!*

The receptionist at the hotel seems rather high, and I don't mean tall. We eventually persuade her that the only services we require from her is to be pointed in the direction of our rooms. Gibbie is sure that she is on drugs, his usual explanation for any strange behaviour patterns that he encounters.

'Did you notice if her pupils were dilated?' he enquires.

'I don't know, I wasn't looking at her pupils,' says Ian.

Getting to our rooms is easier said than done. Upstairs is a maze of stairways and passages and blind alleys. Having found Gibbie's room quite easily Ian and I explore three passage-ways before eventually encountering ours. I close the door behind me, hoping that there will not be a fire in the middle of the night. The rooms are basic but clean and comfortable. A quick coffee and freshen up is called for before we 'hit the town'.

We try three pubs looking for Real Ale but have to settle for something more pasteurised. Our own hotel has a cosy lounge and we end the night there, producing souvenirs from past Island Hops: my bit of Tiree pier that I've been carrying around in my leather jacket for some bizarre reason and Gibbie's stone from Strontian car park. He now definitely hopes it is not radioactive as he has been carrying it in his camera bag for over a year.

Day Two – *A Big Circle*

We are down for breakfast at 0730 and share the early start with ten working men and only one waitress. We wait a while for service, keeping an eye on the time as our taxi will soon be arriving to take us to Claonaig. An Irish chap whose head is one huge ball of tously, brown hair sits adjacent to me and in the space of fifteen minutes consumes three cigarettes in accompaniment to his poached eggs and coffee. One of our fellow guests gives up waiting and disappears into the kitchen. He emerges a few minutes later with a plate of sausages. This reminds me of yet another *Fawlty Towers* sketch.

Our breakfast arrives eventually. 'Sorry for the delay,' says the waitress, 'I've been waiting for a new toaster!'

We eat quickly and then meet up with our taxi which has been waiting for us outside. As we leave the dining-room our Irish companion is lighting up again – at this rate he will puff his way through a hundred today.

In glorious sunshine and with all our gear stowed in the boot we speed our way across Kintyre to the ferry point at Claonaig, some five miles away. A cool north-easterly breeze greets us there and for the rest of the day the sunshine is intermittent.

Claonaig, on the eastern side of Kintyre, overlooks the dark mass of Arran and is connected to it by the half-hour ferry crossing to Lochranza. The ferry is the *Loch Tarbert*, a new vessel for an Island Hop and we can see her making her way across to us. She is due to leave our side at 0905.

The *Loch Tarbert* is a broader version of the original 'Loch class' of ferry. Her extra breadth gives her an extra lane for vehicles, allowing her to carry eighteen instead of twelve cars. Due to increased traffic on this route in recent years it has been necessary to provide a bigger vessel.

We depart Claonaig on time and the crewman scrutinises my Rover ticket as if looking for some discrepancy that might render it invalid. In which case he is disappointed.

I recall sailing this route in 1989 on board the *Loch Ranza* when there was a good going south-westerly swell. That day it was quite exhilarating. Today it is rather cold and noisy. We plan a quick coffee in the Lochranza cafe at the head of the pier before taking the bus to Brodick at 1010. To our dismay, however, the cafe has vanished and a house is being built in its place. On reflection this is not entirely surprising considering our last experience there (c.f. Hop 1991). Ian retires to the Tourist Information Office to see if he can find it. No luck. Perhaps the bellicose waitress had finally driven the last of the customers away with her congenial charm. We stride out towards the castle and sit out next to it in the returning sunshine to await the arrival of our next mode of transport.

The bus is five minutes late and the tickets we receive are longer than the vehicle. It bumps us the fifteen miles to Brodick and we peer out of the window looking for deer in Glen Chalmadale. No luck today.

Our plan is to catch the 1140 cruise ship out of Brodick but we want to check our baggage into our hotel and grab that much sought-after cup of coffee first. As we reach Brodick, however, the *Caledonian Isles* is preparing to leave and so in true Island Hop tradition sustenance comes second and we hurry up the pier for photographs.

The *Caledonian Isles*, known locally as 'The Big Mac', is the largest ferry ever to serve the Clyde. At 300 feet long she is twelve feet greater than the *Isle of Mull*, to which her likeness is more than superficial. She is even longer than the famous MacBrayne paddle-steamer *Columba*. We will be sailing on her later in the day, if all goes to plan, but for now we watch as she eases herself away from the recently refurbished Brodick pier and swings round towards Ardrossan. As she passes we can make out our next ship approaching from Garroch Head. We quickly dump our bags in the hotel and await her arrival, now suffering from acute caffeine deprivation syndrome.

The new route from Gourock, Dunoon and Rothesay to Brodick is only two weeks old and we peer out to sea to identify which ship is on the route today. It is the *Pioneer* which brings a smile to most of our faces (Gibbie doesn't like the *Pioneer*), as we have never sailed on her before on any of our trips. Gibbie's criticism of her stems from the fact that her deck space is somewhat fragmented. This is undeniably true but her steeply flared bow and considerable speed combine to give her a good bow wave and purposeful look which make her very photogenic to avid ship photographers like us.

My personal memories of her go back to my first trip on her in 1978, from Kennacraig to Port Ellen, and to sailing on her in a stiff wind from Mallaig to Armadale in 1985. She has taken on a new lease of life this year as the secondary Rothesay vessel and as the cruise ship to Brodick and Holy Isle on Mondays and Thursdays.

The *Pioneer* docks at Brodick and eighty passengers disembark – but no cars. Some twenty-two of us get on board and we sail some ten minutes late at 1150. The reason for the delay is unclear. The crew stroll the length of Brodick pier as if they are out to enjoy the afternoon sun. Eventually we set off turning southwards out of the Bay towards Holy Isle which we pass to starboard.

As you have probably gathered by now I am one of those poor unfortunates who count things. My two colleagues are used to this affliction. 'That's eighty people who just got off that ship. You know chaps this is the forty-third sailing we've taken since we started Island Hopping. Whew, that was quite a climb to the top deck, fifty-six steps no less.' My mother said it started when I was a baby – my first words were: 'That was one hundred and twenty-three contractions, you know.'

On towards Whiting Bay, where the pier, that was once a regular calling point for numerous Clyde steamers, has long since fallen into the sea.

During the cruise, which lasts one and a half hours, we try the catering facilities. These are minimal, but hot rolls with scrambled egg are available – which is what Gibbie and I had for breakfast in Tarbert. At least the coffee is generous. Ian asks for one cup and gets two! Unlike catering on the Western Isles, the Clyde routes could do with upgrading.

Back on deck we meet Mike, an English chap who has taken Island Hopping a stage further than us. He has bought an eight day car Rover ticket at £150 and had apparently sailed down with us on the *Isle of Arran* last night (his was the one car travelling from Oban to Kennacraig). He is doing a whirlwind tour of almost every Hebride. The timetables of the upper Clyde routes have him baffled however. He asks Gibbie for assistance, 'Go and speak to the expert,' says Gibbie.

'But the purser's office is closed,' replies Mike.

'No, not CalMac,' replies Gibbie. 'Ask Stuart!'

He wants to get from Brodick to Dunoon with his car which is still in

Brodick meantime. I advise him to take his car onto the *Pioneer* at Brodick and change ships at Rothesay where one of the 'streakers' will take him up to Dunoon. This he apparently does before taking his car up to Oban again. He is even madder than we are!

On the inward part of the cruise we pass between Lamlash and Holy Isle. We call back at Brodick where we load our eighty passengers and Mike's car (no I didn't count them again).

When we depart again at 1320, on route now for Rothesay and Wemyss Bay, the *Caledonian Isles* is waiting to berth. We will be seeing more of her later as we are now off on a big circle of the Clyde.

Downstairs for a refreshment and to discuss how exactly we are going to get from Wemyss Bay to Ardrossan for 1800. I had, in fact, ordered a taxi to meet us at Wemyss Bay but from there we have three options. We could taxi to Largs and either take the bus or the train to South Beach, Ardrossan. Or we could taxi all the way to Ardrossan harbour.

A glance at the train timetables reveals that the combination of taxi-train-train is ideal. We will be in Largs in time to catch the 1650 train to South Beach where we can take a second train to Ardrossan harbour, arriving before the 1800 sailing to Brodick. This option appeals to us, for if it works out, we will be using public transport in the best tradition of Island Hopping!

Our brains now well and truly confused with studying timetables, we emerge back on deck and find ourselves off the shores of Kilchattan Bay on Bute. Another old calling point for steamers. As we speed into Rothesay Bay the *Jupiter* crosses our path.

All passengers, including us, disembark at Rothesay in beautiful sunshine, this town always seems to glow when we visit it. Nothing better to do than stand around on the pier, grateful that most of our bags are safely in our Brodick hotel and we don't have to carry them around.

The *Pioneer* sits out, awaiting the arrival and departure of the *Juno*. She has been filling in for the *Pioneer* during the latter's cruise. She is due to arrive in from Wemyss Bay and will head for Dunoon and Gourock with most of the cruise passengers and Mike and his car. The *Pioneer* is then going to revert back to her Wemyss Bay/ Rothesay schedule for the remains of the day. We are going to join her on her first crossing to the mainland. The *Jupiter*, meanwhile, is the main Rothesay ferry today. I hope you've got all that.

As we wait, the puffer *Old Vic 32* approaches and berths at the pier. Billowing black smoke belches from her lum. It is a nostalgic sight, although if it had billowed from a modern vessel we would call it pollution. We eye the puffer's resplendent tattiness – searching the crew for 'Dan'. Dan isn't there, however. The vessel is now used for holidays, hammocks strung across the coal bunkers?

The *Juno* arrives and departs with Mike, who has decided to spend his last night in Barra. We wish him well. I am just glad that he did not ask me how to get from Dunoon to Castlebay. He will have to work that out for himself.

The Pioneer berths again and we get on board for the 1515 sailing to

Above: Looking for tea-break, but which way to go?

Below: Driving across Scalpay

Bottom: Dalmation House, Tiree

(G Anderson)

Above: Kilt Rock, Skye

Below: Island of Canna from the deck of *Lochmor*

(G Anderson)

Above: Stuart and Ian feeling cold en route to Lismore

Right: Gibbie and Ian on board *Lord of the Isles*

Below: Three CalMac ships at Oban, *Lord of the Isles, Raasay* and *Isle of Arran*

(G Anderson)

Above: *Hebridean Isles* sailing into Uig Bay, Skye

Right: *Hebridean Princess* sailing up Broom Loch

Below: *Waverley* at Tarbert, Loch Fyne

Above: Keppel leaving Dunoon pier

Below: Pioneer powering her way across to Rothesay

Above: *Suilven* gliding up Loch Broom

Below: *Claymore* in Campbeltown Loch

(G Anderson)

Above: The Mountains of Rum

Below: *Glen Sannox* arriving at Kennacraig Ferry Terminal

Bottom: *Claymore* early morning, West Loch Tarbert

Above: Kyleakin at Kyle of Lochalsh

Right: Counting us off and counting us on at Staffa

Below: Sailing off to the island of Lismore on the *Eigg*

(G Anderson)

Wemyss Bay; she has reverted to her ferry role now. It has been an interesting half hour on Rothesay pier, with all the comings and goings. But now it is our turn to go.

Another cup of tea and a bun later and we are at the 'Bay' where our taxi duly waits for us. As we head the six miles south to Largs we try to map out our movements to the taxi-driver.

'Where have you boys come from?' he asks.

'Brodick.'

'I see, and where are you headed?'

'Brodick.'

He falls silent after that. How can we describe our journey from Brodick to Wemyss Bay and then explain to him that we are off to Ardrossan to catch the ferry back to Brodick and expect him to understand us? He drops us off in Larg's Main Street and sets off to find his next batch of nutty passengers.

How can we kill twenty minutes in Largs except down at the pier? The *Loch Linnhe* is serving Cumbrae alone and the *Second Snark* (tomorrow's ship) is approaching.

We compare the 1990s style of architecture of the new Moorings Building on one side of the street with the 1960s featureless fabrication of the Cumbraen Amusement arcade on the other. Gibbie thinks one of them is *kitsch* but I'm not sure which one he means.

On the way up to the railway station we have to physically drag one of our number out of the photographic print shop otherwise we will miss the train. Scotrail don't let us down but as we trundle out of Largs Station a group of foul-mouthed louts behind us are a reminder that we are back on the mainland again. It is with some relief that we alight at South Beach only fifteen minutes later. This is not to say that there are no louts that swear on the islands. If I lived on one or two of them that I've seen I might take to the odd curse myself. Those islands will have to remain anonymous.

A tangible feeling of loneliness always descends when one steps out onto an empty platform and watches the train pull away into the distance.

'Where are we?' asks Gibbie, 'I know we are in South Beach but where are we?'

We have thirty minutes to hang around until our next train arrives from the opposite direction and so we seek out the beach, which turns out to be as deserted as the station. I've got to say that Ardrossan is not my favourite Clyde resort. (I use the term *resort* loosely).

Our connecting train arrives on time at 1736 and we almost get on the wrong end. If we had we would have ended up in Glasgow with our pyjamas in Brodick. That would have been an embarrassing one to explain: 'Hallo dear, I'm home a day early. I got on the wrong end of the train.' However, we get on the right end and feel pleased that our clever bit of timetabling has worked out well.

Ardrossan Harbour has two ships in evidence. The *Caledonian Isles*, is loading up for the last crossing of the day with a fairly hefty load. At the inner berth the *Claymore* is moored in readiness for her inaugurating sailing to the Isle of Man which is due on the forthcoming Saturday.

We board the *Caledonian Isles* and give Ian a guided tour of CalMac's latest ship. He is unsure whether he likes her, he takes a lot of pleasing. She is similar, internally, to the *Isle of Mull* but has her restaurant and upper observation lounge further forward. Her bar is consequently astern and both sides of her main deck are divided into various forms of seating. Most important of all she has a view over the bow! The decor is an unfortunate shade of blue. But the worst thing about her is her name. Who has ever heard of the *Caledonian Isles*? There are no such islands. What is wrong with just *Caledonia*? A fine traditional name for a Clyde steamer. The popular choice would have been *Glen Sannox*. Such is the continuous build up of traffic to Arran that a bigger ship has to be provided roughly every ten years. So by the middle of the next decade there might be another new vessel, probably called the *Myth'ty Isles*' or something like that. Today's ship will then be geographically displaced. To where? The Caledonian Isles?

The departure from Ardrossan is slightly delayed by a lady who arrives late at the barrier with her car and frantically gesticulates that she would like to come on board. The ramp is re-lowered for her.

During the crossing we have our evening meal and on arriving at Brodick we have merely to stroll a hundred yards up from the pier to our hotel to be reunited with our baggage. As simple as that. We have completed our circle. Our rooms are even more basic than last night but they do overlook the promenade. It appears that breakfast will not be served until 0900 and as we hope to sail on the 0820 ferry back to the mainland this seems to present a problem. We decide, therefore, to break the golden Island Hopping rule which states that route changes should never be made halfway through a trip! (this rule was laid down after 1992). We have a re-think. I note that on this trip we have yet to bag a 'new' island, but can amend this, however, by taking an early morning trip to Holy Isle and then catch the later 1105 sailing from Brodick and meet up with our target ship, the *Second Snark*, at Largs instead of Rothesay.

Our day could still 'work' well. Apart from bagging a new island the other advantages are that we will not have to get from Largs to Wemyss Bay and, more importantly, we will be able to have our breakfast. As there is no obvious disadvantage in this change the amendment is unanimously approved. Everything will work out as long as our taxi can get us to Lamlash and back in time for 1105. As the first ferry for Holy Isle leaves Lamlash at 0930 we book a taxi for 0910. Our plans settled, we bring a smile to the hotel manager's face by assuring him that we do not require breakfast until 0845.

The evening is beautifully calm and tranquil. The wind has dropped to nil and hardly a ripple breaks the surface of the water in Brodick Bay. We strike out to explore the village but on spying the aptly named Duncan's Bar (Ian is confusingly also known as Duncan. This hails from his days in Stephen's Shipyard where he was re-christened Duncan to distinguish him from all the other Ians. There was only one Gibbie, however) a mere hundred yards from our hotel and noticing that it dispenses Real Ale we decide that we are tired after two days heavy cruising and that a reward is called for.

The evening in Duncan's Bar ranks among some of the best evenings we have ever had on any of our trips. The Boddingtons helps. Ian has been searching for a Real Ale house since we left Oban and his eyes light up when he sees the sign. Gibbie is happy too. In his hotel room he was watching a television programme on early whiskies. It influences him so much that he decides to have a gin and tonic.As we leave to stroll home some time later the twinkling lights of Fairlie, Seamill and Ardrossan are clearly visible many miles away across the sea.

We've been there today – and we're going back there tomorrow.

Day Three – *Holy Intervention*

Friday 0730 after a great night's sleep, must have been the Boddingtons. Breakfast is adequate with none of yesterday's delays. It is served in a rather grand dining-room by a rather large waiter who looks as though he would rather be somewhere else. Gibbie is certain he is from Kilmarnock. We have slightly more time this morning in which to gather up our possessions. Our taxi arrives at 0915.

It is another beautiful day – we are really seeing the Clyde at its best. Another hectic day of transportation beckons.

Our taxi is a VW Passat and apart from ourselves the only passenger is a black and white mongrel called Sally who sits in the rear compartment and licks Ian's neck all the way to Lamlash.

At Lamlash pier, which is only three miles from Brodick pier, we enter into a three-way summit conference with the taxi-driver and Jim, the boat-owner. All three parties are very helpful. We are to wait a few more minutes until the tide advances in a few more feet and then Jim will take us over to Holy Isle and back again in time for our taxi back to Brodick. Such convoluting itineraries are what makes days like this rather exciting. Would our taxi return for us? Will we reach our next ship in time? Will Jim get the engine of his boat started? The taxi driver asks us why we do all this. When we explain our travels to him he gives us that bewildered look that we frequently see on the faces of the people that we meet on our travels. He gives an approving nod. 'I'll be back for you.' The rest of the day's plans depend on that assurance.

Ian decides that he does not want to cross to Holy Isle but would rather take a stroll around Lamlash as he has never been here before. He leaves Gibbie and me on the stone jetty watching Jim who has rowed out to his boat and is struggling to start his engine.

Lamlash is the administrative capital of Arran and its bay is effectively sheltered from the rest of the Clyde estuary by the presence of Holy Isle, a mile and a half offshore. The mountainous lump that embodies the island rises to over a thousand feet high, although the island itself is only two miles by half a mile. It resembles a huge shark's fin sticking out of the sea. In recent years a group of Buddhist followers have used the island as a retreat from the pressures of modern living. The pressures that the rest of us have to put up with.

Jim's engine roars into life across the still waters and he arrives at the slipway, which is aptly named due to the layers of green, mossy seaweed which cover it. The tide is still very low but Jim turns his boat, the *Nordic,* around and we climb in. He guides us slowly over the shallow water that only barely covers the sandbanks which lie just out from the jetty. I ask him about the Buddhists.

'Oh they're all right,' he replies. 'Just kinna weird.' As we clear the last of the sandbanks and shallows, Jim opens up the throttle. 'OK boys, off we go !'

It is an eight minute exhilarating ride across the bay to our new island. The *Nordic* has now replaced the Ulva Ferry as the smallest craft we have sailed on. The engine seriously disturbs the peace of Lamlash's morning as it churns up the surface of the water and spews it out behind us.

It is twenty years since I first set foot on Holy Island. A visit which stands in my mind as I was attacked by a swarm of herring gulls with a strong parental bond when I had strayed too close to their nests. Squadrons of them came swooping down on my head like *stukas*. At the last second they would pull up and fly off just as I was preparing myself to have a four-inch beak embedded in my scalp.

Several of the island's inhabitants are coming down to the jetty to meet us. All are young and some wear orange gowns which makes them look as if they've been *Tango-ed*. A few also have their heads shaved. We are greeted with smiles as we step ashore, feeling as conspicuous as Captain Cook must have felt, for a visit which will last all of five minutes. One of the girls on the beach gives out a loud 'Gee!' as she recognises the logo on Gibbie's blue sweatshirt. Gibbie is rendered speechless in admiration at the girl's powers of perception, so much so that he still talks about it to this day.

Holy Isle is the only 'new' island on this year's trip. There are not many new islands that can be visited on a Clyde-based Island Hop such as this. Wee Cumbrae was an unlikely option, Ailsa Craig would have been impossible to reach and the sugar-boat stuck on the sandbank off Helensburgh would have a nice view but nowhere to eat. Holy Isle fits the bill well, however. It is not often that we get the chance to step ashore on an island that has a different religion. We just have time for a walk up the stony beach to look at the strange looking sheep penned into a small field. Perhaps they are Buddhists too.

Jim is soon calling us back and we are joined by a half dozen other passengers for the return trip. One of the girls is a resident of the island and is off to do the weekly shopping in Lamlash. The others are visitors, returning to civilisation after spending some time on the island.

'How did you spend your time?" I ask one of them, a bulky-looking chap in his late twenties who comes from Surrey and whose head and face are a mass of unkempt hair.

'Oh. . .' He thinks for a sufficient number of seconds for me to wonder whether or not he is going to continue. 'Oh . . . birdwatching, building drystone walls and studying Buddhism,' he replies.

'Were you forced into total abstinence during your stay on the island?' I ask out of sheer unadulterated nosiness.

'Eh, yes,' comes the reply, which is tinged with a hint of regret.

'And how long have you been over there?' I ask. From the condition of his hair I expect him to say six months.

'Two weeks.'

Gibbie gets chatting, like he does, to a chap from California who is wearing a plastic elasticated duck's bill on his face. My mind returns to the sea-gull at Oban who could have done with it.

'Where did you stay on the island?' Gibbie asks the duck-bill.

'They gave us our own cave each!'

If we seem intrigued by our fellow passengers then they are fascinated by us. Our travels and circular routes seem to interest them.

At Lamlash pier, as we approach, Ian is standing in amazement at the sight of the robes and the duck-bill. He is glad he remained in the relative safety of Lamlash. We say farewell to Jim and our Holy Isle friends who have made the trip both possible and enjoyable.

The chap with the hairy head from Surrey shuffles forwards. 'Eh – is there anywhere in Lamlash where I can buy a bottle of wine at this time in the morning?'

Our taxi arrives on time – without Sally this time, much to Ian's considerable relief – and we climb back over the hill to Brodick in plenty of time to pick up our bags at the hotel.

Our next ship is approaching. As this is the start of a holiday weekend the incoming *Caledonian Isles* is very busy. We watch as hundreds of people stream down the pier, many being met by relatives and friends.

Watching them embrace, Ian remarks that he feels as though he should be kissing someone. I am not sure if he has anyone in particular in mind but Gibbie and I back away from him. He must be feeling homesick.

Eventually we get on board and watch from the bow as, still in glorious sunshine, we pull away from Brodick pier for the third time in twenty-four hours. We have breakfast number two in the restaurant. To be perfectly honest, whenever we get on a ship which has catering facilities before noon we always have a second breakfast. It kills time prior to lunch.

We have to talk about how we are going to get from Ardrossan to Largs (again!) in just under an hour. Yesterday we had been puzzling over how to do it in reverse. I consult the encyclopaedia of timetables in my bag and suggest that if we stride out from Ardrossan harbour to South Beach we can take a train to Largs that will arrive in good time for our 1300 sailing on the *Second Snark*, our next little cruise ship. At the thought of walking a mile in around twenty minutes Gibble visibly pales. As we pull into the berth at Ardrossan, however, relief spreads over his face as the solution to the problem, in the shape of a bus, pulls up at the gangway. A quick enquiry reveals that for the cost of 47p we can ride to the train station at South Beach. Flexibility is the name of the game – one must always look for opportunities to link one sail with the next. If all else fails – get a taxi! It seems like cheating when we use a taxi but fortunately we have kept taxi journeys to a minimum.

We leave the *Caledonian Isles* to load up another huge queue of holiday traffic and rattle off on our wee bus to South Beach. As we stand on the station platform we are embraced by a strong feeling of *deja vu*. This time Gibbie knows where he is.

The train must be punctual and I confidently announce that one can set one's watch by the time-keeping of the trains on this line. I count down from ten and as I reach zero, to everyone's astonishment, our train appears from around the bend. We are back in Largs with fifteen minutes to spare before the arrival of the *Second Snark* from Rothesay.

The *Second Snark* was built in 1938 by Denny of Dumbarton as a tug-cum-tender. Now, she is operated by Clyde Marine Motoring as a neat little cruise ship sailing to all the main upper Firth resorts. She has covered deck space with an open lowered deck at the stern. Below, there are two saloons – one with a tiny bar. Today we are going to join her on her cruise to Millport, with time ashore, and then back up river to Dunoon, via Largs and Rothesay.

As the little ship ties up at Largs pier, an elderly man shouts to the crew: 'Can I go to Tighnabruaich? Can I get a single ticket? Can I get a pint aboard?'

As the reply to the first question is negative he declines to come aboard. We jump on and are soon off towards Millport, capital of the Isle of Cumbrae. Gibbie is dispatched to buy our tickets (our CalMac Rover tickets are not valid on this leg of our journey). The purser looks at Gibbie and enquires if it is three senior citizen tickets that he requires. And so it is that for £3.25 each we get the bargain of the trip. Even more so because the ticket includes a free cup of tea. Meanwhile I ponder on how I can make myself look like a senior citizen for the next few hours.

Millport, a new pier for an Island Hop, has been bathed in Mediterranean sunshine for a whole week now and friends of mine, Sharon and Alex, who have been on holiday here during that time, are down at the pier to greet the ship, looking as tanned as if they had spent the week on the Bahamas. We have an hour and a quarter to spend and, as the catering facilities on the *Snark* are limited, lunch seems like a good idea. After all, it is barely 1400 and we are on our third island of the day, having been on three vessels, two taxis, a bus and a train and have only had two breakfasts. We look no further than the George Hotel at the head of the pier, where, over our chilli, Gibbie gives us a history lesson to add to those he gave us at Tarbert, Lamlash and Ardrossan.

In the few minutes before our departure I hastily purchase four sticks of rock for my children – an act which I have previously declined on account of their dental health. I surreptitiously position my purchases behind my back as if to hide them from my conscience when, to my horror, I discover that a patient of mine, Murray Dobson, is standing behind me. 'Hallo Stuart – what on earth are you doing here – buying rock for the children?' I almost drop the forbidden foods in embarrassment.

We wave goodbye to our friends, and anyone else who is standing in the glorious sunshine on Millport pier. We then stretch out on the stern deck, only a couple of feet from the swirling water, as the *Second Snark* speeds on her way towards Largs again. We feel as if we are on a private yacht – and all for the price of a pensioner's ticket. After Largs we set off across the Firth to Rothesay. In mid-channel, a sleek, speedy cabin-cruiser overtakes us on the port side and crosses over our bow.

'Well, Gibbie, what are the regulations regarding such a manoeuvre?' Ian asks.

'Give way to ships to starboard unless you're overtaking,' he acclaims in his official naval voice. Then, adopting his more usual tone: 'But I'd ram the bugger up the a....!'

The *Jupiter* is pulling away from Rothesay pier and this gives us cause for a burst of decision making. As this 'streaker' is on the Wemyss Bay/Rothesay run with the *Pioneer* then the back-up ship is likely to be the *Juno*. This 'back-up' vessel will be performing a run from Gourock to Dunoon, then sail from Dunoon to Wemyss Bay and then take up the Rothesay service in place of her sister. Now, we have never sailed on the *Juno* before on an Island Hop and, what is more, we have never sailed Dunoon to Wemyss Bay direct. In just over an hour's time the *Juno* will be doing that very route. Furthermore, as Gourock railway station is closed for repairs, by sailing direct to Wemyss Bay we can catch a direct train home to Glasgow Central.

Another option is to ignore all this and stay on the *Snark* to Helensburgh or Greenock but we dismiss this. Look at all the fun we'd be missing. The 1715 sailing from Dunoon by the *Juno* therefore becomes the target for our last sea crossing of the 1994 Island Hop.

All seems well. The *Second Snark* is running on time and is due to reach Dunoon pier fifteen minutes before the *Juno* is due to leave. Our optimism is, however, short-lived. As we sit at Rothesay pier an official looking gentleman in a suit and carrying a briefcase comes on board.

'Oh-oh here comes trouble,' predicts Gibbie who reckons the chap is from the Department of Transport. Unfortunately he is absolutely right and the unannounced spot-check on the *Second Snark* is to delay us by twenty minutes. Inspections like this are carried out from time to time and without prior warning on all passenger ships, to check on safety equipment and facilities. This is all very reassuring but why did he have to pick this moment when we are rushing to get to Dunoon?

He inspects every nook and cranny onboard while we constantly inspect our watches. It is no use, by the time he leaves the ship, apparently satisfied, and we pull out of our berth we know that by the time we get to Dunoon the *Juno* will have been and gone! We settle down to our free cup of tea and ponder what to do. Not to be out done I approach our skipper and ask if he can make haste. As we pass by the ruined pier at Innellan, however, we can see the *Juno* arriving at Dunoon pier way ahead of us. The skipper is game for a bit of sport and offers to radio the CalMac ship to see if she can be held up for us. This seems rather bold but desperate times require desperate actions and if you don't ask in this world . . . anyway, I'm a cheeky bugger sometimes. The only way that we are going to catch her is if the skipper of the *Juno* agrees to our request. We are not too optimistic. *Juno* will be sailing light to Wemyss Bay and will, therefore, have no cause to be delayed. We near Dunoon but are still ten minutes away as the *Juno* looks ready to depart.

'Hallo *Juno, Juno*, this is *Second Snark* here.'

'Go ahead *Second Snark* this is *Juno*.' The reply bounces quickly back through the ether.

'We have three passengers who wish to join you. Could you possibly hold up for a few minutes?'

'Ehhh, I think that will be okay but we don't have a lot of time 'cos we have a quick turn around at Wemyss Bay.'

Gibbie and Ian are amazed when I relay the good news. This is certainly the first time that CalMac have held up a ship for us. But then it is the first time that we have asked them.

By the time we arrive at Dunoon we are aware that the *Juno* is now seven minutes late and the rope handlers are standing around shaking their watches and their heads. We race up one gangway, along the pier and go up another gangway to board the *Juno*. This is our quickest ever visit to a pier. We've made it ! The skipper of the *Juno* is waiting to greet us, after all we are his only passengers.

'This is a right Irish way of getting to Wemyss Bay!' He grins. 'Why didn't you get the ferry from Rothesay?'

The answer is too complex so I decide just to smile nicely back at him. A smile that probably makes the guy think: 'This chap is off his rocker.'

The *Second Snark* departs the pier first – her skipper blowing his horn whilst her passengers wave in unison as if they are all pleased for us. We set off for the Bay on the last leg of what must be the most exciting end to an Island Hop that we have ever had.

The ship is practically empty and our cameras and tripods are set up on the upper deck in time honoured fashion for the Annual Toast to the Island Hop. The weather has dulled but it hasn't darkened our spirits as we pose for lenses with our glasses full – well pleased with our day's journeying.

The *Juno* has taken our total number of Island Hopping ships or boats to 34 over the years. Although we had achieved only one new island in 1994 we had sailed on no fewer than six new vessels, including Jim's *Nordic*. By sailing on the trio of *Caledonian Isles, Pioneer* and *Juno* we have now sailed on all of CalMac's major ships.

Meanwhile the *Juno* arrives at Wemyss Bay and we disembark. As she loads for Rothesay her sister ship *Jupiter* approaches and sits off the pier. I film the two of them swapping over at the linkspan and then make haste up the recently refurbished station to our train.

The Victorian ironworks of Wemyss Bay Station have been repainted in a vivid green and baskets of flowers hang above the pillars of the central atrium. It looks nicer than I can remember seeing it.

Our train departs at 1818 and a taxi from Central Station takes us back to the southside of Glasgow. It has been a very convoluted trip, yet again. We have certainly achieved our targets of new ships and many hours on the Clyde. The weather has been the best to date, the difference that sunny days make to such a trip is immense.

For the statistician we have reached seven islands and sailed on eight vessels. Eighteen ports have been visited in three days, thirteen of them on the Clyde. We have had six taxi journeys, five train journeys and two buses.

Ian's highlights were the Mull crossing, sailing between Millport and Largs, and finding a pub that sold real ale. My highlights were the trip to Holy Isle and holding up the *Juno*. When asked Gibbie says his highlight was Tuesday! This is surprising as our trip did not start until Wednesday.

Next year? I think the Outer Hebrides and some new islands are beckoning.

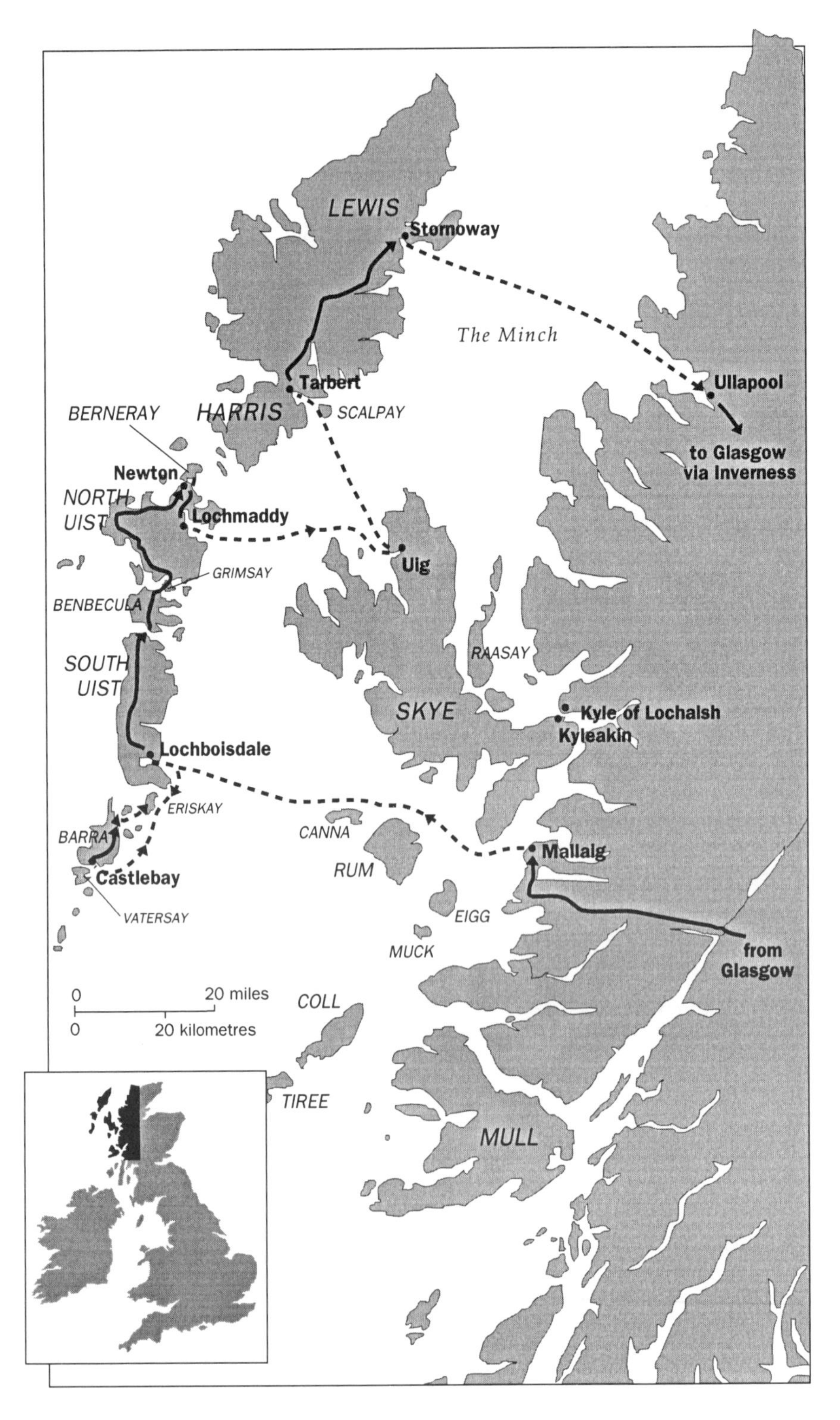
LEWIS
Stornoway
The Minch
Ullapool
to Glasgow
via Inverness
Tarbert
HARRIS
SCALPAY
BERNERAY
Newton
NORTH
UIST
Lochmaddy
Uig
GRIMSAY
BENBECULA
RAASAY
SOUTH
UIST
SKYE
Kyle of Lochalsh
Kyleakin
Lochboisdale
ERISKAY
CANNA
BARRA
Mallaig
Castlebay
RUM
VATERSAY
EIGG
MUCK
from
Glasgow
0
20 miles
0
20 kilometres
COLL
TIREE
MULL

1995 Linking The Long Isle

The Plan

The term 'Long Isle' can be used to describe the entire archipelago of the Western Isles, or Outer Hebrides, from Berneray, Mingulay and Barra in the south to Harris and Lewis in the north. The people of Lewis and Harris, however, will tell you that it is a collective term for Lewis and Harris alone. For the purpose of our trip I will choose the former meaning.

A return to the chain of the outer Western Isles for our 1995 Island Hop was considered way back in 1993 when we loosely planned the trips for the next two years. It had been our ambition, then, to travel the length of the 'Long Isle', without a car, from the south (Barra end) to the north (Lewis end). We planned to link as many of the Western Isles as possible on the way, using ferries, taxis, buses, anything that would secure our line of advance.

At the planning stage in January 1995 only one realistic option seemed possible; a route starting at Mallaig and finishing at Ullapool was chosen. We would try to visit 'new' islands on our way north. Eriskay, Vatersay and Berneray were targeted in addition to the main jewels on the Western Isles chain: Barra, the Uists, Harris and Lewis.

CalMac had returned to direct Mallaig – Barra sailings the previous year and planned to use the elderly *Iona* on this route for 1995. The *Lord of the Isles* and *Hebridean Isles* were vital ships in linking our overland travels and the *Suilven*, in her last few months of service before being replaced by the new *Isle of Lewis,* would convey us back to the mainland. For this epic journey four days were allowed.

The route offered us new islands and the chance to sail on *Iona* and *Suilven* for what was likely to be the last time. On the negative side long and expensive train journeys were necessary to get us out and back to our starting and finishing positions.

Day One – *the 'Modren Young Man'*

My journey starts two minutes before the others at Langside Station in Glasgow on Tuesday 16 May. Ian and Gibbie join my train at Pollokshaws East, the next station down the line on the Cathcart Circle.

At Central Station we split up immediately – before our journey has even seriously begun. Ian and I stride out for Queens Street Station but Gibbie opts for the wee linking bus. He likes to cram in as many types of transport as possible. Needless to say, we arrive first and spend a couple of anxious moments waiting on number three to arrive. Will we go without him? Our train to Mallaig is due to leave in ten minutes.

Arrive he does, with five minutes to spare, and we depart on a five-hour train journey on the threatened West Highland line. In actual fact the train is delayed ten minutes as we ironically await the arrival of passengers from Central Station! We try telling the BR guard that Gibbie is now in fact with us.

We have reserved our seats, which is just as well as the train is busy and stifling hot. Across the Clyde, as we hurtle along the north bank, we can see the new *Isle of Lewis* fitting out at Ferguson's Yard in Port Glasgow. She is due to enter service on the Ullapool – Stornoway route in July and is the largest ship ever built for the Western Isles services. From this distance she looks like a cross between the *Suilven* and *Lord of the Isles*.

The familiar scenery whizzes past, the waters of Loch Long and the Gareloch glisten in the welcoming sunshine. A row of brightly coloured boats way below us on Loch Long look like toy boats tied together with string.

Gibbie produces a sealed envelope from his bag and secretes it in his jacket pocket. It is his traditional 'fairin' pocket money from his mum. She has been giving him this annual holiday spending money for the past fifty-nine years. The amount contained within has to remain a secret.

Most of our fellow passengers are either American or English. The former rather loud, large and looking at maps. The latter with flasks of tea, zip up duffle-bags and barley-sugars.

The train splits at Crianlarich, the front half going to Oban and the other two coaches to Mallaig. Pity help anyone who finds himself in the wrong half. We have now made up time as we climb up towards the bleak Rannoch Moor. On the valley floor a road crosses the fields looking like a grey streak painted by a child. The wooded glens are now giving way to snow-capped mountains and glacial moraine. There may be the evidence of snow outside but inside the train we have to ask the conductor to turn the heat down as my bar of chocolate (emergency rations) is melting.

At Bridge of Orchy Station an outing of West Highland Ramblers disembark. One has his Collie with him, and an orange dog bowl tied to his rucksack. As he strides off it looks like a target stuck to his back. Let's hope there are no deer stalkers about.

At Rannoch Moor Station we encounter our first ever snowstorm on an Island Hop. We hope it will be our last. Further on at Corrour a sign lying on the ground gives our elevation as 1350 feet. Beyond the window it resembles the Himalayas. At Loch Trieg we find a wintry snowstorm at one end and summer sunshine at the other. Such are the vagaries of our Scottish weather.

We have a brief pause at Fort William where I find a pigeon sitting on her nest directly behind a station loud speaker. She seems unperturbed by the announcements of 'the train now departing....' Maybe she's a deaf pigeon. She is likely to be now.

Over the Glenfinnan Viaduct and into South Morar I am granted permission to film from the rear cab of the train. The conductor opens the rear door to reveal the track snaking away from under us.

'Please don't fall out,' he pleads. I almost jump out of my skin when we unexpectedly enter a tunnel.

Despite the beautiful scenery five hours is a long time on a train and we are glad to reach Mallaig at 1545.

Our ship *Iona* and her smaller companion *Lochmor* are at the pier. Now into her twenty-fifth year of service the*Iona* is CalMac's oldest vessel and more than beginning to show her age. Her forward saloon resembles the resident's lounge of a fading Highland hotel but it is comfortable and peaceful. The bar, several decks down, below the car-deck, is also peaceful but spartan and uninviting. Its only occupant is leaning against the bulkhead with his supply of McEwans Export around him. The voyage out to Lochboisdale will take five and a half hours! The atmosphere recalls that of a basement cellar. Red and black plastic-covered seating and only one radiator working. We will seek the warm corner later on.

We sail fifteen minutes late at 1830, held up by a broken-down artic which is eventually secured aboard along with four others and a handful of cars.

The *Iona* lists noticeably to port as she heads out towards the open waters between Rum and Skye. The cold northerly wind seems responsible for this. Never shy to ask, I am allowed to visit the ship's bridge where the mate seems even more interested in the details of our journey than I am in the details of his ship. He praises the sea-handling qualities of the *Iona* and describes the newer *Lord of the Isles* as 'diabolical' in heavy seas. Oh well, let's hope it will be this calm tomorrow night when we sail on her

Past the cliffs of Canna and across the Sea of the Hebrides towards our first port of call – Lochboisdale on South Uist. We arrive there at 2145 and watch from a cold windy deck as we spin around to dock stern first.

Gibbie has been advised by his wife Janette on the night before our departure not to scratch his troublesome elbow or speak with his mouth full. Over a scone and a mug of tea he is doing both as we eventually pull away from Lochboisdale some twenty-two minutes late. Suitably chastised he promises to behave himself from now on. The ship sets off again southwards to Barra.

The cold drives us downstairs to find that 'warm corner' and by now the single occupant is replenishing his liquid supplies with pints of draught, his cans long since emptied.

'Does this ship have stabilisers?' he asks of the barmaid whose knitting has lengthened admirably since the start of the voyage.

'It's you who needs stabilisers, Jimmy,' she retorts as Jimmy gingerly picks his way back to his cold corner.

The barmaid has fallen out of favour with Ian and Gibbie. She has referred to me as '....the young MODREN man' as I had preferred ice instead of water in my whisky. They take great offence to this blatantly accurate compartmentalisation of their fellow traveller, who is clearly able to move with the times. From now on they refer to me as 'The Modren Man'.

We hold the Island Hop Quiz that I had compiled to keep us amused during the longer part of the journey. Gibbie wins, his prize is a Bruichladdich miniature which he hides in the depths of his bag – never to be seen again during our travels, along with his little brown envelope of money. Ian is able to answer only half of the questions correctly which leaves us wondering if he has actually been on any of our previous trips!

Our present situation prompts our discussion on the various positions of bars on Clyde Steamers. On this occasion we are certainly 'down by the engines' (their traditional site) if not right underneath them. This bar is not so much in the bowels of the ship as the rectum of the ship. By the time that we sail into Castlebay we have switched our chat to Harris super-quarries.

As we pull against the pier Jimmy emerges from the bar and commences to hold a conversation with Gibbie, who is retaining his penchant for drawing the weak and feeble-minded towards him.

'You'll be looking for a good screw now!' Jimmy dares.

'Sorry, we're a bit on the tired side tonight,' Ian replies almost apologetically. We make our way briskly up the pier before Jimmy can proffer any suggestions on where we might obtain such entertainment.

We disembark at three minutes to midnight and the *Iona* slinks away into the darkness, back to Mallaig, at seven minutes past. Our beds for the night, at the friendly Castlebay Hotel, are a short stroll up the hill.

It is my first visit to Barra (Ian and Gibbie were here without me in 1991) and I look forward to daylight to see what the place looks like.

Day Two – *Whisky Galore*

Barra is a circular island, about seven miles across, with a circular road around it. The population is about 1400. The only village is Castlebay in the south, where the ferry sails from. Sheltering Castlebay is the neighbouring island of Vatersay – now linked to Barra by a causeway. At the north end of the island is the famous beach Traig Mhor, which is used as the airport runway.

Barra is the archetypal 'Katie Morag' island. A thriving community despite its relative isolation – it is a six-hour sail from Oban. It forms the southern end of the intriguing dipole of religion on the Western Isles. Just as Lewis and Harris are predominantly Protestant, the people of Barra are nearly all Catholic. The statue of Mary and Jesus on a hill overlooking Castlebay stands testament to that as do the numerous Celtic strips sported by the youngsters and not so youngsters. There are three primary schools and a secondary school, several churches and shops and a couple of hotels.

Today we require the weather to behave itself as we are planning an extended visit to the neighbouring island of Eriskay. To that end my first task of the day is a phone call to the Eriskay ferryman Willie Rusk to confirm sailing times. There are one or two doubts. How can we get to Eoligarry, some eight miles away, where Willie's boat leaves from? Is the tide suitable for a crossing? Will his boat be full? The call answers the last two questions. There is plenty of room on the boat but due to exceptionally low tides, our visit to Eriskay will have to be extended to five hours. Let's hope it keeps dry! Willie's boat will depart Eoligarry at 1045. In order to answer the first question we descend the hill after breakfast to the Post Office.

On remote islands, in the absence of a Tourist Office that is open, the Post Office usually has the answer to most questions. I find the two occupants of the Post Office locked in conversation, about some financial irregularity, which interchanges between Gaelic and English for no apparent reason, apart perhaps, from the presence of an eavesdropping tourist like me.

Our timing is excellent, the postbus leaves in ten minutes and will deliver us at Eoligarry in time for the sailing to Eriskay. What accommodating people these 'Barrachs' are.

Castlebay is an interesting collection of buildings that I rather like. A more substantial-looking village than Lochmaddy or Loichboisdale on the Uists. The southerly-facing bay is flanked on almost all sides by land and, to complete the scene, the small and well preserved Castle Kisimul sits a few hundred yards off the village shore on a tiny islet. This castle is the ancestral home of the MacNeils of Barra. The present castle has stood on this rock since the 1400s but was restored this century.

The postbus, an invaluable link to intrepid island hoppers like us, arrives, driven by Hamish, on time. We are soon being bumped along Barra roads on his morning round, turning northwards towards our destination at the tip of the island. Each post-box on route is visited and the contents duly sorted into first and second class. A few miles into the journey we pick up one other passenger who points out the statue of St Mark, standing on a small tidal islet, for our attention.

By the time that we stride up the jetty at Eoligarry our next line of advance is tying up. The *Brendan* – Willie's boat – seems well equipped for the bumpy six-mile ride over to Eriskay. With four other passengers we set off immediately. Although our fellow travellers are bound for Ludag on South Uist as the next link of their own intrepid challenge – walking from Barra to Stornoway (Gibbie shudders at the thought) – Willy offers to take us over to Eriskay first: 'We'll go the tourist route,' and he points his bow towards the south of Fuday Island.

On Fuday's shores seals sunbathe without a care in the world and a dozen fulmars sit vigilantly on their nests. A solitary gannet dive-bombs into the sea a few yards from the boat and a cluster of common terns overhead suggest that the local fishing is rewarding.

'There are a pair of golden eagles with chicks on Eriskay just now,' Willy volunteers when he notices my ornithological tendencies.

Eriskay is not big, three miles by two, and is one of those evocatively-named islands that everyone has heard of but few know exactly where it is. It sits snugly below South Uist in the Sound of Barra. Barra itself is to the south of it. A couple of hundred people live there, crofters and fishermen mostly.

We pass the western beaches of Eriskay where Bonnie Prince Charlie first set foot on Scottish soil in 1745. It had been raining then but the weather today is more favourable.

Due to delays caused by excessively low tides we will have to spend five hours on Eriskay. As we step ashore on what is a new island to all three of us, we ponder just how we are going to pass the time. Well, there is the church to visit, the hill to be climbed, the eagles to be observed and, of course, there is the pub – opened in 1988 and named the *S.S. Politician*.

The politician referred, of course, to the T and J Harrison cargo-liner of the same name which foundered off the north-east corner of Eriskay on the night of 5 February 1941. She was on her way to join a convoy bound for Jamaica. Her cargo included 264,750 bottles of whisky. The islanders, whose whisky supplies had been interrupted by the war, had a field day. The ship was towed round to a point midway between Eriskay and South Uist where it sank. Willy was succinct: 'The wreck's still there but the whisky's all gone.'

The local priest at the time, Father Calum Morrison, was even less subtle: '....nothing was done agriculturally while the Politician was accessible....it's a gift from God.' The modern day value of the cargo has been put at £8.2m.

The story was eventually immortalised in the 1948 film of Compton McKenzie's novel *Whisky Galore* which was actually filmed on neighbouring Barra. For the American audience it was renamed *Tight Little Island.*

We go in search of our own Politician and find that we have to wait an hour until it opens. In the shelter of its garden, however, we don't care and sit back in the sun watching our local eagles performing their acrobatic display in the blue skies above; holding talons and diving with wings held back. It has to be the most marvellous sight I have ever seen from a pub garden. Next door is a cottage aptly named 'Celtic View'. Its wooden fence railings are painted alternately in green and white. Everything else in the garden is also painted green and white. Even the grass is green. When we eventually gain entry to the modern looking bungalow that serves as the only pub on the island we are able to see at close quarters a couple of bottles of whisky that have been salvaged from the wreck, their contents now cloudy and evil looking. This doesn't stop Gibbie from wanting to sample a nip. He is advised against it.

We spend the remainder of our five hours on the beach, delighted that the weather has held out for what could otherwise have been a wet experience. Across the water on Barra we watch a plane take off from the beach runway at Traigh Mhor. It must be the only airport where scheduled flights are governed by the tide.

There are two items of nautical interest in the little church which sits on a hill above the village commanding a superb view of the Sound of Eriskay, the narrow strip of sea between South Uist and Eriskay, where the retreating tide is exposing a long spit of sand just out from the jetty. The altar has below it the white painted bow of a small wooden boat which apparently was one of the lifeboats from the aircraft-carrier *HMS Hermes.* This had been lost overboard during a storm.

Outside the church hangs a large brass bell which has also been salvaged, this time from a German Battleship of World War 1 vintage, the *S.M.S. Derfflinger.* I give it a sharp dong to see if it still works. It rings out loudly.

By 1630 the tide is returning and so is Willie and the *Brendan.* We deliver a teacher to South Uist who visits Eriskay on this particular weekday. I ask her what subjects she teaches.

'They get a lot of French on a Wednesday!' Lucky them.

We pass the Western Isles ferry *Eilean na H'oige* and weave a convoluted path around the treacherous rocks and reefs of the Sound of Barra back to

Eoligorry. What we imagine is a school of porpoises breaking the surface of the sea to our right turns out to be the tips of black rocks just penetrating the surface. The boat swings from side to side as Willie avoids other potential hazards unseen by our eyes.

Willie's assistant, John, is interested in how we had spent our time on Eriskay. 'Did you go up to the church?'. I nod. 'I hope you didn't ring the bell.' My expression betrays the answer to that one. John points to one of the other passengers in the cabin. 'That chap is the Eriskay priest. He wants a word with you. The bell is only rung to summon his parishioners to mass.'

On our way across, our skipper radios a taxi for us as there will be no connecting bus to get us back to Castlebay. We have three hours before *Lord of the Isles* arrives there to take us on the next sea leg of our journey and we have another island to get to before that.

Donny Sinclair is the man who has answered our Mayday for a taxi. He immediately gets into the spirit of things. Not only will he get us to Vatersay, the island just south of Barra, and connected to it by a causeway, he also suggests that we go around the west side of Barra, thus completing the circle, as we have seen the eastern shores already. What a charming chap. We sit back and enjoy our own personal tour guide. Features of interest are pointed out en route from the beach at Traigh Mhor, to the roadside boulder that looks exactly like Queen Victoria's profile. He answers our probing questions. 'Is the population of Barra stable?'

'As stable as it can be – nobody has a job.'

He wouldn't move from Barra though, even if he 'won four million on the lottery.' I would love to suggest that he buys himself a new set of windscreen wipers should such fortune look kindly upon him, as his corroded ones have seen better days but he, like the others we have met on our visit, has been so pleasant and kind that I wouldn't dare emit a single word of criticism.

Vatersay is a beautifully peaceful island once served by the ferry from Castlebay but now linked to its northern neighbour by a causeway. We cannot resist a quick dash over in order to add it to our ever growing list of islands.

Donny supplements his already overflowing ashtray while we step out onto the fourth island of our trip and fight off the amorous advances of two Vatersay dogs. It is rather a shame that we cannot see the real Vatersay but the village is spread out between the sand-dunes a couple of miles away and time is now of the essence. The *Lord of the Isles* is less than two hours away and we have not eaten for hours.

As we re-cross to Barra a huge hole on the hillside above the causeway is proof of the ease with which the quarrymen were able to supply materials for the road link to Vatersay.

Dinner at the Castlebay Hotel and arguably the best view that we have ever enjoyed from a dinner table. Our hosts suggest that we stay another day and take a trip to Mingulay – one of the southernmost, uninhabited islands of the Long Isle chain but the *Lord of the Isles* is rounding the corner into the Bay and regretfully we have to go. She spends a mere six minutes at the Pier – long enough to load us – and we are on our way to South Uist – again!

The long, sunny day and friendliness of all of the people we have met today leaves us with a warm feeling towards Barra. The chilly northerly wind, however, forces us to seek shelter in the nether regions of the ship. Just over an hour later we are sailing into Lochboisdale for the second night in succession. This time we are getting off and our beds are literally a heaving-line away from the pier.

Day Three – *That Bloody Harris Man*

The following morning reveals drizzly rain and a disappointing view of the South Uist capital. I find myself starting each day with the weather report. But it is important. Let's face it, the first thing that comes to mind on opening one's eyes in the morning is: 'What time is it?' The next thing is: 'What's the weather like?' When Island Hopping, another question springs to mind somewhere between the first two: 'Where the hell am I?'

Situated at the end of a picturesque narrow sea loch, (the ship seems to pass very close to the surrounding hills) the charm of Lochboisdale seems to melt away the further from the pier one strolls. This morning Lochboisdale is literally a building site as land is being hacked away by a bulldozer and an old crumbling building is in the process of being re-roofed right behind our hotel. A dumper truck driver sings a Gaelic ballad loudly as he unloads another ton of rock. We will not be here long, our next mode of transport is the reliable 0950 bus to Benbecula but the link after that could prove troublesome for several reasons.

Firstly we have to reach Newton, on the northern shores of North Uist fifty miles away, by 1315 in order to catch the ferry to Berneray. If we can't reach Newton on time we cannot reach this target island. Unfortunately the bus from Benbecula to North Uist will not get there on time and so an alternative is necessary. This will have to be a taxi and Alda McKaskill is the man recommended to us by the nice lady at the Lochboisdale Tourist Office. He promises us that we will be at Balivanich Airport on Benbecula to meet the arrival of our bus from South Uist.

Another potential problem is looming. The timing of our proposed ferry to Berneray is critical. Although we seem certain to reach Newton, the ferry point, in time for the 1315 sailing, we also need to be off the island and at Lochmaddy Pier by 1610 for our sailing to Harris. Yesterday the tide held us up on Eriskay but we can afford no such flexibility with our time today. If we are to miss our sailing from Lochmaddy the rest of the trip will be completely scuppered. What's more – having returned to Newton from Berneray we have no means of getting the eight miles to Lochmaddy for our sailing.

The waitress in the hotel dispels the worries about the tides, Berneray is not Eriskay and we are assured that the sailings of the ferry are not normally affected by the tides. She should know as she comes from Berneray. The other problems can perhaps be resolved later.

Our Hebridean Coaches bus trundles along the twenty odd miles to yet another island, Benbecula. We have of course experienced this part of the journey before – in 1990. The road has been improved, a little, since then.

The scattered crofts and bungalows of South Uist have an almost continental look about them. A new house sits next to the previous house which in turn sits next to the ruins of the house before that. Consequently a third of the buildings look new and another third derelict. The people around us look happy enough, however. All, that is, except our walkers from the Eriskay ferry. We pass them in the persistent drizzle as they plod on with heads slightly bowed. Poor souls, I cannot think of a more exposed and boring road on which to get soaked.

We take one detour from the Trans-Uist Highway in search of more passengers, but to no avail.

A Uist fly is buzzing around Gibbie's ear in front of me. It resists all of his headshaking and arm flailing. It obviously knows that it is onto a good thing. Perhaps it is in search of the sugar-lumps that Gibbie keeps in his camera bag: 'In case I meet a friendly horse.'

The wildlife outside the bus is equally absorbing. Greylag geese, tufted duck and redshank are common sights upon and around the mosaic of shallow roadside lakes. To me the landscape of South Uist seems totally unique.

By now we have increased in number to four. Mavis Pilby has joined our bus and been overheard enquiring of our driver how she might get to Berneray. We step in to rescue her and offer her a seat in our taxi, should it be there. This she accepts gladly.

Alda, the taxi-driver, is true to his word and he solves the first and last parts of our North Uist/ Berneray problems. Not only will he take us to Newton in time to catch the ferry but he will also collect us on our return in time to make our Lochmaddy sailing. Obviously a man fully understanding of the needs of an Island Hopper. Taxi-drivers in the Western Isles seem to be particularly obliging. Perhaps they feel slightly sorry for us. They probably all go home at night and say to their wives: 'Those sad ship-spotting loonies are back on the island again.'

Our visit to Benbecula is brief, in actual fact a fifty-yard dash between bus and taxi. If our previous taxi-driver Donny had been a good storyteller then Alistair is a true Hans Christian Anderson. A North Uist man, his gentle brogue is a delight on the next twenty-seven miles of our journey through the lakes and bogs of his native island. As he speaks a Hercules transport plane touches down onto the RAF base at the northern end of Benbecula. I have to interrupt him to point out that we are now leaving Benbecula by causeway and are crossing yet another tidal island, Grimsay. One further linking causeway and we are on Alda's home island. 'At one time there were 3,000 horses on North Uist,' Alda informs us. Gibbie's sugar may yet come in handy.

It is now noon and we realise that we are going to miss lunch as we wait at Newton for the ferry to Berneray. There is no cafe of any description at Newton, only a small waiting room and nothing else. Alda refuses money at this stage 'That way you'll know I'll be back for you!' At least he also knows that we can't exactly go very far either.

We chat to Mavis, who consumes a succession of chocolate bars, fruits and drinks which make us feel even hungrier. All we have is a custard cream and a small carton of pineapple juice between us. Never mind – Berneray, which now lies one mile offshore, has a cafe.

Mavis works for the British Museum. She is on a working tour of the Western Isles. It seems like a good way to earn a living. Her subject is Japanese art and she has conducted two lectures in Stornoway on this subject. The first night attracted an audience of five, including the local museum curator. Sadly, on the second night poor Mavis was on her own. She seems unperturbed -at least she had no hecklers. The people of Lewis must consider Japanese art low down on their list of cultural pursuits. As we have a further wait of three-quarters of an hour Mavis produces an apple from her pocket and strolls off for an exploration of the shoreline.

We study the map of the island that we are striving so hard to reach. Berneray is four miles by two miles. The east side accommodates most of the settlements and is low-lying and grassy. The west side is composed of a rich seam of machair, almost uncultivated and its shore is one long sandy beach. The island reached the newspaper headlines in recent years when Prince Charles visited, on two occasions, seeking solitude. On his first visit his presence was kept a complete secret by the islanders. Not even their neighbours on North Uist were privy to the identity of their royal guest. Eventually, when the word leaked out that Charles had been on Berneray for a week, a large posse of pressmen assembled at Newton requesting to be taken over to the island. By some strange twist of fate their visit was coincident with the ferryman having difficulty with the gear-box on his boat. One thousand pounds was offered to anyone with a boat who would take the press over to Berneray. There were no takers and Charles eventually left by helicopter. The cottage where Charles stayed on his visit was pinpointed for us on our map.

On his second visit to Berneray, Charles brought Selina Scott and a BBC film crew with him.

Our ferry is having no such gear-box troubles. To our surprise it is not the Western Isles Council vessel but CalMac's 'Island class' *Bruernish*. This is good news for us as the *Bruernish* is one of only four CalMac ships that we have never sailed on. (*Rhum, Loch Linnhe, Loch Dunvegan* are the others). Berneray is not a 'CalMac Island' but today it is, and one of their little ships that was going to take us there.

'Splash' McKillop appears on the slipway. He is the man who had 'put up' Prince Charles in his cottage during the Royal Visit. I was too shy to ask him why he is called 'Splash' but had a quick peep into his van to see if another Royal Prince was hiding in there. No such luck.

On studying our map we could see another slight problem – well for one of us anyway. The village on Berneray is a mile from the slipway and Gibbie's Scalpay Nightmare beckons yet again. The solution, in the shape of a five-ton lorry, stands waiting on the concrete slipway.

'That's for me,' says Gibbie. A quick negotiation and reciting of the now infamous Scalpay Tale to the driver, Finlay, secures a lift in the cab for Gibbie to the village of Borve. The heart-rending Scalpay saga must have tugged at Finlay's magnanimity.

While this is going on, I am involved in discussion with another vehicle driver, who pulls up at Newton looking a bit bewildered as to why his pocket compass points west instead of north. He accepts my tongue-in-check assessment that the delinquency of the compass is due to the natural magnetism of the rocks. Apparently satisfied with my reply he turns his vehicle and drives off south – or is it east ?

The *Bruernish* chugs across to get Ian and me, Mavis and her fruit and Gibbie in his lorry. Our skipper is none other than the cheery Angus McInnes whom we remember from one of our Clyde trips in 1991 when he skippered the *Keppel*. His old charge is, as I write, beginning a new lease of life in Malta.

To our delight the rain has now gone and the weather window which we hoped for appears. The sun shines from the moment that we step on to Berneray until the minute that we leave. It is still unseasonably cool, however. We have one and a half hours on the island. First stop is the cafe. Gibbie and Finlay roar off along the narrow road while Ian, Mavis and I stride out to rendezvous with him at the only eating place. Half a mile further on who should be coming down the hill to meet us but Gibbie. Having allowed Finlay to drive him to the far end of Berneray he then ask: 'Where is the Cafe, Finlay?'

'The Cafe! Och it was the very first building we passed half a mile back!'

Scalpay revisited. Our footsore companion fortunately seems to see the funny side of it – this time ! Ian and I have no reason to be smug either – we have walked right past the cafe ourselves.

Mavis says her goodbyes to us. She is off to find her Bed and Breakfast accommodation, just as Prince Charles had probably done.

After all these shenanigans we find the Cafe is closed – but the shop isn't. A loaf of bread, a packet of sliced ham, as we sit on a plank of wood outside, goes a long way. Dessert is a packet of Tunnock's Caramel Wafers.

While Gibbie recovers from his hi-jacking, Ian and I stroll out to the village at Borve from where we have a stunning view over the machair towards the island of Pabbay and the Atlantic Ocean. Berneray looks very peaceful.

Our short visit is over and we sail back to North Uist on the *Bruernish*. Alda is waiting with his taxi and we listen to part two of his Hebridean folklore. His family roots on the island can be traced back to the early fourteenth century and the days of Robert the Bruce. Finally he has some advice for our future Island Hop plans. Hearing that we are ultimately on our way to Lewis he explains the popular story going around the island at the moment regarding the new ferry, *Isle of Lewis*, soon to replace *Suilven*. The famous Brahmin Seer, an early day clairvoyant, is alleged to have predicted that the Isle of Lewis would one day sink. The people of Lewis, of course, believed that it was impossible for their island to founder. With the naming of CalMac's new ferry to serve Stornoway, however, the connotation has changed. The Seer was of course referring to the ship, not the island.

'Be warned,' says Alda, 'the only survivor in the tale was wearing red shoes, make sure you have them on when you take your first sailing on the *Isle of Lewis*.'

We do not, of course, believe in such superstition – but, just in case, I make a mental note to order three pairs of red shoes for future trips.

Alda delivers us in good time at Lochmaddy. He is a fascinating chap and his handshakes, to the three of us in turn, are very genuine. This time he takes the money.

The sun is still shining over the North Uist capital as we set up tripods and cameras to film and photograph the *Hebridean Isles* sailing into the bay. Little has changed in Lochmaddy since our last visit here during Island Hop number two in 1990.

My favourite ship sails on time at 1610 for Uig, Skye, and eventually our own destination – Tarbert, Harris. We are sailing on two legs of the Uig triangle today.

We have a meal and then stretch out in the sun on the upper deck where we find shelter from the north-easterly wind. After a busy day this is a very relaxing part of the trip. The views of Vaternish on Skye are stunning.

The stop at Uig on Skye is brief and we are soon heading back across the Little Minch to Harris. It is difficult to identify the various land masses to the west of us as the peaks of hills, rising above the invisible flat plains of the Uists, resemble distant islands. What looks like Rum turns out to be South Uist. We can make out the highest mountain, Hecla, more than forty miles away. The flatter land is beyond the horizon.

We reach the narrow sea loch at Tarbet on Harris and disembark. Our hotel is a few hundred yards away and because it is full we have been given a family room with three single beds in it. We have known this in advance and have placed a ban on lentil casserole or bean hotpot from the supper menu accordingly.

The hotel brochure has some interesting advice on pets: 'We would appreciate if they were not allowed to foul the front lawns. Flying Flymo-ed Faeces Foul Faces.' I am glad that I have already eaten when I read this. We choose to descend to the attractive and bustling bar where we can each choose a different malt for our collective palates to savour. Gibbie takes the precaution of shaving before we start in case things get out of hand and he slits his throat later on.

A Glenkinchie chosen by Gibbie, a Talisker by myself and then things really do get out of hand – a Courvousier for Ian! We will have to educate this man. Meanwhile in the corner of the lounge the old lady with the wig breaks wind very loudly.

As the night wears on we are joined by Mr Morrison, the owner of the hotel, who gives us a brief history of the division of the third largest island in the British Isles into Harris and Lewis. The split originates from the division of the land between two brothers but as no roads passed between Lewis, in the north and Harris, the two areas evolved socially into two communities. In more recent years when two farmers argued over the position of the boundary they dug down and found the charcoal remains of the original Harris/Lewis border. The boundary, therefore, seems to have been an amalgamation between historical and geographical influences and in modern times now runs south-eastwards from Loch Resort to Loch Seaforth.

Mr. Morrison has been influential in preventing the Sunday sailings by CalMac to and from Harris. CalMac are always keen to run their ships 7 days a week but the strong feelings in the predominantly Protestant Harris, Lewis and North Uist towards the preservation of the integrity of the Sabbath as a day of rest is very stoic. For the time being Morrison`s views have won the day. 'CalMac call me "that bloody Harris man",' he chuckles proudly.

Day Four – *The Final Link*

Our last day dawns bright but still cool. We are completing our journey through the Long Isle today but, as our bus is not due to leave Tarbert for Stornoway until 1145, we realise that the spare morning will allow an additional unscheduled sailing opportunity which cannot be missed. Our old stamping ground of Scalpay, last visited in the heatwave of 1992, beckons. We can easily reach it and get back to Tarbert in time for our Stornoway bus. Gibbie is negative about this at first. Once we have promised him that he will not actually have to walk on Scalpay he relents.

At the breakfast table we muse that the only difference between my 'sausage and bacon' and Ian's 'full mixed grill' is that Ian has a fried tomato – which he does not like anyway.

I approach the reception desk gingerly with cheque book in hand and a request in mind. The proprietor's gaze follows me with a mercenary eye. 'You're a marked man as soon as you walk in here,' he grins.

My request is granted. A taxi is telephoned to take us to the ferry at Kyles Scalpay. There is no connecting bus. 'Hallo Donald, could you come to the hotel to collect three scallywags for Scalpay?'

Morrison considers our craving for new islands rather eccentric. He is completely correct, of course. 'Come back next year and spend two days here.' Where have we heard that before? 'You'll be able to visit Taransay, Pabbay, Ensay, Killegray, Scarp.' I vow to look these ones up on the map later.

So the three 'Scalpay Scallywags' set off in yet another taxi on the six miles to catch the wee CalMac ferry to one of the most densely populated of the Western Isles – Scalpay, island number eleven.

A bridge is being planned to link Harris with Scalpay and thus CalMac will sail to one island less. We ask our driver Donald what he thinks of the bridge proposal. 'It will mean a few changes to the islanders, they'll have to get MOTs for their cars and their children will have to stop driving them.'

As he deposits us and drives off back to Tarbert the only sounds that reach our ears are the lapping of the waves, a calling cuckoo and Gibbie muttering something about '...I'm not walking to Mrs McTavish's!'

The *Canna* is the ferry – just as it was in 1992. Due to our tight schedule, we have to catch the 1145 bus to Stornoway to complete the last link of our Long Isle trip and we can only afford an hour on the island.

Ian and I stride off to the village to supplement the profits of the local grocer's – but not by much. We find it closed but the owner comes running across the road from his house. 'Sorry – I was having my morning cup of tea,' he humbly apologises. I then apologise for the 18p purchase of a carton of orange juice.

'Oh don't worry – I'd open just to sell a box of matches.'

Scalpay is as quiet and peaceful as Berneray had been. We never make it to Mrs McTavish's for a cup of tea but turn back to meet Gibbie who has followed us out along the winding road. After all the fuss he has made about his 1992 visit here, he claims that '. . . the road now doesn't seem as long!'

We re-cross to find our connecting bus waiting to take us back to Tarbert. We are well into our fourth day and are due back home tonight but still have forty miles to cross of another island, Lewis, before reaching the end of our trek along the length of the Long Isle.

The bus twists and turns along the single-track road which winds its way across the barren, rocky hills of south-east Harris. All around the scene resembles a lunar landscape – the bare gneiss penetrating the thin soils to such an extent that there appears more rock than vegetation. The resulting pattern is completely different from the landscape of the Uists and Benbecula. The people of Harris show how much they respect their fragile environment a mere five days after we return home. They vote against the proposed conversion of one of their mountains at Lingerbay into a superquarry. The resulting hole in the landscape would have been visible from space.

As we arrive back in Tarbert the *Hebridean Isles* is returning to the berth she vacated at 0730 the same morning. We are not boarding her again, however. We step off one bus onto another to complete our journey to Stornoway.

Now we climb up amongst the highest mountains of the Western Isles. The bus labours uphill beyond Ardhasaig and drizzly rain begins to trickle down the windows. By the time we reach the top of the pass the mountain vista outside recalls the Land of the Giants. Meanwhile, inside the bus, my two companions are in the 'Land of Nod'.

We speed downhill now, along the shores of Loch Seaforth with its mountainous island rising from its depths. Imperceptibly we pass from Harris into Lewis. Like our crossing to Vatersay, Grimsay and Benbecula we can pass from one island to another without the use of a ferry.

The scenery is suddenly quite different. Mountains and bare rock give way to a softer, peaty land dotted with numerous houses. Lewis, the largest Scottish island, sustains a sizeable population and its capital Stornoway contains the administration centre of the Western Isles chain.

Our bus reaches Stornoway just as the *Suilven* is berthing at the pier. I had hoped the she would be running late as this will be my one and only chance of filming her arrival at the port. We are anxious to get off quickly to get a photograph but there is a queue down the central aisle of the bus as passengers wait to pay. Gibbie is at the head of it and having communication problems.

'Three from Tarbert, please.'

'That's three times £2.95, now let me work that out...' says the driver.

Gibbie tries to be helpful. 'Three times £3, then subtract fifteen pence.'

The driver is now confused. 'No no, two ninety-five plus two ninety-five then another....'

We wait patiently. A chap behind me points to Gibbie and offers his opinion. 'He talks just like one of these MP chaps, doesn't he?'

'Yes,' I reply, 'and he has a degree in mathematics as well.'

Gibbie is exasperated by all this. 'That guy behind us has a screw loose. Or in proper engineering-speak: he is one section off the full manual.'

By the time we get off the bus there is no time for any pictures, we have to get on board. The ship has already berthed.

Stornoway must surely have many attractive features about it – but today we do not see them. Perhaps we are in too much of a hurry. We hurry from bus to ship. Going up the gangplank of the *Suilven* Gibbie shows his run-around ticket to the crewman. 'It's a Rover ticket,' Gibbie volunteers.

'Just as well it isn't an Escort you've got or it wouldn't be much use to you,' the crewman erupts into laughter at his own joke which seems rather well rehearsed. Gibbie gives him a stony look.

The *Suilven* is due to finish service on the route that she has made her own for twenty-two years in just two months time. Although of an attractive appearance and considerable car-carrying capacity her passenger accommodation is inadequate when compared to her more modern consorts. The notice requesting passengers not to be recumbent in the lounge is being ignored by a couple of supine sleepyheads.

During her career with CalMac the*Suilven* has only once strayed from the Ullapool/Stornoway route and then only for two weeks, when she replaced the *Isle of Mull* on the Oban – Craignure service in October 1989. Her successor, the *Isle of Lewis*, with her superior speed, will hopefully take an hour off the crossing time, which today would be three and a half hours. We have sailed on the *Suilven* during the course of our 1992 Island Hop and today, as on our previous trips, we take the Annual Toast. Unlike on that occasion, we do not enjoy Mediterranean temperatures but as we make our way eastwards across the Minch the rain gradually abates. The sea is calm.

I film from various vantage points around the deck and then descend to a reclining chair for a snooze – well it has been a busy day. By an amazing stroke of luck Glbbie finds my prized *Royal Yacht Britannia* badge, which I am not aware I have lost, upon the deck rail of the upper deck where it had fallen out of my jacket as I leaned over for an astern shot a full hour previously. It had caught his eye while he was up top taking the air and he had almost flicked it into the sea. 'Where did *you* get a *Royal Yacht Britannia* badge from anyway?' he demands.

'Oh, I found it on the road on Berneray,' I tell him. 'Someone important must have dropped it.'

The *Suilven* enters the fjord of Loch Broom and Ullapool juts out in the distance. I ascend to the bridge to do the filming that has been approved by the mate and find our jovial crewman relating his joke about Gibbie's Rover ticket to the skipper, John Norman McDonald. '...and I said to him it's just as well it's not an Escort you've got....' Much guffawing as I leave the bridge, having a bit of a giggle myself.

Ullapool is enjoying some sunshine as we dock, stern in at 1700. We bid farewell to the *Suilven* as this will certainly be our last ever look at her. As I descend the gangway back to mainland Scotland the crewman collecting tickets nudges the purser and points at Gibbie.

'That's him there. I said to him just as well it's not an Escort . . .'

By now the entire ships crew must have heard the tale.

Another bus. We can take our pick between several coach companies. Inverness is an hour and a half away and our filming terminates there. On the express train back to Glasgow's Queen Street Station we reflect on the highlights of the trip as we are speedily and almost noiselessly conveyed through the beautiful verdant scenery of Inverness-shire.

The trip has certainly been a success – a record twelve islands with four good lengthy sea crossings on major ships. We have been successful in attaining Eriskay and Berneray as important links in the chain of the Western Isles. The route, we felt, has been a good one with the highlight probably being the *Hebridean Isles*. The weather has been sunny and dry just when it needed it to be, though unseasonably cold.

Another drunk latches onto Gibbie as we pass Pitlochry. At Stirling the inebriate (not Gibbie) staggers off to relieve himself and never makes it back again. The doors slam in his face as he tries to retrace his steps to the carriage. We have to suppress our urge to wave goodbye to him. He is the last of this year's 'Island Hop' characters. We have certainly met a few of them – most of them taxi-drivers.

As we pull into Queen Street Station at 2330 our final collective thoughts are next year. A few gaps in our collection of islands will have to be filled.

* * *

Postscript: Since returning home Ian has been putting ice instead of water into his whisky – he reckons that he now looks ten years younger!

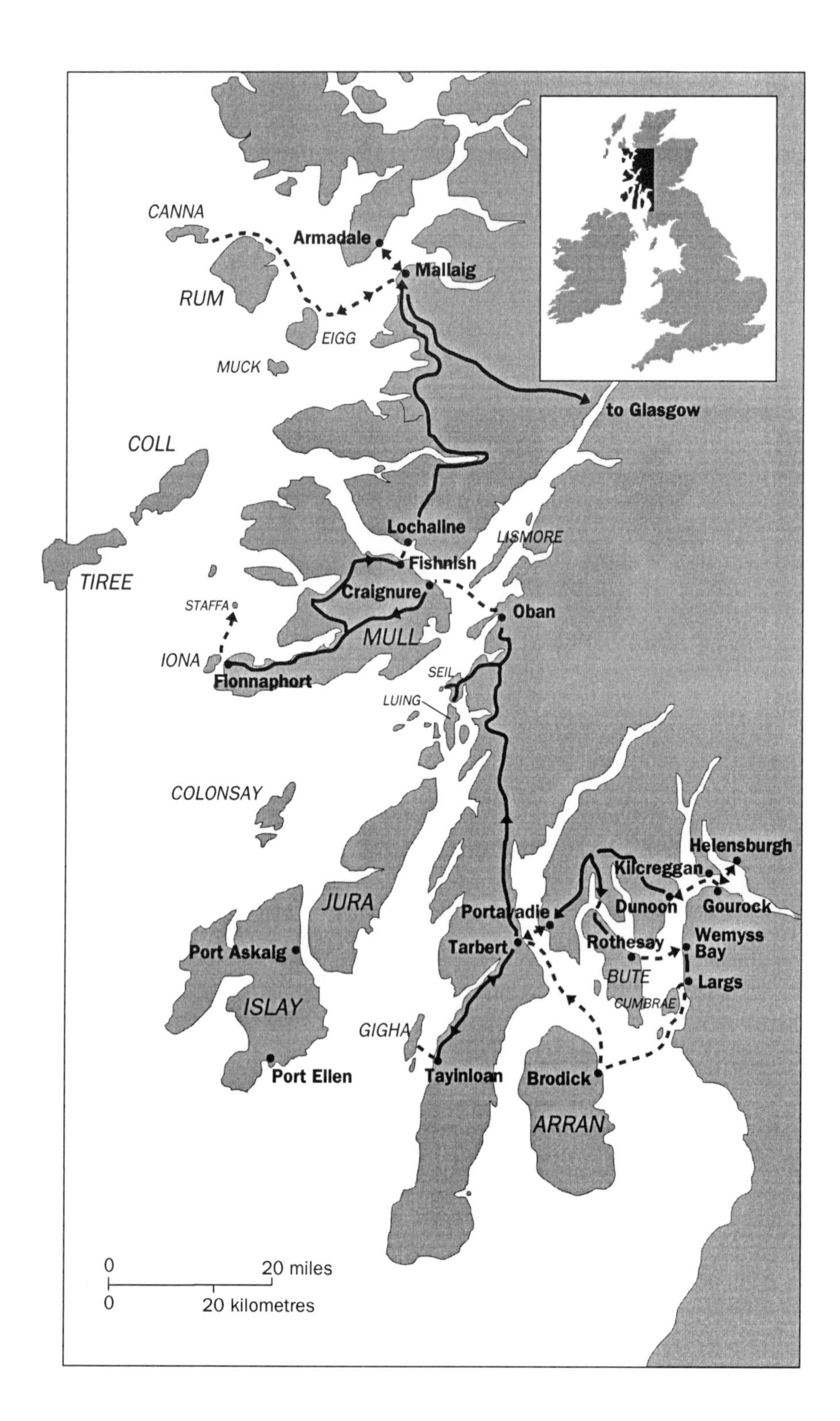
CANNA
Armadale
Mallaig
RUM
EIGG
MUCK
to Glasgow
COLL
Lochaline
LISMORE
Fishnish
TIREE
Craignure
STAFFA
Oban
MULL
IONA
Fionnaphort
SEIL
LUING
COLONSAY
Helensburgh
Kilcreggan
Dunoon
Gourock
JURA
Portavadie
Tarbert
Rothesay
Wemyss Bay
Port Askaig
BUTE
Largs
ISLAY
CUMBRAE
GIGHA
Port Ellen
Tayinloan
Brodick
ARRAN
0
20 miles
0
20 kilometres

1996 Small Ships For Small Isles

The Plan

After seven years of Island Hopping it would be reasonable to assume that there are no new adventures to seek or ambitions to be fulfilled. In fact in seven years we must surely have repeated ourselves and from now on be crossing old ground and not new. In other words, are we not totally fed up with crossing to Craignure on the *Isle of Mull* or stepping off a train at Mallaig or jumping off a small ferry onto some remote island only to turn around and get back on it again? In actual fact – no! There are always new vessels coming onto the scene and there are several islands on which we have never set foot. This year, instead of choosing new ships, like CalMac's new Stornoway vessel *Isle of Lewis*, unclaimed islands would beckon us on Island Hop number eight.

Looking back at the two previous years, both were planned with a geographical theme. This year there would be no geographical pattern and with one notable exception it would not be a quest for particular vessels. This would be pure island bagging.

At the planning phase, a map of the west of Scotland was spread out on the living-room carpet and various islands were pinpointed. Islands that could be easily reached. Islands that we had not visited before. A way of linking them had to be worked out. A path had to be woven, loosely linking them to available ferry sailings. To do this timetables had to be poured over and connections between various routes considered. Ideas sprang to mind, were considered and then discarded because they would not link up in the time available. But eventually a way of linking the target islands developed, and the Island Hop was born. This is how all the Hop plans evolved. The islands chosen for 1996 were dotted randomly along the west coast of Scotland with nothing in common other than the fact that the three of us had never been on them together as part of an Island Hop.

There was Gigha in the south. It was almost claimed by us back in 1991 on Hop Three but was forsaken due to the cost of the necessary taxi.

There was Staffa, visited by Gibbie and me in 1989 but missed out due to bad weather in 1993 and still to be graced by Ian's presence.

The trio of Luing, Easdale and Seil were easily accessible but had never been considered before.

There were of course, the Small Isles of Canna, Muck, Eigg and Rum. We had almost reached one or two of them, back on Hop Four in 1992 but missed out because we altered our plans at the last minute.

Finally, there was Kerrera – but we decided to give that one a miss.

To get to all of these islands in three or four days would require the use of a car, for the first time since 1993. Our trips had in the past always taken place in May but due to domestic obligations, which must always take precedence over everything else, our 1996 Hop was to take place in late April. This allowed the possibility of another intriguing option. The paddle steamer *Waverley* was due to give a couple of sailings on the Clyde at the end of April and it seemed likely that we could include her in our itinerary for the first time. We had never sailed on a *real* steamer – mainly because there are none left apart from the grand old paddler.

Looking back, it seems a bit of a shame, or even a downright outrage, that it had taken eight Island Hops for us to get aboard the *Waverley.* She is the most famous steamer of them all and we were only now including her in one of our itineraries. Actually the reason for this is simple. Our Island Hops had always taken place in May – usually the third week. The *Waverley* is normally sailing in English waters then. But this year, because our trip would take place in April we could join her on one of her early season Clyde sailings.

A route was chosen that would take four days to complete and allow us to join the *Waverley* for at least part of her Clyde River Steamer Club charter on the Clyde.

The Clyde River Steamer Club was formed by a group of steamer enthusiasts in 1932 and is still going strong today, even though steamers are a bit thin on the ground, or should I say water. Over the years they have organised Club charters of many of the most famous of the Clyde steamers, from the old paddle-steamer *Lucy Ashton* in 1948 to the modern car-ferry *Caledonian Isles* in 1996. The *Waverley* has obviously featured heavily in recent times and the timing of our Island Hop coincided with the 1996 Club charter of her – an opportunity not to be missed. The destination of the *Waverley* was Ardrishaig on Loch Fyne. We would take her some of the way. On Saturday 27 April she would sail from Greenock and Helensburgh to Largs, Brodick, Tarbert and Ardrishaig. This would be Day Two of our Island Hop and would mean that Day One would involve a bit of car positioning. In reality this meant taking a car to Tarbert (Loch Fyne) and leaving it there. We would return to it on Day Two via *Waverley* and then have the means to continue northwards on our quest for islands new. Clever? Without a car, we could never reach some of our far-flung destinations in the limited time available to us. In fact there were long stretches of this year's trip where we would not use the car. We needed it simply as a tool with which to link up the good bits of the Hop.

Day One – *Coke Rustlers*

Friday morning 0845 and, with Gibbie at the wheel of his Rover, we are on our way towards Gourock below skies which are darkening with every mile. It is the start of a fairly hectic day which will involve seven ferry crossings on five different vessels and a car chase around the Cowal and Kintyre peninsulas trying to get aboard them on time. Late in the afternoon the car will be left at Tarbert and we will have to make our way to our overnight berths at Rothesay under our own steam. It seems like a mad scramble but in fact it has been carefully orchestrated and measured.

Prior to boarding the Dunoon ferry at Gourock, we are going to join the

Clyde Marine Motoring vessel on her morning triangular route from Gourock to Helensburgh and Kilcreggan. The only reason for doing this is that we can fit it easily into our schedule and it will add two 'new' Clyde piers to our tally. The vessel should have been the *Kenilworth* but due to a last minute hitch we are denied a 'new' ship and have make do with her substitute, the *Second Snark*. Apparently the *Kenilworth* has experienced problems with her steering chain and had been taken off for repairs.

The rain has started as we pull away from the decaying Gourock pier towards the north bank. Being aboard a low-decked vessel at low tide affords us an unfortunately subterranean view of the rotting timbers of this once great curving pier. It is not a sight for the faint-hearted steamer enthusiast. Nobody seems to have the money or the inclination to prevent this historic structure from turning into dust and falling bit by bit into the Clyde. Whereas the old steamers have all but gone, they have at least been replaced by vessels of a sort, but it is this decaying structure that, more than anything, portrays the end of the golden age of the Clyde Steamer. Once lined with the great paddlers and turbines (and even the odd great motor-vessel) of the past, the changes in the transport scene are no better exemplified than by the long, empty, rotting Gourock Pier. Maybe multi-storey car parks will one day sit abandoned and rejected like this.

The cold, *dreich* (what a great word) atmosphere adds to a general air of depression not normally encountered at the start of an Island Hop. We head below deck to the cosy saloon where Chris, the chief steward, pours us expensive teas and enthuses about his job. He does not have many customers today but at Helensburgh the total number of passengers almost doubles when three intending travellers loom above us from the pier. They remain 'intending' as, to our surprise, boarding is denied to them. Apparently they are 'Coke rustlers'. Not of the cocaine variety but more of the American soft drink type. The skipper has recognised them as the three lads who had stolen a couple of trays of the drink from the bar of the *Kenilworth* a few days previously. A radio call to headquarters confirms that access will be denied and we sail without them. They are left standing in the rain. Serves them right, if you ask me.

The ship has been delayed seven minutes by these capers on a schedule that is fairly tight. We hope that the *Snark* is not to be a bogey ship as far as delays are concerned (see Island Hop 1994). Gibbie claims that he would have let the three raiders come aboard and then hung them from the yard-arm. Unfortunately the *Second Snark* does not have a yard-arm but then there is always keel-hauling. We cast off from Helensburgh pier eventually or, at least, I cast off with some style, I might add.

At Kilcreggan we are joined by another dozen passengers but the heavy rain ensures that the cameras remain in our bags. Sadly Kilcreggan becomes the only pier or slipway that we have visited without taking a photograph. We cannot afford more tea from the saloon, but we will soon be back at Gourock – not that there is much to offer of a culinary nature there. CalMac has recently withdrawn catering facilities on its upper Clyde routes. An incongruous vending machine now replaces the bar staff on the Dunoon and Rothesay ferries.

The Dunoon ferry in question is the *Saturn*. She will take us over to Cowal.

There are now four permanently rostered vessels on the upper Firth. The *Pioneer* is always one of the Rothesay vessels and covers the midweek cruises to Arran. The other three: *Jupiter*, *June* and *Saturn* cover the Dunoon roster, second Rothesay roster and the back-up. This back-up gives additional services to Dunoon, performs midweek sailings to Tighnabruaich and takes over from the *Pioneer* when the latter sails to Arran. The three ships change their rosters on a weekly basis. On this Friday morning the main Dunoon vessel is the *Saturn*. She takes us to our fourth Clyde pier of the morning, Dunoon. It is only 1150 but we don't hang around as we have barely an hour to get across Cowal to our next ferrypoint – Portavadie.

Our route takes us through Tighnabruaich via the high road above the Kyles of Bute. Normally the view from here down the East Kyle is splendid but today the low cloud is filling the glens and we cannot see much, apart from the road ahead of us.

At Tighnabruaich we can only afford the briefest of visits to the local Spar shop to purchase the ingredients for a wholesome lunch. We arrive at Portavadie in good time for our 1300 sailing across Loch Fyne. This route, which was inaugurated in 1994, saves us a long drive around the head of the longest sea-loch in Scotland and sets us up nicely for our trip to Gigha. So off we go on the *Rhum*, vessel number three towards peninsula number three – we have still to reach our first island.

The *Rhum* is the only 'Island class' ferry that we have not sailed on in the course of our years of travel. The crossing of Loch Fyne takes twenty minutes and Gibbie is soon scraping the front valance of his Rover off the Tarbert slipway.

On across the narrowest part of Kintyre. Our next destination is the ferry-point of Tayinloan, nineteen miles away, on the west side of Kintyre. From here the island of Gigha is served by the ferry *Loch Ranza*. We speed southwards as fast as the roadworks will allow and arrive with just five minutes to spare.

Gigha is to be the first island of our trip and a 'new' island as well. 'God's Island', as its name means, is an attractive and fertile little strip some five miles by two. Interestingly, from certain aerial viewpoints it is shaped very much like a map of Scotland – just like Loch Garry! It sits a couple of miles off the west coast of Kintyre and is sheltered from the mighty Atlantic Ocean by the island of Islay away to the west. The North Atlantic Drift (Gulf Stream to you and me) slops right past its shores and offers it a mild climate. So mild that there are several palm trees growing on Gigha. I have bathed in the sea around Gigha – the water still feels bloody cold. The warming effect of the North Atlantic Drift is a subtle one. The island is famous for its sandy beaches and the Achmore Gardens. These were laid out by the late James Horlick, of even-tide beverage fame, in the 1950s.

As is often the case on our trips, the visit to Gigha will be an ephemeral one – in fact for Gibbie it is to be positively fleeting. He elects to step ashore only and then return directly on the ferry to the mainland. Ian and I, however, want to spend an hour ashore to 'take in all the sights'.

Gigha is the twenty-eighth island that we have visited on our Island-Hopping. The hour and ten minutes ashore is not as brief as some of our visits to previous islands: our three minutes on Raasay in 1993, two minutes on Jura in 1989 and one minute driving across Grimsay in 1995 all spring to mind.

As we take our first steps ashore on lush Gigha, the rain finally stops and the sky begins to clear. The only sights we manage are the hotel and the church where a stained glass window dedicated to the aforementioned Mr. Horlick attracts the eye.

On our return we present the less intrepid Gibbie with a new Gigha sweat-shirt as a souvenir – and ask him to pay for it.

Back up to Tarbert. Our arrival coincides with the imminent departure of the *Rhum* back to Portavadie so we chose to join her instead of waiting for a later sailing. Gibbie's car is abandoned at the side of the road where we consider that it will be perfectly safe for the next twenty-four hours. As we stride out along the road towards the waiting ferry Gibbie looks back at it ruefully, like a dog owner who has just told his pooch to 'sit!' while he wanders off – only Gibbie will be gone a whole day.

On the *Rhum* again, nautically speaking, of course, we are accompanied by a few more passengers this time. There are two Chilean fish-farmers crossing to the Norwegian-owned fish farm at Portavadie. There is also an elderly gentleman, equipped with clipboard and questionnaires, who is carrying out a passenger survey for the Tourist Board. He wants to know our reason for travelling, how we knew about this ferry route and details of our final destination. Unfortunately he does not have a category on his questionnaire that in any way fits our journey description. This is perhaps not surprising. Our 'final destination' causes him a few problems as well – Canna!

We now have a bit of thinking to do. We have to get ourselves to Rothesay, somehow, or as Gibbie is in the habit of putting it: 'secure our line of advance'. He has been reading about the Napoleonic wars again. Our first target is to get to the ferrypoint of Colintraive, twenty miles away, without a car. The one and only bus left hours ago and there is nobody on the *Rhum* who looks friendly enough to beg a lift from. Gibbie has gone around the small ship eyeing up everyone appealingly but all he has got back are suspicious looks. It appears that we will have to use a taxi. Fortunately we are no longer in a rush and have no hectic deadline to reach. After a busy day of ferry-hopping, the afternoon pace is slowing down.

The chap at the ticket office at Portavadie offers some assistance in the form of tea and taxi telephone numbers – we accept both. There follows half an hour of that usual Island Hop activity – hanging around. It's something that I actually quite enjoy. There is usually a spell or two on every Island Hop when we are waiting for some form of transport to show up and all we can do is stand around and wait for it. It is usually quite a relaxing experience – as long as the awaited mode of transport actually does arrive on time. The exception to all this is when we have a car with us. Somehow a car destroys all need to hang around. But as the car was hanging around at Tarbert for a day, we have to do likewise across the water at Portavadie – but only for half an hour. I can think of better places to hang around in than Portavadie. The name is synonymous with the oil industry for in the 1970s, during the boom in oil exploration in the North Sea, Portavadie was earmarked as a wilderness worth destroying for the sake of progress. A huge basin was excavated and a village built to house the hundreds of workers who would be descending upon this quiet spot to construct an oil-rig. Unbelievably no oil-rig was ever fabricated as no order for one was ever forthcoming. Like the much lamented Inverkip Power Station chimney, a blot on the landscape stands testament to another white elephant. What a pity one couldn't be buried in the other.

Mr Smith arrives at half past five with his taxi and we pile in. Our journey to Colintraive is aurally illustrated by our driver's chat. He is a former shepherd and he updates us on all the local gossip and history in the form of a cheerful banter that is sustained for the twenty miles to our next ferrypoint. Climbing up out of Tighnabruaich, above the Kyles of Bute, he bemoans the lack of driving skills among the young locals as he slews his taxi yet again back onto the left hand side of the road. He must have enjoyed the ride as much as we have for on reaching Colintraive he sheepishly gives us his price and then gives us a discount. It is more than a coincidence that Gibbie has been instructed to pay for this part of our journey. He never seems to get charged the full rate for anything. Perhaps people feel sorry for him or perhaps he just has an honest face.

Our next little ship, *Loch Riddon,* is waiting at the slipway at Colintraive for the very short crossing to the Isle of Bute. That is all very well but how can we advance from there? Rothesay, our base for the night, lies nine miles away across the island.

The answer comes in the shape of a single-decker coach at the side of the road. Two mechanics emerge from the rear end and enter into a conversation with the blue-blazered driver that is punctuated with much head-shaking and arm-elevating. I seize on an opportunity to further our aims and approach the driver. Anyone as smartly attired as he and in charge of a vehicle such as this just has to be heading for Rothesay. A quick chat with him and so are we!

It transpires that the bus has been suffering from a leaky hydraulic suspension but by a stroke of luck has just been repaired as we arrive on the scene. Ian shakes his head in disbelief at our luck and my audacity for asking for a lift. Onto the ferry it goes, with us tucked cosily inside.

The driver, Alan, is a Newcastle United fan but seems happy enough nevertheless. While giving us his informed opinion on the English Football Premiership he grounds the coach on the ramp, giving us a few heart-stopping moments, but we are soon on our way down to Rothesay.

Outside our hotel on the front of the Bute capital we demonstrate our gratitude to Alan but decide to forego an extra unscheduled sail on the *Jupiter* which is getting ready to depart for Wemyss Bay. We have enjoyed plenty of crossings today already.

In our hotel our individual rooms are playing out the theme of our Island Hop well – they are all named after Clyde steamers. Ian will be retiring to *TS*

Queen Mary II, Gibbie's abode is *MV Loch Fyne* and my dormitory is the topical *MV Jupiter*. It strikes me that if Gibbie had been assigned the *MV Caledonia* he might have checked into a different hotel.

Rothesay is bright but unseasonably cool. The setting sun is highlighting the hills around Loch Striven as we dine surrounded by a vista with which only last year's hotel in Castlebay could compete.

Despite previous visits to Rothesay on an Island Hop, this is our first overnight stay so we take the opportunity to visit a local hostelry. That rare island breed, a pint of real ale, proves elusive. Over a pint or two of whatever else is on offer we settle our financial differences with each other. As usual this seems to involve Gibbie emptying out more of his wallet than the rest of us. As we retire to our respective 'ships', a glance across at the waterfront reveals my particular vessel moored at the pier beside the *Pioneer*. Which of these two ships will take us to Wemyss Bay in the morning?

Day Two – *'Doon the watter'*

I am awakened by rattling windows – the *Pioneer* is leaving. Just why we cannot fathom but whenever this vessel sails in or out from the pier the vibration from her engines or propellers seems to send shock waves around Rothesay Bay on a scale that would register significantly on the Richter Scale. The windows of the hotel are responding. She is taking the 0715 sailing to Wemyss Bay, which means that she will also be taking the 0845 crossing – the one that we will be taking.

Before heralding this news to Gibbie, I take a pre-breakfast stroll to the Highland Boundary Fault. I don't have far to go as this geological landmark between the highlands and lowlands of Scotland runs right through the middle of Bute and meets the sea outside our hotel. Its position on the promenade is marked by a colourful post.

We sail on time, aboard Gibbie's least favourite ship – the *Pioneer*.

'Oh well, it will only be for half an hour,' he complains.

I rub salt in the wound inadvertently by telling him that he looks aggressive this morning in his bunnet. He grudgingly takes it off and it remains in his bag for most of the trip.

For all her faults the *Pioneer* does possess speed and we are swiftly conveyed to Wemyss Bay, passing the *Jupiter* to port off Toward. We arrive on time at 0915 and our connecting bus to Largs can be seen departing ahead of us at 0916 as we are still struggling up the pier with our bags. Bus operators and ferry companies still do not seem to have got their act together.

We hang around (our first today) at the bus stop trying to decipher conflicting timetables when suddenly a bus, of which there is no apparent mention on the timetable, appears, as if from nowhere. It is heading for Largs so we climb in. My suggestion that we now have time for a quick dash over to Cumbrae, to bag another island, before the *Waverley* arrives, is met with an inertia bordering on apathy. But the ferry is just about to depart so after a bit of arm-twisting all three of us step aboard. Unfortunately, the ferry is not the

Loch Linnhe which would have been a new vessel for us, but the *Loch Striven*. The arm-twisting is for Ian in particular. He doesn't want to jump on board in case disaster strikes on our way across and we miss the *Waverley*, which is due to depart Largs at 1030.

We sail across to island number three, with Ian biting his nails, wishing he had stayed in the bookshop. But we are still back in Largs with forty minutes to spare, much the better for the experience.

The *Waverley* comes splashing around the corner on schedule. The sun catches her North British colours as she wheels to port to approach Largs pier from the south. We can sense that on this part of our journey we will be in for a real treat. A new vessel for an Island Hop – but what a vessel!

The last in the line of traditional Clyde steamers, who would have believed when she was sold by Caledonian MacBrayne for £1 on 8 August 1974 to the Paddle Steamer Preservation Society, that twenty-two years later she would still be sailing 'Doon the watter' to Largs, Millport, Rothesay and the rest. At that time the hope was to save the paddler from the breaker's yard. In fact today she looks in better condition than ever. Bits of her have been replaced over the years but that huge, magnificent triple expansion engine remains the same. In those early years under the Preservation Society my father John Craig, recently retired, performed some joinery work for the ship. Perhaps his infectious enthusiasm for Clyde Steamers has rubbed off on me. I think it is the bits that he built that have been replaced.

Today she is full of steamer nutters – like ourselves – all out to support her and the Clyde River Steamer Club and have a fun day at the same time. We are probably the only passengers joining her with single tickets. These will take us on a three-hour cruise to Brodick and on up Loch Fyne to Tarbert.

We depart from Largs with a good number of people aboard. Our route takes us around the northern tip of Cumbrae and south down the east coast of Bute, past the mountains of Arran and into Brodick. It is perfect paddling weather, a fair wind under a bright sky combined with the gentle swell to give us the experience that we are on a *real* ship.

We do not know where to go first. To see the engines? A tour of the ship for the benefit of Ian, who hasn't been on her for years? The cafe? The bar? We end up doing all four but not necessarily in that order. The bar is in the bowels of the ship (as it is traditionally)and the portholes on either side, just on the waterline, splash with water in such a way that it is hard to believe that we are not in a launderette.

Just upstairs, the three cranks of the massive steam engine hiss and thump in unison, driving the ship onwards with impressive power. The air is heavy with the smell of steam and hot oil. Aromatherapy for steam engine enthusiasts.

After Brodick (island number four) the rain arrives and we head for the restaurant for lunch. Unfortunately everyone else aboard has the same idea and by the time that we return on deck we are entering the mouth of Loch Fyne.

At Tarbert an old green and red MacBrayne's coach waits to take a score of passengers up to Ardrishaig to meet up with the ship. This is reminiscent of past years when steamers of the same company name made daily visits to the ports on Loch Fyne.

The bus, the *Waverley* and ourselves are all heading independently for Ardrishaig. Bus and steamer will then be retracing their route but we will be heading north in the quest for more islands. It is not yet two o'clock but we still have three new islands to reach today. All of this, however, depends on whether Gibbie's car is still parked on the main street of Tarbert.

A few hundred passengers, a good percentage of whom are wearing woollen hats in the black, white and red of the paddler's funnels, spill from the ship's decks at Tarbert pier and we are among them. Cameras click away as we watch the ship depart and swing to starboard in a tight arc in order to regain the open waters of the loch. A rocky outcrop lies ahead of her bow and from our position it looks as though her tight turning circle is not going to be sufficient to clear it. I keep the video camera running in case it should be useful for 'News At Ten' but thankfully the paddles stop turning, go into reverse and forward again as *Waverley* performs a nautical three-point turn. She looks a glorious sight in the glistening sunshine as she heads up Loch Fyne. A living, breathing, working museum.

Gibbie's car is where we had left it and we pile in to chase the steamer and the MacBrayne's bus up the loch side. We overtake both but do not pause at Ardrishaig to watch the ship berth – we have to push on. Our next destination is the island of Seil.

A cluster of islands lie just off the west coast to the south of Oban. Seil is the nearest to the shore, so close in fact that a short, single-span, stone bridge links it to the mainland. The bridge was built by Thomas Telfer in 1792 and is popularly known as 'The Bridge Over The Atlantic'. Seems like a bit of an exaggeration to me!

We reach the bridge at about 1500, nicely on schedule, and drive over Telfer's bridge to island number five. Below the narrow channel, sea water swirls menacingly in the tidal race. We speed on, with the idea of having a closer look at the bridge later, towards the ferry-point at the south end of Seil which provides a link to yet another island, Luing.

Seil looks a green, prosperous little island – apparently the mother of Diana, Princess of Wales has a house here. Its wilder neighbour Luing is only a few hundred yards away across the turbulent Cuan Sound. The small, blue-hulled, council-owned ferry, the *Belnahua* is ready to leave. On we stroll and dig into our pockets as the ferryman shakes his head at our CalMac Rover tickets. That makes two ships in a row on which they are not valid. Gibbie will be looking for a refund.

Luing is famous for slate quarries, now disused and red-haired cattle. There is no sign of any cows but the slate beach provides evidence of the former workings. Today it looks like a peaceful little haven but as we have not brought the car with us we are not going to see much of it. Another 'island ticking' visit. We are soon back across on Seil.

Off now to the west coast of Seil for yet another ferry crossing to the last island of the day, and another new one – Easdale, which is even more famous than Luing for slate. It was quarried on this tiny island until the great storm of 22 November 1881 which flooded the workings. Easdale must go down in the annals of Island Hopping as the smallest island that we have visited. Even today, as a result of the slate workings, it has a carved out appearance, as if much of it is missing – which of course it is, covering the roofs of buildings all over the country.

At the crossing point on the western flank of Seil, at Ellanbeich, Gibbie and Ian sit out in the sun, waiting for the ferryman to finish his tea while I retrace my steps to the Luing ferry to recover my camera-bag which I have foolishly left on the *Belnahua*.

On returning to Ellanbeich I find Gibbie preparing to ring the bell to summon the ferryman, who lives on Easdale. With a blast that would waken the dead, the klaxon bellows out and, within a couple of minutes, a small motorboat is bouncing across the waves between Easdale and Seil. On the other side we wander among the whitewashed cottages, many of them holiday homes, on a grassy island, a quarter of a mile square, that has no roads and no cars. It is very quiet, in fact the only resident to put in an appearance, apart from the ferryman, is an irate dog who comes out to bark at us. I become the object of two other acts of belligerence this time from my fellow travellers. One from Gibbie, who is complaining that the sun is burning his cap-less brow and the other from both of them when we discover that the coffee shop is closed. As it is now 1655 we abandon the sight-seeing and jump back into the motor boat to return to Seil. If the only cafe in Ellenbeich is also closed then I am in serious trouble. We are its last customers of the day.

Back at the 'Bridge Over The Atlantic' we set about searching for the fairy foxgloves (*erinus alpinus*) which reputedly grow on the bridge walls in the month of April. Not being able to tell a fairy foxglove from a Californian Redwood we soon give up and take an interest in the stone structure itself. Narrow and very high arching, it is not, despite our initial thoughts, the first bridge that we have crossed to reach an island. The new Skye Bridge still awaits us one day but the islands of Benbecula, Grimsay, North Uist and Vatersay have all been attained in a similar manner.

Just after six o'clock we arrive in Oban and make straight for our hotel. It is now a beautiful sunny evening. Over dinner we discuss our contingency plans for the following day.

Tomorrow we hope to get to Staffa. Ian has never set foot on the famous little island – our plans were wrecked by the weather in 1993. The pressure is on me, for not only have I still to finalise the plans for getting us there but my two colleagues are convinced that I have contingency plans in the event that we can't. Gibbie even goes so far as to offer his opinion on what those contingency plans might be:

'If it involves Kerrera then you can stick it!' I am shocked at his outburst – he doesn't even have his bunnet on when he says it.

The man with the key to the success of our visit to Staffa is Gordon Grant, who is most likely to be the one who takes us out there in his boat. He lives on Iona. I go off nervously to telephone him.

The news is good. I have no need to invent a quick contingency plan. We can cross to Staffa on one of Gordon's boats at 1215 and be back in time to catch the last sailing off Mull from Fishnish.

A successful day is rounded off very nicely in Auley's Bar, an establishment that we have frequently been drawn to over the years.

Day Three – *Ian keeps his date with Mr Fingal*

At 0945 on Sunday morning we are standing on Oban pier waiting to board the *Isle of Mull* for the crossing to Craignure. This ship has featured in every Island Hop except 1990 and 1995 and we are almost on first name terms with the crew. Gibbie flashes his Rover ticket and manages to get his Rover aboard without any jokes from the deck crew.

We're off on time, as usual, at 1000 and are actually able to sit out in the sun on the upper deck, sheltering behind that hideous funnel. This is the first of only two sails on the west coast on large CalMac ships this year, so we want to make the most of it.

At Craignure I drive the car off and we have to wait for Ian to stroll off with the foot passengers. We wait for a while – he is at the back of the queue. Then it is a scenic drive across Mull to Fionnaphort where we find Gordon Grant, his son Paul and his motor launch *Ossian of Staffa* waiting for us, plus a coach-load of tourists, for the strip to Staffa.

Staffa lies ten miles out to sea from Fionnaphort in exposed waters – the weather is therefore crucial in determining whether day trips such as this can go ahead. Fortunately the strong south-westerly winds of the last two days have moderated, although the sea is far from being flat calm.

'It will be a bit splashy,' Pal says. He is going to be our pilot and promises us a landing provided the seas around the shore are not too rough.

Ian is following some very famous footsteps on this, his first visit to Staffa: Sir Walter Scott went in 1810, Keats in 1818, Felix Mendelssohn in 1829, William Wordsworth in 1833, Queen Victoria and Prince Albert in 1833, Jules Verne in 1859, David Livingstone in 1864, RL Stevenson in 1870 and, of course, Stuart and Gibbie in 1989.

On the deck of the powerful little boat we soon get soaked from the spray that showers us by the bucketful from either side as we literally bounce across the wave tops. It is all very exciting. Gibbie puts his bunnet back on, muttering: 'I don't care if I look aggressive or not.'

As Staffa draws nearer, the black hole of the entrance to the famous Fingal's Cave grows to cathedral proportions. Out at sea I scan the waves looking for puffins, whales and dolphins.

'We might get a good view of some cetaceans,' I prompt my two colleagues.

'We have a better chance of seeing Alsatians!' says Ian. What natural history Philistines I have to travel with!

By the time we are halfway across to the island Gibbie has managed to engage everyone aboard the boat in conversation. Most of our sixteen fellow passengers are European: a German couple on their first visit to Scotland, some Dutch on an island hopping trip of their own. There is also an English couple who had been to a wedding in Oban the day before but have come for a sail today to 'clear their heads'.

We draw nearer to the island and motor close to the shore. Our skipper has promised he will try to get us ashore on this tiny island whose fame seems disproportionate to its dimensions. We pass at close range to the sixty foot high entrance to the Cave. The promised landing is gingerly made and we scramble along the black basalt columns to Fingal's Cave. There, in glorious sunshine we toast Mr Fingal and island number nine with a drop of Highland Park in a polystyrene cup. I drop the lid of my hip flask into a puddle of sea water and joke about how it will flavour the whisky – a curiously portentous act, as we shall see.

We have twenty-five minutes on Staffa – not enough time to experience this truly spectacular place. We are all herded back aboard the *Ossian of Staffa*. Like some expedition from the Falklands War, our skipper counted us off the boat and counts us all back on board again. Spectacular the island may be but being left behind on it would not be much fun. Off we sail, back to whence we came, leaving the sheep to their isolation.

We sit out on the open deck on the way back. The sea has moderated. The German woman looks round at us and smiles in a toothy, gold-capped grimace: 'I smell viskie!'

The *Ossian* takes us to Iona next, island number ten, and after a quick 'tea-and-a-bun' we stretch out on a small beach of white sand. At the waters edge a pair of herring gulls are doing their bit to ensure the propagation of the species.

Two more ferries lie ahead of us. Soon we will be on the *Loch Buie* over to Mull and then, after a forty-two mile drive across the island, the penultimate crossing of the day on the *Isle of Cumbrae* back to the mainland. Gibbie suggests that we could make a mad dash and reach the ante-penultimate crossing but that sounds too complicated and the rest of us are not too sure that there is such a thing as an ante-penultimate crossing.

The *Loch Buie* is the thirteenth vessel of our trip. We take the 1515 sailing from Iona and I drive across Mull. We stop on the bleak mountain road to film the car passing as part of a linking shot for our travelogue video. I get out of the car, having issued instructions to my two companions. I then carry my camera and tripod a few hundred yards to a suitable spot to film the desired scene. As I am bending over to lock the camera onto the tripod Gibbie drives past!

We are at Fishnish, on the east coast of Mull in time for the 1720 sailing over to Morven. Will Jean's Tea Bar still be at Lochaline? With a long drive across Morven ahead of us we are in need of further refreshment. We are in luck, not only is Jean's Tea Bar there, it is open and, what's more, it is Jean herself who is in attendance. Gibbie is beside himself with joy and quickly stuffs his bunnet into his pocket.

'Why were you not here when we called three years ago?' he enquires.

'Oh I was probably in Majorca,' replies Jean, who in between preparing tea for us is manhandling half a dozen of the largest live prawns I have ever seen.

'I don't see prawns on the menu,' I enquire.

'Oh no – these are for me,' she announces proudly.

What concerns me is that although she was not here in 1993 she has heard about us and our visit from the lady who had served us then. We are probably infamous as the three nutters who tour the island every spring.

From Lochaline Ian takes the wheel for the first time for the scenic but tedious drive to our next hotel, at Morar, a distance of some seventy miles. The road across this large and empty part of Scotland is almost completely single-track and frequently tortuous. After the thirty-seventh stop at a passing-place it is all becoming a touch wearying.

We are tired when we finally arrive but are now a mere two miles from Mallaig, from where we shall be sailing in the morning. As none of us are particularly keen on Mallaig we have chosen Morar as our stop-over.

A new by-pass has been built since our last visit to Morar and the village, now virtually traffic free, has been restored and spruced up. The tiny railway station with its neat fencing and painted lamp posts now resembles something from Noddy's Toytown. There is even a chap with big ears standing on the platform.

The hotel is empty but for ourselves and a young honeymooning couple. We have a bar supper where Gibbie demonstrates his gastronomic versatility: *moules* yesterday, mutton pie today. The rest of the evening is pleasantly spent sipping a malt or two beside a large open fire with a couple of deer heads looking down at us in resentment. It is like being guests in a large private mansion. Ian starts off the synchronised yawning and the three of us are tucked up in our beds by eleven o'clock – which is half an hour earlier than the honeymooners.

Day Four – *Water in your whisky, sir?*

It may have been the mutton pie, but whatever the reason, Gibbie sleeps in. Ian and I are well into our kippers and there is no of sign him. There is no sign of the young couple either, but then they have an excuse. We are just drawing lots to see which of us will go up and break down his door when he appears, bleary-eyed and apologetic. He manages a rushed breakfast before we make a swift exit and dash the two miles to Mallaig.

Our next ship, the *Iona* waiting for us. Despite the new bridge we can sail over the sea to Skye. We are having a quick return trip on the *Iona* to Armadale on Skye, prior to our sail on the *Lochmor* around the Small Isles.

The *Iona* is now in the twilight of her long career with CalMac. She has served most of the routes in the Western Isles now and each year we have sailed on her we announce confidently to ourselves that this will be our last ever trip on her. Now, in 1996, she is still here and we are more confident than ever that this will be our last sail on her.

Gibbie and I have seen a lot of the *Iona* recently. We had taken a sail on her from Gourock to Campbeltown, then Kennacraig, just a few weeks earlier and I had also joined her during her recent relief sailings on the Clyde – unusual duties for her.

At Armadale the linkspan has been constructed since our last visit in 1993 and the ship now berths at right angles to the pier, stern-in. This means a quicker turnaround time and therefore Gibbie misses out on a visit to the craft shop yet again!

Back at Mallaig it is a case of jumping off one ship and onto another. The *Lochmor* is loading planks of wood and wheelbarrows for Eigg by means of her deck crane. Why couldn't they have used the wheelbarrows? Her route today will take her out to Eigg firstly and then on to Rum. At both islands a tender will motor out to the ship and exchange intending passengers. She will then sail on to Canna where there is a proper pier. This will allow us to step ashore and claim yet another new island.

As we wait to sail, a nosy seal pops its head up in the harbour. What a great life seals have, we muse, lounging around all day, going for a cool swim whenever the notion comes. And then, when hunger strikes, it's a quick dive under the surface to catch a sea-trout or two. I decide that in the next life I want to come back as a seal. Gibbie announces that in the interests of an easy life he has already decided to come back as a CAD draughtsman.

We chug out past the moored *Iona* at 1035 and turn south-westwards towards Eigg, our load of wheelbarrows glistening in the sun. The skipper is Roddy Morrison, who like us, has jumped off the *Iona* and onto the *Lochmor.*

We settle ourselves on the small upper deck on a seat sheltered from the breeze. During the course of our seven-hour cruise today this spot remains sheltered no matter which way the ship turns. We almost have the deck to ourselves after we leave Eigg as most of the passengers for the island are tradesmen who disembark, with their wheelbarrows, onto the tendering motor boat *Ulva*. They look as though they are off to dig a big hole somewhere.

Eigg is a thriving little island which the islanders are soon hoping to purchase. This will give them better control of their livelihood and their destiny. It is regretful that we cannot actually land, but we would have to spend the rest of the Island Hop there. Perhaps one day.

The transfer of passengers and cargo is a cheery affair with Captain Roddy coming down a deck or two to banter with the crew and passengers in a discordant amalgam of English and Gaelic. The crane swings back and forth and the *Ulva* bobs up and down alongside on the gentle swell. Above us the Sgurr of Eigg looms – a giant thumb-shaped piece of rock which dominates the southern end of the island.

The *Ulva* turns around and heads back to the island. Instead of straightening her bow, however, she completes the circle and returns to the side of the *Lochmor* to collect a parcel which has been left behind.The parcel is dispatched through the air between the two vessels – let's hope it isn't antique china inside – and off we sail for the next island, Rum.

It is a glorious day now and if it were not for the slight coolness of the air it could be the Med we are cruising on. Gibbie takes a photograph of the approaching island of Rum and later shows it to friends, telling them that it is a picture of the Greek island Skyros. He is believed.

Rum is a big, round, wild island whose mountainous form rises quite dramatically from the sea. It is owned by the Nature Conservancy Council and most of the people who live there are employed or connected with them. Tourism used to be discouraged, as it was the domain of deer and eagles. Now visitor access is more relaxed. Unfortunately, we cannot land here either, or else we would have to spend the rest of the week here. What kind of Island Hop is this?

We pass close to the barren southern shores of Rum and turn north to sail up the eastern side. The *Hebridean Princess* appears, as if on cue, and adds welcome colour to the bare grey rockscape of Rum behind her. As we munch at our lunch we gaze at her decks through binoculars but can see no one out in the open. It is obviously lunchtime aboard her as well. Ian shakes his head: 'What have they got which we don't on such a lovely day as this?'

'Cup-a-soups and cheese sannies for lunch – that's for sure,' Gibbie mutters.

At Rum we sit out in Kilmory Bay and look over at the castle and the half dozen cottages which prove that there is life on Rum apart from midges and sea-eagles. The tender boat *Rhourma* comes out and the process of unloading and loading is repeated with similar efficiency. When we leave the bay I go up to the bridge to chat to Roddy. He seems to be enjoying the cruise as much as we are and even breaks into a few bars of 'Mull of Kintyre'. I don't know why – it must be his favourite song or perhaps he always sings it when he sails away from the island. Perhaps he chants: 'Yo-ho-ho-and a bottle of rum' when he sails around Kintyre. The *Lochmor* chugs on at ten knots.

The pier at Canna appears suddenly around a rock cliff face which is daubed with graffiti. Someone had apparently painted his girlfriend's name on it years ago and nobody wanted to stop the practice from then on. GIBBIE, STUART & IAN – ISLAND HOP 1996 would look good if there was the space for it. At least we can step ashore here.

On the pier itself the local dogs outnumber people and they are soon involved in a right stramash – the dogs that is, not the people.

We jump ashore onto the eleventh island of the trip. None of us has ever set foot on Canna before. The bay forms a natural anchorage, much favoured by yachtsmen and is dominated by the church standing on its own on the other side of the bay from the pier.

The ship picks up three passengers and one of the dogs, which just about doubles the passenger complement.

As we sail away from Canna it is judged to be time for the Annual Toast and I am dispatched to study the whiskies available from the bar. It is One Hundred Pipers or nothing. I buy three miniatures and carry them up to our favourite deck spot, pausing at the toilet tap to add a drop of water to two of the cups. Our leering smiles for Gibbie's camera turn to expressions of aghast horror at the realisation that the water I have added is *salt* water! Ian and Gibbie's laughter is ringing in my ears as I descend to the bar for replacements.

'Finished them already – that was quick,' the barman comments. I don't have the heart to tell him.

The weather is glorious and brings us additional glow. As the afternoon sun beats down on us Gibbie puts his bunnet on again. Somehow he does not look aggressive any more. In fact as we lie back on our seats, enjoying the sunshine we have not a care in the world. Not even a low-flying RAF Tornado, which has dipped over us on its way north, can interrupt our relaxed feeling of accomplishment.

The *Lochmor* with Roddy at the helm, drones on towards Mallaig at her steady ten knots. The only thought on our minds: what next year. . .

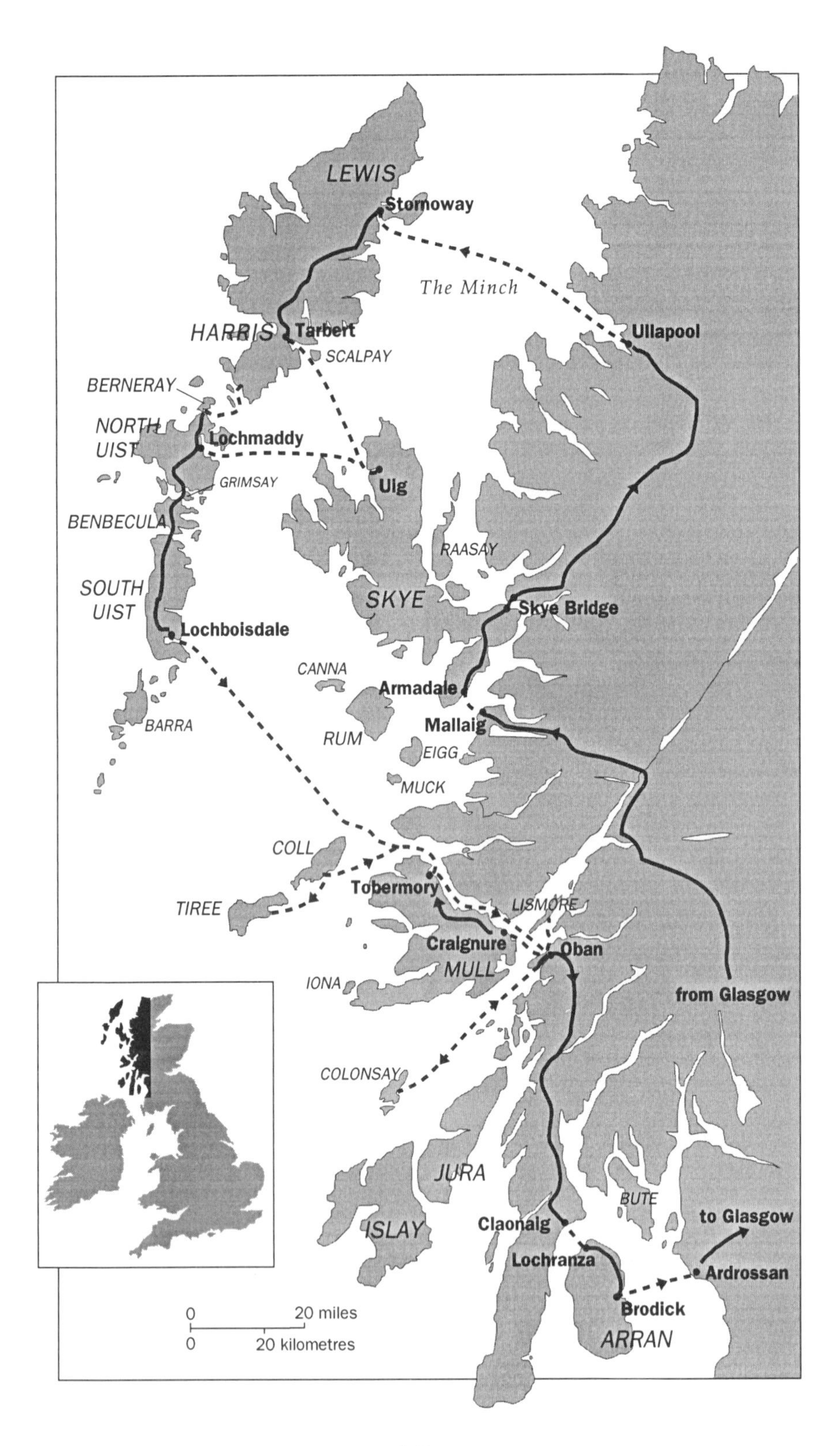
LEWIS
Stornoway
The Minch
HARRIS
Tarbert
SCALPAY
Ullapool
BERNERAY
NORTH
UIST
Lochmaddy
Uig
GRIMSAY
BENBECULA
RAASAY
SOUTH
UIST
SKYE
Skye Bridge
Lochboisdale
CANNA
Armadale
Mallaig
BARRA
RUM
EIGG
MUCK
COLL
Tobermory
TIREE
LISMORE
Craignure
Oban
MULL
IONA
from Glasgow
COLONSAY
JURA
BUTE
ISLAY
Claonaig
to Glasgow
Lochranza
Ardrossan
Brodick
ARRAN
0
20 miles
0
20 kilometres

1997 The Nights of the Long Sails

The Plan

This was the first Hop since 1993 that had to be planned from scratch. In the intervening years we had a fairly strong theme that we wanted to pursue i.e. in 1994 – Clyde sailing, 1995 – crossing the length of the Outer Isles, 1996 – reaching some of the smaller islands we had never sailed to before. For 1997, however, we had no strong theme, merely a few ideas on paper. So the drawing board had to be brought out of retirement in order to invent an entertaining four day Hop. This meant hard work for the tactician while the strategist could rest on his laurels.

It was becoming quite hard work keeping Ian and Gibbie happy with itineraries for Island Hops. They would express the wish to use a car: 'Too many long train journeys.' So the next year we would take the car. This was then met with: 'Can we not go back to our traditional ways of getting around – like using buses and trains?' The following year they would want the car again. It was the same with the sailings. 'We've been a long sail on that ship, why don't we get to new islands next year?' After doing just that in 1996 they were moaning again. 'What we need are some long sails, we haven't done that for years.' And so the theme that developed for the 1997 Island Hop was – Long Sails. As most of these were in the evening...The Nights of the Long Sails.

Of the various ideas for the trip, perhaps the most exciting idea of all was that of taking overnight berths on the *Lord of the Isles* out of Lochboisdale on the second evening. We had never stayed overnight on any of the ships before but the notion of this filled at least one of us with a degree of trepidation. Ian was most concerned that he might not sleep well!

Another touch of innovation was the idea of sailing to Colonsay, in the evening, aboard the *Isle of Mull*, which serves the island two evenings a week. Despite several brief visits to the island we had never sailed there on that particular ship. Thus the 'Nights of the Long Sails' evolved.

Furthermore, a new ship beckoned, *Isle of Lewis*, on the Ullapool – Stornoway service. She would have to be included somehow.

When the first draft of the itinerary was produced, it became obvious that the use of a car would make life easier and give further sailing opportunities. Although we had used a car in 1992, 1993 and 1996 on selected routes to link up the mainland points of our departures we had never before bought a Car Rover ticket and sailed on most of the routes with a vehicle. This was another new aspect of Hop '97.

And so it was that we drove off from Glasgow on the first day, heading for Ullapool, with the prospect of at least three new vessels to sail on. We had to get to Ullapool by 1700. As to *how* we got there, we had several options. Having complete ferry freedom due to our car ticket, we could choose whatever route or routes we wanted on our way north. One such route seemed to be more enticing than the others. The decision to go via the Mallaig – Armadale crossing and then the Skye Bridge was made the evening before our departure. An evening cut short due to the demands of an early start the next morning.

Day One – *Speed bonny bridge . . .*

Up at 0650 and looking forward, eagerly as ever, to the drive north. Having the bulk of our overland driving at the beginning of the Hop is definitely more attractive to us than finishing with a long drive or train journey. So it is a carful of cheery Island Hoppers that sets off at 0728 on the first day, Wednesday 21 May 1997. Cheerful may be an inappropriate word as by the time we join the M8, heading west towards the Erskine Bridge, Gibbie is describing himself as 'cantankerous and...irascible' and Ian is claiming proudly that his wife Hilary had recently described him as: '. . .getting more like Victor Meldrew every year.'

After a half an hour on the road it is becoming clear that Gibbie's car is only capable of two speeds, twenty-nine or seventy-nine miles per hour.

Crianlarich at 0843. My two temperamental companions are now humming wistfully to 'Nessun Dorma' and disagreeing as to which tenor can deliver the best rendering. It could be worse. They could be discussing their kidney stone experiences, again. Twenty minutes later, speeding across Rannoch Moor, they are doing just that.

The road is surprisingly empty. This suits us as we have to make good time to Mallaig to catch the 1210 sailing to Armadale on Skye. Pockets of snow are still clinging to the highest, north-eastern slopes of the mountains surrounding Rannoch Moor. We pass a boulder, eight feet in diameter, with a ten-foot tree growing out of a crack in it; nature's tenacious hold in such a bleak environment.

Into Glen Coe and in the morning sunshine I have never seen the Glen in such an optimistic mood – a bit like ourselves, including Victor in the front seat. At 0928, exactly two hours into our journey, we are crossing the Ballachulish Bridge and are well on schedule. We have covered ninety-five miles. I reckon that we can spare the time for a cup of coffee when we get to Fort William. How well I can remember as a child queuing for the Ballachulish ferry in my Dad's Ford Anglia. We would sit there for what seemed like ages, shuffling forward six car lengths whenever the ferry left our side. After about half an hour of boredom we would end up driving around the Loch via Kinlochleven.

The sky is by now clearing from the north-west, exactly as forecast. Ian cannot believe it. Yesterday, he and Gibbie, making full use of their Rover tickets, completed a round trip of Bute and Cowal, using three ferries, in unabating torrential rain. I have told them before that the sun never shines when they go without me (cf 1990 and 1991 Hops) but they never listen.

We are in Fort William two and a quarter hours after leaving Glasgow. A late Highland breakfast is what is wanted. Bannocks and porridge? We have to make do with a 'Bacon and Egg McMuffin' from McDonalds. It's amazing the shape that these Americans can grow eggs into. Over the late breakfast, which is rather good, Ian complains in his Victor Meldrew manner that one of Gibbie's cats attacked him in his bed in the middle of the night. Gibbie shrugs as if it were an acceptable risk when staying the night at his house.

Before setting off on the road again I am despatched to a telephone to secure our line of avance. I have to make sure the ferry can accommodate our car on the 1210 sailing from Mallaig. If not, we will have to head directly to Ullapool. The news is good, there is plenty of space for us.

On the road again at 1015 for the winding, unpredictable forty-six miles to Mallaig. Apart from talking about the condition of the road the chat has now developed from kidneys to teeth. I find it difficult to contribute.

At a set of road works, where the traffic is controlled by traffic lights, a German registered Volkswagen slews past us, ignoring a red signal.

'*Vorsprung Durch Tecknik* my arse!' Growls Gibbie. He has an irrational dislike of Volvos as well.

We arrive at Mallaig at 1125, in plenty of time for our first ship, *Iona*. This will surely be our last sailing on the old lady as she is soon to be sold out of the fleet – due to her age. The twenty-seven year-old former Caledonian Steam Packet Company ship is nearing the end of her useful life in Scottish waters. Although apparently a good sea boat her limited passenger accommodation now makes her a poor country cousin to the newer, more luxurious ships in CalMac's fleet. So with greater agreement that this will definitely be our last Island Hopping sail on the *Iona* we walk aboard, except Gibbie who drives aboard. For once we have been able to film the ship's arrival at Mallaig but any filming on deck has to be restricted due to the noise from her air-intake fans. We make for the cafeteria for a bowl of minestrone and film that instead.

Very much a booming tourist route for those still wanting to sail 'over the sea to Skye', the ship is busy, particularly with young travellers who look as though they are going to spend longer on the island than us, judging from their backpacks and heavy boots.

Thirty minutes later we are on the large island itself, passing Gibbie's favourite craft shop. We have a farewell look at the *Iona*. Not a beauty but a very itinerant ship. I think back to my first view of her, sailing up the Sound of Mull. Since those early days in the 1970s I have sailed to fifteen different piers on her. Now, she has had her time.

We join the end of a convoy of cars heading along the single-track, gravelly road towards Broadford. The Red Cuillins loom in the distance, looking like giant termite mounds in the bright sunshine. After Broadford the road, to Kyleakin, improves considerably. A van embellished with 'Hairy Coo Backpacker Hotel' breezes past us. An image of a hotel bar packed with Highland cattle with rucksacks springs to mind.

We are now approaching the infamous Skye Bridge. This is the first time any of us have seen it, let alone crossed it. Much controversy has been created by its construction. The majority of the people of Skye wanted the bridge but were unprepared for the one-way toll imposed on them for the privilege of using it. To compound matters, the Scottish Office has denied CalMac the right to continue to run a ferry service and the recently constructed ships *Loch Fyne* and *Loch Dunvegan* have had to be removed. They are reputedly unsuitable for any other route and will be sold. Since their lay-up in 1995 the two ferries have lain in dock at Troon, awaiting a buyer.

Going over the bridge, I am actually quite impressed with it. To my architecturally uncultured eye it merges well with the landscape as it arches steeply from the Skye side onto the island of Eilean Ban, owned in the 1960s by *Ring of Bright Water* author Gavin Maxwell. As well as an abutment for the bridge it is home to a conspicuous lighthouse and the grave of one of Maxwell's famous otters. We can surely claim this small island as another conquest, at least *I* can as I walk across the bridge. If Grimsay counts as an island then Eilean Ban must also. It will beat Easdale as the smallest island yet visited. From Eilean Ban a shorter, straighter span then completes the link to the mainland. Within an hour we have sailed over to Skye and left it by the bridge. Our first island has been briefly blessed with our presence, for a mere fifty minutes.

At the toll booth we stop to film, despite me urging Gibbie to drive straight through in protest at the charge, and thus give some good substance to the film i.e. Gibbie being frog-marched off in handcuffs, not to be released until next year's Island Hop.

We continue on our way to Ullapool, another eighty-four miles, on this long short-cut to the next ferry terminal. Soon we are skirting the southern shores of the strikingly beautiful Loch Carron. The road and railway run together for several miles. They part when the gradient forces the road upwards or downwards and come together again to cross streams by a communal bridge or to burrow under the hillside in a communal tunnel.

More road works ahead – this time a bulldozer digging a new ditch and holding up both lanes of traffic. We still have time on our side, however, and at Aultguish we pull up at the Inn.

'Tea and a pee,' orders Gibbie. Both will have to wait as in true Highland hospitality the Inn is shut. It intrigues me what foreign visitors to our beautiful country must think when they arrive at hotels or restaurants at half past two in the afternoon and find them closed. They must think the whole country goes for a siesta until six o'clock. If you have not had lunch by 1430 – forget it.

We push on past the dammed Loch Glascarnoch. 'Not full but nearly full,' observes Gibbie. Just like my bladder.

Relief comes soon at Corrieshalloch Gorge where I have a long pee – down all two hundred feet into the gorge. The roadside scene adjacent to the gorge is following the script of a true tourist attraction. In the car park is a fast-food van and two coachfuls of Lancashire sightseers who are forming a procession down to the gorge with huge ice-creams in one hand and video-cameras the size of bazookas in the other. Sipping a cup of refreshing tea, I watch as they march back to their buses, holding only their cameras now, their faces showing no change in expression despite the wonderful natural wonder they have just witnessed.

The gorge was created between ten and fifteen thousand years ago by melting glacial waters and is one of the best such features in Scotland. Now, the River Droma trickles through the wooded cleft, two hundred feet below the road. A precarious suspension bridge spans the fifty-foot width of the gorge but we feel safer on the firmly anchored viewing platform. Standing on the platform with my tea and camcorder I suppose I am one of the tourists myself. But at least I am smiling – more in relief than anything else.

A few miles further on is Ullapool and we have time to send a few postcards before taking up camera positions to record the incoming *Isle of Lewis*.

The new, impressive ship has been much lauded by the people of Lewis, which it serves. She is gliding up Loch Broom and comes round to dock stern-in at the linkspan at Ullapool. The longest of CalMac's ships, exceeding the *Caledonian Isles* her most obvious features to me are the large, rectangular picture windows of her forward restaurant and observation lounge. The twin funnels are positioned well astern and the black tops to them are angled upwards at the back. She looks a fine ship and we are eagerly looking forward to our first sail on her.

As soon as we are on board we set off to have a good look around. On a wall in the observation lounge we come across a framed photograph of her predecessor, *Suilven*. She is now in inauspicious retirement, conveying sheep between the main islands of New Zealand. Just imagine, all those sheep lounging around in the cafeteria and bar, like we once did, being asked repeatedly to take their feet off the seats. A caption proudly boasts that she arrived at Wellington on 13 October 1995 having sailed 12576 miles.

The accommodation on the *Isle of Lewis* is impressive. Her restaurant is enormous and tastefully decorated in soft pastel yellows and blues. Above all this the large windows lend a very spacious feel to the largest observation lounge I have ever seen. The view forward is quite superb but leaves Gibbie wondering how such large windows would fare in a Minch storm. With a separate TV lounge, shop, bar and playroom, and a good amount of open deck she seems ideal for her role linking Ullapool and Stornoway. My only criticism, apart from there being no view over the bow, is the lack of imagination in the name. A friend of mine was recently heard to say that an appropriate name for her might be 'Sabbatarian Isles', bearing in mind the refusal of the islanders of Lewis to let her sail into or out of Stornoway on a Sunday. That would have been better, but better still would have been a Gaelic name.

We set off up Loch Broom at 1730 having chalked up two hundred and fifty miles in Gibbie's car which is now safely tucked away on the car-deck down below. Down to the restaurant for our fish and chips as the ship pitches slowly in the north-easterly swell. Ian asks if there will be a 'happy-hour' in the bar but by the way that everyone is staggering around the unsteady ship it looks as though the 'happy-hour' has already been.

In my usual shy way, I seek permission to visit the bridge. This is granted and I ascend to be met by the mate Calum Campbell who is happy to let me film and wander around this glass tower as the ship ploughs across the Minch at 16.8 knots. The instrumentation and equipment at the Captain's disposal look very impressive, like a floating airport control tower. One major advantage the new ship has over the *Suilven* is speed. On arrival at Stornoway we have taken fifty minutes off the older ship's normal crossing time. Our time today on passage is a mere two hours and forty minutes.

With me at the helm of the car we drive off onto our second island, Lewis, on the final leg of today's journey – the thirty-eight miles to Tarbert on Harris. As the sun gradually settles across Lewis, the mountains of Harris rise ahead of us, turning a deep mauve in the fading light, beckoning us to our final destination.

Although joined together, Harris and Lewis are considered as two distinct islands. We cross a small stone bridge marking the boundary. The landscape now certainly looks different. The only thing that appears to grow on Harris are grey boulders. The hillsides and mountains are strewn with them.Past Loch Seaforth, after which a famous MacBrayne's steamer was named, up over the mountain pass and down to Tarbert, stopping only to film a true Hebridean sunset.

At the hotel, at Tarbert, we are recognised by the now retired hotelier who shakes hands with us. Two years ago he had introduced himself as '...that bloody Harris Man'. His daughter now runs the hotel.

We are tired, having been travelling for fourteen hours. Gibbie has, however, one last mission, to find out the winning lottery numbers, for the ticket he bought at Ullapool.

'I want to know if I have to go home at the end of the trip.'

My mission is a phone call home to my daughter Julia. She is delighted that I have survived the *Isle of Lewis* sailing. She had taken to heart the clairvoyant prediction, by the Brahmin Seer, that the Isle of Lewis would one day sink. Modern day thinking is that this now refers not to the island but to the new ship.

'Did it not sink Dad?'

'No,' I reassure her. 'Not even once.'

I fall asleep with a full moon casting a ghostly glow into my room.

Day Two – *I'm* not *going on this again!*

Up at 0750 and down to a breakfast made almost unpalatable by my colleagues' chat about bowels and cholesterol. Their bodies seem to be becoming an obsession with them. It must be their age.

This morning we are off to the island of Scalpay, with the car, where we intend to create a cinematographic re-enactment of the march we took in 1992, in Mediterranean temperatures, to the far side of the island. This is purely for the benefit of our video diary.

This is another of these 'last chances' as a bridge to Scalpay is due to be completed in November 1997. This will be our last sail over to the island and this time, instead of the *Canna*, the ferry will be the *Rhum*. Gibbie seems most under-whelmed by this last detail so I take the necessary photographs. As we drive off across Scalpay I inadvertently leave my camera bag on the ferry – as I do most years!

We drive to the end of the road of this thriving little island, whereupon I get out and stride back the way we came. It is such a lovely day it seems a shame to spend much time in the car. The sea around the rocky shore is a deep ultramarine and indents the island into numerous small sheltered bays, each holding a couple of small fishing boats. It is a true picture postcard scene.

The camera is set up in Cecil B. DeMille style as we film the famous Scalpay March epic outside the relevant bungalow. Gibbie totters along a hundred yards behind Ian and me, mopping his dry brow with a handkerchief and shaking his head in an anguished acting performance not seen since John Mills in *Ice Cold in Alex*. He seems well pleased with his performance and has at last purged his soul of memories from that experience five years ago.

'It was just like the filming of the raising of the American flag at Iwo Jima,' he proclaims. I didn't realise he had been there as well.

Ian's comments are more mundane, as he nods towards the guest-house:

'With all this activity outside her house she's bound to have put the kettle on.'

We move on to the Post Office. Nearby, Mrs McKay, one of fourteen weavers on the island, is working her loom in a small, cluttered hut beside her cottage. It looks hard work. The twenty year-old loom has to be hand operated.

'You can use your feet when your hands get tired,' she says reassuringly.

Mrs. McKay is from '...the mainland of Harris' and is happy to chat as she feeds bundles of wool, of a deep blue colour, into the machinery.

'It takes a lot of hard work to make a living,' she concedes with an air of sadness.

This old, local working tradition contrasts vividly with the multicoloured lycra-clad jogger skipping past outside, in the direction of our favourite guest-house. Five minutes later she is running back again, more slowly. Clearly the distance was too much for her as well.

An incredibly hairy maned dog strolls up to us and makes me start. It is fawn coloured and looks just like a lion. A good shearing would supply Mrs McKay with a couple of days more raw material.

Back at the ferry slip, my camera bag has been kept in safe custody by the skipper of the *Rhum*. He shrugs ruefully and silently when I ask him what he will do when the bridge is completed. Back to the fishing, I suppose.

We sail over to the mainland of Harris for the last time ever and observe the bridge construction work on either side of the narrow Sound. The expected completion date seems a bit optimistic.

It is back to Tarbert now, six miles away, for the sail on the ship which both Ian and I have nominated as our favourite, the *Hebridean Isles*. We now have a four-hour sail on her from Harris to Lochmaddy (North Uist) via Uig on Skye. This involves crossing the Little Minch twice, but none of us is complaining about that. It is a very scenic crossing aboard a very comfortable vessel. As far as Ian is concerned this route is Island Hopping's *raison d'être*. He anticipates he will pass the next four hours in a hedonistic haze. By the time we reach Lochmaddy, Gibbie and I anticipate having to prise him off his seat on the stern deck.

As we prepare to board the ship, in the car, Gibbie unflinchingly informs the officer in charge of loading that we will be staying on board at Uig for the sail to Lochmaddy.

'Does that cause problems – where on the car-deck should I leave the car?' From the look on the crewman's face you would think that Gibbie had just asked him to scratch his back.

'Reverse over there.'

We sail away from Harris across a calm sea, our second sailing of the trip over to Skye. Ironically, we will be sailing back to Harris again, later in the day, on another vessel.

The *Hebridean Isles* has always been a favourite with us. Her accommodation is compact and she also has plenty of open deck space. Today, as the wind is coming from the north-east, we make for the sheltered stern deck to enjoy the midday sunshine. On each occasion that we have sailed this route the sun has never failed to shine. I eventually haul myself way downstairs to look for an officer – we have a new mission to fulfil. We have never been in an engine-room on any of our previous trips. This has to be put right and permission is sought from the chief engineer. While we await a response I glance at the *Whales, Dolphins and Porpoise Field Guide* on the wall. The sperm whale (*physeter macrocephalus*) can be identified by its forward spraying blow-hole as it characteristically gives 'a forward blow with a sharp angle to the left'. Off we go to the engine-room to see if we can see one.

It is now Gibbie's turn to be 'in his element' as he fires off esoteric questions to the chief Robert Ritchie. It brings back memories of his days at Stephen's Shipyard in Govan. He even discovers that they have a mutual friend. Gibbie has friends all over the world – even on the Little Minch. Outside the air-conditioned, sound-insulated control cabin the noise from the twin banks of Mirrlees Blackstone diesel engines, delivering 2315 shaft horse-power, is deafening. Inside, Gibbie is a happy man.

Back upstairs again. The Shiant Islands way out to port rise like jagged teeth on the horizon as we push onwards, safe in the knowledge that the engines, four decks below us, are in capable hands.

At Uig we stay aboard and as the ship empties of passengers the skipper Roddy Morrison descends from the bridge to chat to us. We remind him that he took us out to Canna on the *Lochmor* last year. To Gibbie's disappointment he cannot remember! Gibbie then quizzes him for the way he has brought the *Hebridean Isles* into Uig.

'You do it different from the others.'

Roddy looks puzzled. 'How do the others do it?'

Gibbie explains that Roddy has swung the ship around to berth stern-in very tightly to the pier, thus denying those ashore of a photographic opportunity of a rear-end shot. Gibbie has to explain that it is only rear-ends of ships he likes. 'If every skipper took their ships in like you do I would never get a blunt-end shot.' Roddy looks back at him and just smiles. He has probably just remembered us from last year.

After Uig we move into the bar where Ian, who also served his 'time' at Stephen's, and Gibbie swap engine stories. Tales of torque converters, crankshafts and horsepower ratios. Looking out of the window, as I feel my concentration waning, the only horses I can see are the white ones dancing on the crests of the wind-whipped waves. But no sperm whales and no water spouts with a sharp angle to the left.

The fish course beckons – herring in oatmeal for me – served by a sad-eyed girl who doesn't seem to be enjoying the crossing as much as we are.

We are now well across the Little Minch, sailing towards Lochmaddy on North Uist. This will be island number five of the trip. Out on the forward deck area one of the Uig passengers is sporting a beard of such huge, overgrown proportions that it is all I can do to stop myself from going over to him and tugging at it to see if it is real.

At 1530 we are about to sail into Lochmaddy for the first time (we had previously sailed *out* of Lochmaddy) and we still have three more vessels to sail on today.

A potential moment of stress is looming. On leaving the *Hebridean Isles* at Lochmaddy we are taking the car ten miles north, to the top of North Uist, to the ferry-point of Otternish. There, firstly, we will be taking a visit over to the island of Berneray, just offshore. Then, after that, we are planning to sail on the *Loch Bhrusda* across the Sound of Harris to Leverburgh on Harris and back again. It is on our arrival back at Otternish, after this, that we will have our moment of stress. We will only have two hours to drive the fifty-two miles of single-track road to Lochboisdale in South Uist where we have to catch the 2300 sailing on the *Lord of the Isles*. It isn't simply that this ship is essential to the further progress of our journey – our beds for the night are on it as well! Provided the *Loch Bhrusda* is running to time, we decide to go ahead with this plan and hope that we can cover the journey to Lochboisdale in the 2 hours. We will not have any margin for error or mishap.

The sailing on the *Loch Bhrusda* is going to be a new experience – a new route and a new vessel. In order to placate CalMac should we be pushed for time in our rush to reach Lochboisdale, I decide to telephone them at their South Uist office to explain our predicament. When I explain apologetically that we may not make the check-in time for the 2300 sailing, the office manager returns reassuringly:

'Oh that's bad. That's very bad!'

Fortunately, I sense from his soft Hebridean tone that he is joking. He reckons we have 'bags of time' for the drive to Lochboisdale.

Off we go, feeling slightly less stressed, across the soft green machair and grey moorland of North Uist. As we near Otternish, brilliant turquoise bays and dazzling white sands merge to provide a truly beautiful, maritime scene. Lapwings flash black and white overhead and ringed plovers, golden plovers and redshank flutter out of our way, seemingly startled to see a car in the midst of their breeding ground. I can imagine this place being desolate and bleak in winter but today, in late May, the overhead sun illuminates the land and sea around us in an array of blues, greens and greys more vivid than any landscape painter could portray.

Even stronger blue is the hull of the *Eilean Bhearnaraigh* which is going to take us over to Berneray. Owned by the Western Isles Council, she is now operated by Caledonian MacBrayne. Despite this change in management she still retains her blue hull, not yet surrendering to the black and white hulls of the traditional CalMac ferry. She is another 'new' ship for us and looks just like a squarer 'Island class' ferry.

Gibbie reverses onto her – he is beginning to get better at it – but need not have bothered as there is a turntable on board. In ten minutes we are on island number six, visited by us on Island Hop 1995. Having the car this time, we decide to take in the whole island. First stop is the cafe – yet again it is shut. Gibbie puts on his 'Cafe – Closed' music, which we are becoming quite familiar with by now on the trip. Off we go to the outer extremities of Berneray – half a mile away. We pass the guest-house where Prince Charles had stayed on more than one occasion. Two men are working in a field, close by the road as we pass. We drive slowly past to get a good look at them – but neither has the ears.

At the school a group of recently ruined cottages form an intriguing cluster which seems worthy of a visit. They resemble an abandoned village and one of them still has an armchair and old range in the remains of the living-room. The torn wallpaper is quite fetching.

Out to sea in the distance, our next vessel, the *Loch Bhrusda* is picking her way through the rocks and reefs which litter the Sound of Harris. Her black, white and red colour scheme looks familiar.

'She looks like the *Waverley* out there,' I find myself saying. Ian and Gibbie shake their heads at me.

Our hour on Berneray is up. We return to the slipway and obtain some excellent pictures of the *Eilean Bhearnaraigh* and *Loch Bhrusda* passing each other. At Otternish our ship waits while the *Loch Bhrusda* discharges her load and retreats into the Sound to let us disembark. She then returns to the slip. We drive off one ship, park the car and walk onto the other. A glance at the watch confirms that the *Loch Bhrusda* is indeed running to time.

'We're only getting onto this ferry if you promise to run to time,' I broadcast to the purser. 'We've got to catch the *Lord of the Isles* at Lochboisdale tonight.'

The purser fails to see the connection. 'But that's in the other direction!'

The new route from Otternish to Leverburgh, on Harris, is quite unique among sea-routes to the isles. Due to the fact that the islands of Berneray, Killegray and Ensay, as well as numerous rocks lie in the way, the path taken by the little ship is a tortuous one, out to the east before swinging north towards Harris. Looking at the map, a safe route around these obstructions seems virtually impossible. As far as Gibbie is concerned a safe route is impossible. He is not a happy man as the ferry takes the first of twelve separate turns to avoid submerged reefs. A pathway of specially laid green and red buoys highlights the route for the skipper but that is no consolation for our man.

'I'm not going on this again,' he declares.

The sky has greyed somewhat and the cold breeze from the north east has intensified. These factors combine to give us an air of silent resignation on our fifty minute journey across the Sound. All the twists, turns and detours will add about four miles to the trip. At one point the vessel takes a left turn of more than ninety degrees. Gibbie shakes his head.

Things are not too great downstairs in the small saloon either. Two user-unfriendly vending machines are causing us grief. Both refuse to take our money or deliver the goods. After much trying Ian eventually manages to obtain a bar of chocolate for 2p.

I go up on deck again to watch the ship's performance. It looks like a one-man show as our skipper, John Webb, steers from the glass bridge using a control wheel in each hand to give direction to the water thrusting propulsion units. He appears to know what he is doing but I decide to pay him a visit later, just to make sure. I am rather enjoying the experience but wish it was a little warmer. The vagaries and absurdities of our travels bring a smile to my face. Having already sailed twice over to Skye from different ports, here we are sailing back to Harris, having left it this morning, while our main direction in a few hours time will be south out of Lochboisdale sixty miles away. Meanwhile, downstairs, to add insult to injury, Gibbie has just paid for a cup of vegetable soup from the temperamental machine.

The ship is still sailing to time, thank goodness, and at Leverburgh I jump off to obtain a photograph. The sun has come out again but there does not appear to be much to photograph apart from the ferry. A couple of small fishing boats are moored nearby and in an adjacent field four young children in white jumpers and sweatshirts are running and jumping around. From this distance they look like springing lambs.

I have my eye on the watch again as we pull away from the slip at Leverburgh. We are exactly on time. Suddenly the vessel stops dead. Ian and I look anxiously around to see why. Gibbie looks suspiciously down into the water. A car has driven up at speed to the slipway and, as this is the last sailing of the day, the skipper has brought the ship to a halt to check if the driver wants to board. Five minutes will be wasted if he does. But to our relief the driver is just looking for a parking space. On we go again. The skipper's magnanimous actions have nearly given me heart failure.

I must meet this skipper and so go up to the overhead, central bridge where a very gentlemanly Captain Webb is happy to explain the workings of his charge. Sitting on his pedestal in the centre of the bridge, with his arms extended, he is working away at the two steering wheels, like a smug chef stirring two pots of soup. I commend him on his time-keeping. He laughs.

'Our Operations Manager was just criticising me for my time-keeping last week. I don't care. I was Best Man at his wedding.'

I ask if he has to make a written note or record of each buoy as he passes it.

'No need – I know every one intimately.'

I get the impression that he can steer the vessel with his eyes closed, but in the interest of Gibbie's nerves, do not ask him to. 'What happens if it gets misty?' I ask tentatively.

'We don't sail.'

I refrain from asking the obvious question; what happens if it gets misty when we're halfway across the Sound?

I return downstairs, where life is still revolving around the bellicose vending machines, to try to reassure, or at least console, Gibbie. He is looking with diffidence at the next set of jagged rocks passing close by. 'What happens if the engine breaks down?' he mutters.

At 2055, as timetabled, we are back at Otternish. Sailing on the *Loch Bhrusda* has been an experience. The next experience is the fifty-two miles to Lochboisdale, along narrow roads and across the islands of North Uist, Grimsay, Benbecula and South Uist. We have exactly two hours in which to do it or the rest of our Island Hop plans will fall apart. I volunteer to drive, more for the sake of my fingernails than anything else.

I need not have worried – the drive is easy and it soon becomes apparent that we *do* have 'bags of time' in which to do it. But we still do not feel easy enough about the time to stop on the tidal island of Grimsay – just to say that we have now actually stood on it rather than just driven across it. So we push onwards.

The road is quiet. We go from one causeway onto the next, in fading light. Away to our right, beyond the flat fields and moors of Benbecula, and then South Uist, a deep orange sun is dipping into the Atlantic Ocean. The houses and crofts are silhouetted by its glow.

Two miles north of Lochboisdale a curving line of car headlights snaking towards us heralds the arrival of the *Lord of the Isles* at the South Uist pier. We pull up a few minutes later alongside the ship. It is 2209, we have taken only one hour and thirteen minutes to travel the length of the Uists and there are smiles all around, especially on the face of the CalMac office manager who welcomes us: 'You're early!'

We board our seventh vessel in two days. Two matters have to be dealt with urgently, concerning the car and the cabins.

As the ship will be docking at Oban at 0500 and then sailing out to Tiree, with us aboard and hopefully asleep in our respective bunks, the car might present a problem as the crew would want to unload it at Oban. As we will not need the car at Tiree, and as none of us wants to get up at 0500 to shift it, Gibbie agrees to the suggestion that he hands his keys over to a crew member who will kindly move it off the ship and park it in Oban. He has only one misgiving: 'I just hope my mint imperials are still there when we get back from Tiree.'

Next the cabins. The steward shows us to them, three in a row, level with the car-deck and promises not to wake us up at Oban. Everything seems to be going too well. The cabins are small but comfortable. There is a bunk bed with a bedside cabinet and private WC and shower. I feel that I will sleep quite happily but Ian imagines that he will remain awake all night. In all of our Island

Hopping over the years this will be the first time that we have had an overnight stay on a ship. It is also likely to be our last, for the new ship due to replace the *Lord of the Isles* on this route will not have cabins on her.

We sail out of Lochboisdale at 2300 and go below to look for some supper. Before joining my two companions around the table I return to my cabin to put away my camera. When I return to the restaurant the two of them are deep in thought.

'Difficult decision,' says Ian. 'Don't know whether to go top or bottom.'

I look concerned but they assure me they are talking about which bunk they will sleep on in their respective cabins! I'm a bottom man, myself.

Out on deck, just after midnight, on what is now Friday morning. The sky is starlit with the added bonus of a couple of planets overhead (Saturn and Jupiter?) and the full moon hiding behind a yellow-grey cloud. The pitching of the ship has lessened as we are now in the shelter of Skye, although it is many miles away to the north-east. I can see no other ship lights at all. It is cold.

Feeling suitably sedated after a whisky with Ian and Gibbie in the bar, I descend the three flights of stairs to Cabin C. The cabins are tucked away behind three separate spring-loaded doors. I don't know if they are to keep me in or the sea out in the event of an emergency.

Lying on my bunk in total darkness, trying to fall asleep, my mind recounting the events of another busy and fascinating day. The ship is moving very little now and the constant drone of the engines is not unpleasant. I reckon I will be up and wide awake at 0500 when we arrive in Oban.

Day Three – *Cool mints and warm wine*

I'm out of my bunk and straight into the shower at 0800, having slept fitfully but otherwise comfortably. I am keen to find out where we are and so get up on deck as soon as I can. Emerging from the bowels of the ship on a new day, bound for a new island, I find that the sun is shining once again. I am even more delighted to find that we are off the coast of Coll. Not half as delighted as Ian, though.

Over a breakfast of bacon, sausage and rolls we swap nocturnal notes. All of us were aware of a drop in engine noise around 0500, which must have coincided with our hour long stop-over at Oban, but we have all slept reasonably well. For Ian it has come as a relief to find that the ship is so far on her way towards Tiree. He had expected to be walking the decks watching the ship load at Oban at 5am.

Other things around us are new, apart from the day, which adds to the occasion. The crew have changed and all the passengers are different. They are all prospective Tiree and Coll passengers now instead of the inward bound Outer Isles lot. The young, boisterous crowd on board last night have been replaced by woollen-clad, newspaper-reading, middle-aged types – and that is just the crew!

I meet a smartly attired, woollen-clad, elderly couple from Sutherland who have joined the ship at Oban at 0600 this morning for a 'cruise to the isles'. They are thoroughly enjoying the experience and are peering over the side, pointing at passing islands like schoolchildren on a geography trip.

'What islands are those?' they ask me.

When I point out the island of Coll, the old gentleman erupts into a lengthy tale about a farmer friend of his from Coll who, many years ago, had been observing the loading of his cattle onto a MacBrayne's steamer at Coll pier. A sling was being used to hoist the beasts up and over, onto the ship. One particular animal was behaving cantankerously. The cow was eventually cornered and the sling positioned under her. As she was being lifted high into the air, the farmer, pipe in mouth, nodded in encouragement. 'There you go now, you fractious bitch.' At that the cow opened her bowels and the farmer was on the receiving line of everything that she had to offer.

A stroll around the deck, bemoaning the lack of deck seating on this otherwise cosy ship, results in an encounter with the crewman who had moved Gibbie's car. He unceremoniously hands over the keys with brief instructions as to where Gibbie will find it. I note that he is sucking a mint imperial.

Another breakfast before Tiree, well, we have four more islands and a whole day of cruising to go and we have to keep our strength up.

At Scaranish pier, Tiree, I get off to see if anyone is there to meet us. Three weeks ago a patient had come down from Tiree for treatment and, on hearing of my proposed visit, promised to come down to the pier to meet the ship. He is not there. Ian is succinct: 'Either he's forgotten or else the last lot of fillings you did for him have fallen out.'

On now to Coll and our brief visit here is even briefer than our visit to Tiree. On the way back down the Sound of Mull towards Oban we decide it is 'velvet' time – our newly acquired, esoteric expression for a pre-lunch pint. As we pass Craignure, the *Isle of Mull* pulls away from the linkspan and sails off ahead of us. As she is obviously going to reach Oban before us, the *Lord of the Isles* reduces speed and we continue at a slow pace. We wonder why the skipper did not reduce speed earlier as it was clear from the moment we left Coll that we were running ahead of time.

On our approach to Oban we are on the lookout for another CalMac ship. The *Claymore* soon to be sold for service on the new Campbeltown- Ballycastle route run by the Argyll & Antrim Steam Packet Company, is due to pay a visit to Oban from Northern Ireland either today or tomorrow. We keep an eye out for her as we round the northern tip of Kerrera but she is not there. We last sailed on the *Claymore* back in 1991 and it seems unlikely that we shall sail on her again, unless we choose to include Northern Ireland in the future. When I bounce this idea, Gibbie quips that we will need 'Irish Rover' tickets for that.

We sit out in Oban Bay for five minutes to let the *Isle of Mull* load up again for Craignure. From our position, we can see Gibbie's car in the CalMac staff car-park. Even from here we can see a white piece of paper stuck under the windscreen wiper.

We disembark from the *Lord of the Isles* after over fifteen hours on board: our longest ever continuous cruise on an Island Hop. We will be seeing more of her later but for now we only have forty minutes before sailing off to Lismore on our next vessel. First we have to retrieve the car. The ominous notice on the windscreen reads: DO NOT PARK IN THE STAFF CAR PARK – USE THE PUBLIC CAR PARK. I reposition the car nearer our Oban hotel and am back at the pier as Gibbie and Ian are boarding the Lismore ferry *Coll*. The *Lord of the Isles* is still at the pier, loading for Barra.

On board the Lismore ferry, we share the deck with five cars, two bicycles and a handful of fellow passengers who *look* like Lismore folk – whatever they may look like. One of the cars is pulling a trailer, full of what appears from a distance to be a mobile rocket launcher, with multiple warheads. In fact it is a trailer full of short, upward-pointing, wooden fence posts.

We have nowhere to sit. Several boxes of bananas and a large case of Bowmore whisky are tempting seats but we elect to stand and lean against the bulwarks. Off we go, on the fifty-minute crossing, heading for the sheltered island of Lismore for the first time since 1991. Access to the upper deck, which used to have seats, is no longer allowed on these small ferries due to an unfortunate accident a few years ago when a small child fell down the steep stairs.

At the Lismore side, the rusting hulk of a landing craft, which we had christened 'the relief ferry' six years ago, is still at its final resting place on the stony beach. It has deteriorated noticeably since 1991 but then we probably have as well.

The great pity is that we do not have the time to spend exploring this lovely, green island. We could even have marched Gibbie the two miles to the cafe. On the way back to Oban we are joined by eighteen multi-national cyclists who are returning, wearily, from an organised trip. I start chatting to a chap from Switzerland. 'Vee haff a cycling tour today and tonight vee haff viskey-taste evening.' Sounds good to me. I ask him if he has a favourite whisky. 'Isle of Jura,' he replies unequivocally.

Off they pedal at Oban, all in gaudy, embellished lycra shorts stretched over a diverse assortment of backsides, looking forward to their evening of imbibition.

Our next ship, the *Isle of Mull*, leaves in just over an hour on her evening cruise to Colonsay. We check into the hotel and dump our bags. As we are going to have 'dinner with wine' while aboard this evening cruise to Colonsay and back, Gibbie decides to shave.

'I don't know how much I'll have to drink tonight.'

Downstairs we learn from the hotelier that the *Claymore* is not due at Oban until 1700 tomorrow (Saturday). The hotel will then be filled with Irish Rovers.

We are back on the pier just before the sailing time of 1800 in very relaxed mood. The sun is still playing by the script and we have a glorious five-hour cruise ahead of us. We wait to board as the ship unloads her latest consignment of Mull passengers. There is a large crowd disembarking slowly down the steep, covered gangway when a man momentarily loses control of the wheelchair in which his wife is sitting, with near disastrous consequences. The poor woman is flung head first onto Oban pier. Anxious looks all around until, with the aid of CalMac staff, she is re-united with her chair. She is wheeled off, reassuringly with a smile on her face, by her sheepish-looking husband.

The ship casts off and heads down the sound of Kerrera. We head off downwards ourselves, for our pre-'dinner with wine' drink. Then it is straight into the steak-pie with warm white and chilled red wines.

It is a beautiful, warm, sunny evening and we all have a touch of the 'feel good' factor as we pass the numerous islands. The rocky, western faces of the Garvellachs are highlighted by the sinking sun and the cracks and fissures etched onto them are exaggerated into deep black lines.

The ship is busy, particularly with English families and their pets heading for a Bank Holiday weekend on Colonsay. Ian remarks that he has never seen so many dogs on a ship. He has obviously never been on a Friday night booze-cruise out of Greenock. In the observation lounge, three young girls are meticulously dividing packets of sweets between them with mathematical precision. Once the deal is completed they bid each other farewell: 'Bye Ursa, see you on the ship next week.'

By now Gibbie's head is rolling as he fights hard to retain consciousness. It eventually falls backwards – his neck muscles unable to resist gravity any more – and nearly collides with the head of the woman sitting directly behind him. She gives him a look of indignation and shuffles six inches further up her seat.

The sun is streaming in through the low windows of the lounge as we arrive at Colonsay. Our arrival wakes us from our slumbers and stirs us into a flurry of activity. I want to film our arrival but Gibbie has spotted the *Hebridean Princess* off our port side, which is worth a photograph. With a call of nature urgently required I do not know what to do first. The *Princess* is resting just out of the bay, probably awaiting the arrival and departure of the *Isle of Mull* before berthing overnight at the pier. She is putting in her annual Island Hop appearance.

As the *Isle of Mull* is running late I dare to jump ashore only very briefly lest the ship sails without me. Back on board a quieter ship – the cackling children and their incontinent pets have all left – we can now grab the best seats in the house for a sunlit passage home. Our third Hebridean sunset in a row is disappearing behind the mountains of Mull and casting a golden glow over the shimmering sea. When it is gone I head down to the shop to see if I can find anything of interest for my children. A book catches my eye, its title: *Missing Dad!* Appropriate, I hope.

We arrive back at Oban at 2315. We have spent twenty-two of the last twenty-four hours at sea and we are tired. Off we head for our one large room at the hotel and we are quickly asleep – like three little bears all in a row.

Day Four – *Tobermory Swansong*

1000 on Saturday morning and we are on the *Isle of Mull* again, this time over to Craignure. We are heading, eventually, for Tobermory, as this will be the last time we can ever sail out of the Mull capital, for reasons that are described later. This is the notorious '1000 ex-Oban', the busiest sailing of the week, compounded by the Bank Holiday traffic, which conveys the Mull, Iona and Staffa tourists over to their first island. At times the *Isle of Mull* can be filled to her thousand-passenger complement. This morning the pier is buzzing with people, like bees around a hive, watching the ship berth, running after tickets and ultimately forming the inevitable queue. American is the dominating language as we shuffle aboard. They are analysing everything:

'I feel fine today.'

'Why are they all going to the front of the ship?'

' Observation Lounge – do you think that's inside?'

'Do we sail back to Ohbaan?'

'Martha, have you ever seen so many dogs on a ship before?'

We find a less crowded spot on the starboard deck to watch our departure and to reconcile our debts to each other. We all owe Gibbie money – which is very unusual as it is normally the other way round.

As we have no car with us now we will require a bus for the next section from Craignure to Tobermory. With so many aboard the ship this could present a problem. What if they are all going to Tobermory? Most of them are talking about Iona – where a celebration of the 1400th anniversary of Saint Columba's death is in full song. Being naturally cautious, I head us down to the exit doors, in my role as acting tactician, in order to be off the ship in the first batch. We should then be able to procure a bus.

As it turns out, we are more successful than we thought – we are the very first off the ship. We are also the first on the bus to Tobermory. It turns out to be prudent planning, however, as the bus leaves full, before the ship has even discharged all her passengers. A very broad American chap plants himself down beside Gibbie – well, it was the last available seat!

'Sorry,' he says, apologetically. 'I'm a big guy.'

'Your mother must have fed you too well,' Gibbie returns.

The bus turns down to Fishnish, where the *Isle of Cumbrae*, coming over from Lochaline, is only five minutes away from the slipway. With a full bus, the driver is not interested in waiting, so he turns his vehicle round and we carry on towards Tobermory. Seems like a pointless exercise. In all the years that we have been on a Mull bus we have yet to pick up a single passenger from Fishnish.

At the Mull capital, we have the nearest thing we have ever had to a shopping expedition. Gibbie even buys a new bunnet. In one shop window is a cake made in the shape of the *Isle of Mull*. Its purpose is to draw tourist attention to the impending loss of the direct ferry link from Tobermory to Oban. Twice a week the Coll/Tiree ship calls at Tobermory both outward and inward to load foot passengers. The proposed new ship, which will replace the *Lord of the Isles* next year will, apparently, be too big to berth at Tobermory pier. This has, understandably, been met with local voices of opposition, the more cynical of which would argue that Caledonian MacBrayne have been looking for an excuse to terminate the service for years. Soon a historic and restored pier will lie under-used, no longer the call of ships bearing the name 'MacBrayne'.

Today we are going to board the *Lord* for the last time, for the sail back to Oban.

While we wait for our ship I try to phone home – without success. A contractor in Glasgow has cut through a British Telecom cable supplying 100,000 phones in the Highlands and Islands. Of course I do not know this at the time (I read it in *The Herald* the next day) and try three different telephones before giving up.

Into the Mishnish, our favourite island pub. The staff are preparing for this afternoon's Scottish Cup Final between Falkirk and Kilmarnock. A large rectangular television screen has been erected in our 'usual corner' and John Kettley is giving a weather report. A huge sun symbol is placed over Mull. Outside is the proof that his forecast is accurate.

On Tobermory pier at 1300 or, more precisely, the cafe veranda above it, waiting for the ship to arrive. Gibbie in his new skipped bunnet comes up and stands in front of me, face-to-face.

'Are my sunglasses still dark?'

'Yes,' I reply.

Gibbie looks perturbed. 'They're not supposed to be, they're in the shadow of my bunnet.'

I'm not sure if he is complaining about the bunnet or the sunglasses.

The *Eigg* serving Kilchoan on the Ardnamurchan peninsula and the *Lord of the Isles* both arrive at the pier at the same time. We watch our last ever departure from Tobermory Pier from the upper deck of the latter and sail off down the Sound of Mull for the fourth time on this trip. We then adjourn to the restaurant, to add lunch to all the other meals we have had here.

I get chatting to the steward, Andy, about life on board this most hard-worked ship. His shifts are at least twelve hours long, each day for two weeks. He then has a two week break. He pours a fine bowl of soup.

By now we know our way around this ship with our eyes closed. In the reclining-seat lounge after lunch, mine are doing just that. But they are soon open again when the captain announces that we are passing a regatta of classic yachts to port. The steam-powered yacht *Corolla* and other old exotic sailing craft pass us at close range. A drawn out, hoarse whistle from the steam yacht is answered by our ship. It is an ideal photo opportunity, almost as if their passing has been specially arranged for our final arrival from the Western Isles and from Tobermory in particular.

At Oban pier at 1435. A white poodle is being carried off the ship in a shopping basket and a black Labrador is being cycled onto the car-deck on the back of a mountain bike. Ian was right about dogs on ships.

It is decision time again. We are sadly on our way home now – but which way? The notion of waiting three hours for the *Claymore* just for a photograph, is dismissed. With the freedom of our Car Rover ticket we can take in a ferry or two, and maybe another island, quite easily. The choice is between Bute or Arran. The latter is our favourite choice, provided we can get back off the island again from Brodick on the *Caledonian Isles*. This way we will have sailed on all of CalMac's major Western Isles ships, with the exception of the *Isle of Arran*.

A phone-call by me, it's always me, has us booked on the 1920 sailing out of Brodick. All we have to do now is get there. Our route will be via Tarbert, Loch Fyne, and Ian is driving. Ten miles out of Oban, Kilmarnock score the winning goal of the Cup Final. The clientele of the Mishnish will be cheering. Even Gibbie seems happy about it.

At Kilmartin we are driving round a bend and have to slow down to avoid a ginger-haired, kilted warrior wielding two double-headed axes. We nearly have heart failure until we realise that it's the town's Gala Day.

At Tarbert, the town is busy due to the incoming yacht race. Dozens of boats are filing into an already crowded harbour. In amongst them the *Bruernish* the current Tarbert–Portavadie ferry, is arriving and we stop for more pictures.

We are now heading for Claonaig, ten miles south of Tarbert, for the back-door ferry to Arran. On the way we stop at West Loch Tarbert pier to see what the former Islay departure point now looks like. A dozen fishing boats are moored at the pier while, further up the loch, another two are half submerged and disintegrating, as if the sea is exacting revenge on them for all the spoils they have taken.

At Claonaig, delighted that there are not eighteen cars ahead of us in the queue, we look at a stunning view of the northern end of Arran. Wispy cirrus clouds criss-cross the sky but eagle-eyed Gibbie spots a large one which would appear to be over the centre of the island. It is mushroom shaped.

'Good Heavens – they've nuked Brodick,' he comments dryly. Ian laughs and Gibbie continues: 'They've picked the wrong place, my first target would be Rouen in France.' I am left wondering what he has against Rouen in France as he volunteers no explanation.

Onto the ferry *Loch Tarbert* we go and up to the top deck for one of the best views of one of the most beautiful firths. Some white-haired children are running about and giggling on the half-empty car deck. Gibbie eyes them gravely. 'Hamburgers!'

I raise an eyebrow. 'Hamburgers!' he repeats, pointing to the children. 'It's due to hamburgers that we can't get on the top deck of the Island class ferries. Hamburgers make kids hyperactive and they fall over.'

As we drive ashore at Lochranza, onto island number fifteen, we have just one hour to get to Brodick for our last ship of the trip. This time I am driving.

Beyond Corrie and only three miles from Brodick pier, we can see the *Caledonian Isles* slipping gently into the Bay. The sky has cleared completely and matches the hue of the motionless sea in a pale cobalt blue. As Gibbie observes, the ship really does look like '. . .a painted ship upon a painted ocean.'

We reach the pier at the same time as the *Caledonian Isles*. A line of passengers trots out along the pier to her, silhouetted and looking like a line of ants crossing a branch. Gibbie and Ian start counting the cars discharging from her and find that they cannot stop. They have to at one hundred and nineteen. The ship's capacity is one hundred and twenty, which proves how popular Arran is on a Bank Holiday weekend.

On board, it is quite a culture shock. A large crowd of day-trippers are heading home. The restaurant is empty and the bar is full. Up in the Western Isles it was the other way round. Although keen to film our Annual Toast up on deck we decide to have a snack first. A French lad in front of me in the queue at the cafeteria asks for a baguette with his roast chicken. He receives a shake of the head, a raised eyebrow and chips. Meanwhile, three middle-aged, tweed-clad farmer types pass by. Their eyes are glassy and their glasses are empty as they stagger in unison on their slow, deliberate path back to the bar.

The Annual Toast finally takes place on the after-deck. It is a somewhat self-conscious affair as it seems to involve a fair number of the other passengers. When we raise our glasses to the camera, perched high on its tripod, half of the ship's complement seems to follow suit. And why not? It has been a wonderful trip. Fifteen islands on eleven vessels. Everything has gone according to plan, our targets achieved. On the drive back to Glasgow we swap notes on our favourite moments. Gibbie picks this fourth day, especially the visit to Tobermory. I go for our sun-setting arrival at Colonsay. Ian chooses his highlight as waking up on the *Lord of the Isles* and discovering that we were off the coast of Coll and not berthed at Oban pier at 5 am, as he had imagined.

* * *

Island Hop Number Nine – The Nights of the Long Sails – will be hard to beat.

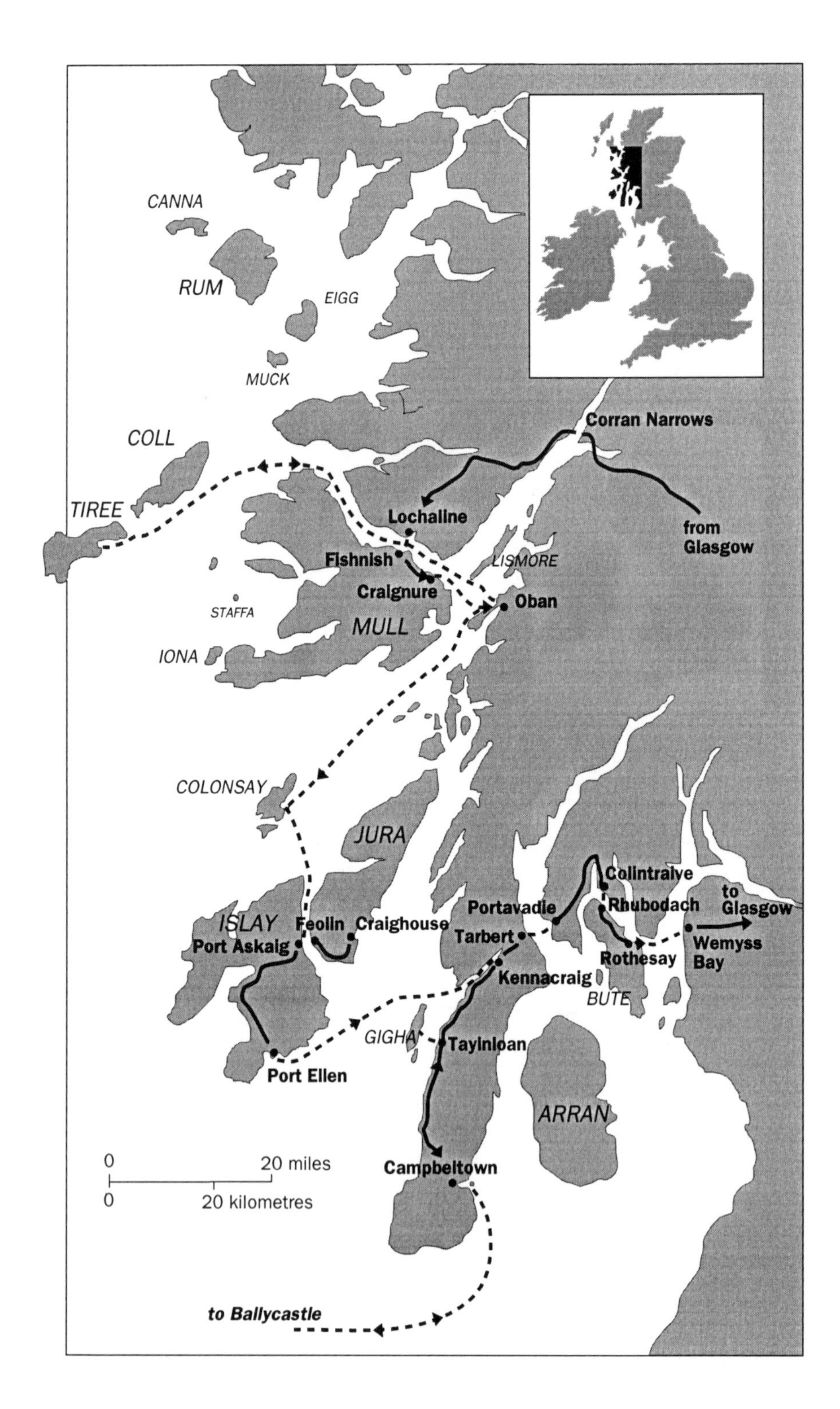
CANNA
RUM
EIGG
MUCK
COLL
TIREE
Corran Narrows
Lochaline
from
Glasgow
Fishnish
LISMORE
Craignure
Oban
STAFFA
MULL
IONA
COLONSAY
JURA
Colintraive
ISLAY
Feolin
Craighouse
Portavadie
Rhubodach
to
Glasgow
Port Askaig
Tarbert
Rothesay
Wemyss
Bay
Kennacraig
BUTE
GIGHA
Tayinloan
Port Ellen
ARRAN
0
20 miles
Campbeltown
0
20 kilometres
to Ballycastle

10 Irish Connections

The Plan

This year was number ten. Hard to believe really. We had to make it a good one – but then, they've all been good. We had no particular theme in mind for 1998 but thought that we had better mop up a few loose ends, such as spending more time on a couple of islands that we had only briefly stepped on before. We could also have one final indulgence – to leave Scotland altogether and sail over to Northern Ireland on the *Claymore*. This, after all, was our tenth Island Hop, and possibly our last. After Number One, the intention had been to have ten trips in all. Now, unbelievably, we were there.

The islands that we planned to see a bit more of were Tiree and Jura. We booked accommodation on both. Hopefully we could also spend a bit more time on Gigha and there might be a chance to add a 'new' island to our list – and a Clyde one at that.

Day One – *The Gaelic Labrador*

I look at my watch. It reads 1010 and I turn to my two friends and announce smugly that my estimation of our journey time from Glasgow to where we now stand is a mere five minutes out. They nod as if they expect nothing less from me.

'Where we now stand' is the east side of the Corran narrows on the shores on Loch Linnhe, just a few miles south of Fort William. The first vessel, I cannot bring myself to call it a ship, of Island Hop 1998, is sitting at her berth in front of us. The *Maid of Glencoul* is more a floating car-ramp than anything else but it will still go down in our records as a 'new vessel' for us our first in what is now our tenth Island Hop. Ugly she may be, but the Council run ferry will save us a drive of nearly fifty miles around Lochs Linnhe and Eil in our efforts to reach the ferry point of Lochaline on Morven. The long narrow sea loch of Loch Linnhe comes to a tight stricture here at Corran and the ferry will take a mere five minutes to cross. Gibbie drives us aboard.

This unconventional route to Oban will add a bit of interest to the usual routine of getting to our starting point; just like last year when we took a convoluted route to Ullapool via Skye. This time we are heading to Oban via Mull. This may seem a bit crazy, but to go the conventional way is too simple for intrepid travellers like us. From Lochaline we will sail over to Mull, and then leave again on the big ship direct to Oban. We must make the 1300 sailing out of Craignure or we will miss our real target of the day – the *Lord of the Isles* sailing from Oban to Tiree.

Our drive down through Morven to Lochaline is pleasant enough. The road is mostly single-track but is not busy. Gibbie pushes on. He is keen to have enough time at Lochaline to sample the culinary delights of his favourite mobile restaurant – Jean's Tea Bar. Needless to say his wish is granted and three of Jean's 'Barge Specials' are soon sizzling away under her canvas awning.

Some three and a half hours earlier we had left Glasgow with the accoutrements of a mobile film crew packed into the boot of Gibbie's new car. It is a blue Citroen Xsara – a detail that has Ian and me a bit concerned. For the previous few weeks Citroen has been advertising their new car with the help of a scantily-clad Claudia Schiffer who proceeds to disrobe as she prepares to drive, the final white under-garment being tossed onto the road as the car moves off. It is all tastefully done but I have warned Gibbie that if he appears outside my house dressed only in his string vest then Island Hop 1998 will be cancelled.

We had left at 0757 – a bit bleary-eyed from last night's eleventh hour final detailing of Hop Number Ten. This is part of the course. Ian always arrives in Glasgow from Surrey the night before we start our trip and we have a get-together at Gibbie's house to finalise our plans. Finalising the plans usually includes a couple of malts and a general reminiscing which goes on longer than expected. Ian always tries to prolong the evening as he has to share the spare room with Gibbie's truculent cats afterwards. Ian is allergic to cats, which do not seem to appreciate the company. On one famous occasion a moggy tried to beat Ian up in the middle of the night.

Gibbie has only had his new car for four weeks but has already christened it 'Andre' after Mr Citroen. He has only one complaint about it – there is nowhere on the sloping dashboard where he can position his corroding and battered old tin of mint imperials. Instead, it sits between the front seats, slumped against the hand-brake. I have no complaints – sitting in the back of the car I can now reach them more easily.

In Glen Coe we see DJ Jimmy Savile's new home – a small white cottage without mains electricity or gas. The only problem is we don't know which little white cottage is his and after half a dozen gesticulations of 'It must be that one there. . .' we eventually give up.

I had estimated a journey time of two and a half hours to the Corran Narrows – thus the smugness.

At Lochaline, the ferry has changed from previous years. The re-introduction of the former Skye ferries *Loch Dunvegan* and *Loch Fyne* has allowed much reshuffling of the smaller vessels of the fleet with many routes being upgraded by larger ferries. Lochaline to Fishnish is one such example. A new vessel, the *Loch Alainn*, was built for this service, but technical problems have meant that she will now be used on the Clyde. Our second ferry of the day, therefore, is one of those former Skye vessels, the *Loch Fyne*. This means a considerable increase in car and passenger capacity on this route. This morning, however, a mere six cars – including ours – board for the fifteen-minute crossing. We have sailed on this vessel before, in 1992 and 1993, the kind of detail that completely underwhelms Gibbie.

Fishnish and Craignure on Mull are a mere six miles apart and as we are booked on the 1300 sailing there is no need to queue. To kill time we head off for one of Mull's best tourist attractions.

The Mull Miniature Railway is the 'Only Island Railway' in Scotland. The narrow gauge track runs a mile or two from Craignure to Toronsay House and Gardens. The small enclosed coaches are hauled by real coal-fired steam engines. As we arrive at the station one of the locomotives, the blue liveried 'Victoria' is wheezing its way along the track, like an old asthmatic work-horse, to its terminus. Crammed inside is its normal-sized driver who looks like a giant Casey Jones.

Gibbie and Ian give the locomotive the 'once over' with their critical engineer's eye. It is a small neat and polished affair which certainly smells like the real thing.

Out to sea the *Isle of Mull* is turning into the Bay – we have to go.

The Craignure – Oban route on the *Isle of Mull* requires no further introduction. Suffice to say that her upper deck is a fine way to spend forty minutes when the sun is shining.

We have about an hour at Oban and decide to spend it no further away than the pier. Two 'Island class' ferries, *Raasay* and *Bruernish*, are manacled together. These ferries are becoming a rare species. Only four from the original eight survive in CalMac's fleet. The *Coll* and the *Rhum* (both sailed on during last year's Island Hop) have been sold to Irish interests. The *Canna* now serves Rathlin Island from Ballycastle in Northern Ireland. The *Bruernish* is now the regular Lismore ferry, the *Eigg* the Kilchoan ferry and the *Raasay* is the spare vessel.

One other point of interest is a small vehicle ferry called the *Maid of Ulva* which is berthed at the Lismore ferry ramp. On her tiny vehicle deck a miniature JCB is taking wooden palettes up onto the pier.

With no other interest of a shipping nature apparent we head for the popular sea-food take-away further up the pier. Here all manner of shelled beasties are available in tubs, sandwiches and platters. Some are so fresh that they are still wriggling. The latter kind attracts Gibbie and he is soon gulping down a slimy oyster from its grey shell. This happens so quickly that I miss capturing it on film so he offers to repeat the exercise provided I buy him another. Down it slithers to join its mate. Gibbie licks his lips like a satisfied cat. It is only then that I notice that a crowd of Albion Rovers proportions has gathered to watch this gastronomic, albeit ephemeral, event. Gibbie sums up the experience: 'It was a brave man who ate the first oyster.' I can easily agree with him but would add that it is still a brave man who eats one for the first time. He goes on: 'The best seafood delicacy of all time is oysters in aspic.' I thought he said 'aspirin'. Alka-Seltzer more like.

The arrival of the *Lord of the Isles* makes us put the cameras away and hustle up the pier. Gibbie has discreetly abandoned his new Xsara on a double yellow line with our confident assurance that it will still be there when we sail back in tomorrow. We board this intrepid ship as foot passengers. We have a three and a half hour trip out to Tiree ahead of us and are looking forward to seeing a fair bit of the island, instead of having one of our flying visits, as we will be staying overnight. The ship sails on time at 1450.

As we sail up the Sound of Mull we join the queue for a late lunch, or an early dinner. The lady ahead of Ian asks the girl serving us:

'What kind of salads do you have?'

'Lamb and corned beef.'

'That's fine, I'll have a gammon one.'

We sail past Tobermory where the ship will no longer call. This is because the new ship for Coll and Tiree, the *Clansman*, will be too long to fit at the pier. The irony is that the new ship is already more than a month late but the *Lord of the Isles* will still not call, even though she fits in at the pier, because the call is no longer in the summer timetable. Due to the late arrival of the *Clansman* other things, such as Clyde cruising, which *are* in the summer timetable, are not happening.

Onwards to the island of Coll. I miss the stop-over because I am having a peaceful snooze in the *Lord*'s reclining lounge. Well, I've seen it all before.

Meet up with my pals in the restaurant – again! It seems that all we do on long cruises is eat. Ian blames it on me but I don't see why. Over a vegetable curry – which consists mostly of carrots and turnip (left over soup?) – Gibbie and Ian discuss reciprocating steam engines with an enthusiasm that imparts a human intelligence to their subject matter. A feminine human intelligence at that:

'She was a bitch when it came to reversing.'

'Yes, but a good slap on her backside would get the reversing gear in place.'

I listen intently as I reluctantly shovel in another forkful of swede korma.

The hairline horizon of Tiree is soon upon us. As the ship ties up two dolphins dance in the water beside it, submerging teasingly whenever anyone raises a camera and showing-off unashamedly when the lenses are lowered. Although we have twice visited the island this is the first time that we will be able to spend more than ten minutes ashore. Our 'look' at the island will be made even better because a friend of mine who lives on the island has deposited her car at the pier for our unrestricted use during the course of our stay. It will be our magic carpet for this evening's whirlwind tour of the island. We find the car parked in the far corner of the car park, an 'H' registration Volkswagen Polo. I am the chosen driver as none of the others look keen. I am quite pleased about this really – until we reach the first junction, where I learn that the perky wee Polo doesn't like to stop. I have been warned that the brakes are none too effective – an understatement! At the first junction a police car is about to cross my path and I am off my seat trying to bring the car to a halt. The police car has already stopped – its driver recognises the car. From now on, Gibbie scans the road ahead to give me warning of other junctions. That way I reckon I will be able to stop in time. We head off, slowly, to find our hotel.

After checking in we set off on our tour, very grateful for the use of the temperamental little car.

Tiree has a population of about eight hundred. Its name is derived from *Tir – lodh* which means 'the land of corn.' This puts doubt on Gibbie's claim that it means 'blue hole in the sky.' Who do we believe? Certainly the billiard table landscape, flat save for a couple of low hills, supports many crofts, but I don't see much corn growing. Crofts mainly provide grazing for the numerous cattle and sheep. Today there is no 'blue hole in the sky'.

The flat interior of the island looks like one giant golf course dotted with dozens of club-houses. All forty shades of green are in evidence. The houses and outbuildings are colourful too. Some red-roofed, a few green-walled and lots of them a white washed stone dappled with black, like over-sized Dalmatians. Some of the cattle are similarly, though naturally, adorned. There seems to be more order to this landscape than there is on that other large crofting island – South Uist. The buildings also seem to be more solidly constructed and in better condition. Trees are conspicuously absent. We pass one garden with a couple of dwarfed, wind-bent conifers but that is all we see.

One feature for which Tiree is now popular is surfing beaches. The island has several lovely beaches of greyish sand which point in all directions of the compass. When the autumn gales blow, from no matter which direction, surfers stream to Tiree to engage in their chosen pursuit. It all looks a bit cold to us as we stand gazing out into the Atlantic from one of the beaches at Balephetrish.

We move on past the school, which serves as both primary and secondary school for the island. The children, therefore, do not have to leave the island to continue their education – unlike those on the neighbouring island of Coll who have to attend a secondary school in Oban. A local tells us later that, traditionally, the children from Coll and Tiree have never got on well with each other anyway. One island looks on the other as a poor relation.

By now I am coping well with our little car. We stop to film a silly sequence about rasping corncrakes, which breed on the island and we immediately cause a three-car traffic jam. It occurs to us that the local people driving past us probably recognise the car as well and may well know about the brakes. Everyone seems to be giving us welcoming smiles and a wide berth.

We skirt the aerodrome and head back to our hotel in the village of Scaranish. The hotel sits above one of the largest sandy bays, Traigh Mhor. The view from my bedroom window is of sand and machair stretching for miles. Below me, the flat, felted roof of the lounge extension is dotted with large stones, strategically placed to hold down bits of roof against the perpetual wind that races across the island. On the table beside my bed is a copy of the local rag called *An Tirisdeach – Tiree's largest selling newspaper.* And it is only A4 size!

Downstairs in the bar we find George, the local (and only BT) man, and his wife. They moved to Tiree from Glasgow five years ago and wouldn't move back. He enjoys his job, being responsible for all the installations and repairs on Tiree.

'You must get quiet days,' I postulate.

'I get quiet weeks,' he replies.

Thinking of the strong winds for which Tiree is infamous, I add:

'But after the gales you will have a lot of overhead wires to fix.'

'No – most of our stuff is underground now.'

George supplements his working week as a barman, taxi-driver and reporter of interesting natural history sightings.

'I'm a whale 'twitcher' – I saw a minke whale off the north coast a few days ago. And there was a goldcrest in a local garden yesterday.' One of the largest and one of the smallest warm-blooded creatures to be found in Europe, and both in the same week!

Another interesting character in the bar is a middle-aged, white-whiskered, black Labrador whose eyes are permanently and passionately fixed on an old and balding tennis ball. An elderly chap is repeatedly kicking the ball up to the far end of the bar and the dog goes charging after it. He then deposits it at the old chap's feet. When I try the same trick (kicking the ball, that is) the dog seems reluctant so I try some gentle verbal coaxing. There is no response from the Labrador.

'It's no good talking to him like that,' says his playmate.

'Why, is he deaf?' I ask.

'No, he only understands the Gaelic.'

Day Two – *New livery and Old boilers*

Despite the light drizzle, I'm off along the beach of Traigh Mhor at 0810 on a pre-breakfast promenade. For once we don't have an early start to our travels, so breakfast can wait.

I'm not alone on my walk – my Gaelic-speaking Labrador friend from last night and one of his pals, another middle-aged but limping Labrador, both picked themselves up from the hotel foyer as I passed through and are now following faithfully behind me, their tails wagging in unison. As I glance back at the one with the white whiskers and the other with the slight limp I am reminded of Ian and Gibbie.

The three of us set off across the damp, pale sand. The tide is out and small ripply waves lap gently to my right. The grey of the sand and the turquoise waters of the shallow bay merge imperceptibly. The beach is spotlessly clean. No plastic bags, bird corpses or washed-up unmentionables here – Tiree sits too far out into the Atlantic.

A flock of thirty dunlin feed feverishly just a few yards ahead of me. They let me approach to within ten yards before rising with their piping alarm call and settling again further away. Half a mile further on my two canine companions are still tottering along. I can almost hear the limping one mutter under his breath just like Gibbie. When I eventually turn to head back to the hotel I notice a distinct look of relief on his face.

Breakfast is not one but two kippers. Then it is off we go. The car is deposited back in the village and we are on the pier just as the *Lord of the Isles* is turning into the bay.

To our dismay the days of standing innocently at the end of a pier with a camera seem to be coming to an end. On our travels this year we have noticed that piers are being chained off and intending passengers 'cattle-penned' into a safe corner. This seems to be in the name of what I call 'safety paranoia'. People have been strolling up piers for years but now this is suddenly a dangerous thing to do. Flying 'throw lines' can be sore if the end of one hits you on the head but in my experience anyone standing on a pier when a ship is coming in has behaved sensibly and stood well back. So when I am standing half way up Tiree pier behaving sensibly, filming the ship coming in, I am rather annoyed when a pier-hand starts ranting and raving at me. We must have arrived before he had time to put up the chains. Anyway – I get my photograph.

At 1035 we are sailing away from the forbidden pier on our way to Oban via Coll. This means it is time for our second breakfast. We are back on deck later to watch our departure from a thinly populated and chained-off Coll pier.

Down the Sound of Mull, just as many times before. Ian has the snuffles. He is understandably anxious as he fears he is becoming allergic to beer. When he voices his fears , Gibbie noticeably pales.

'Oh my God – imagine if I became allergic to whisky!'

As we pass Tobermory, our old friend the *Hebridean Princess* turns out of the bay and follows in our wake down the Sound. With the Kilchoan ferry *Eigg* following her we are heading a miniature convoy. The *Eigg* pulls into Tobermory, the *Princess* anchors off Duart Castle and the *Lord of the Isles* turns in towards Oban. For the next hour the events in Oban are quite hedonistic for a bunch of ship-spotters.

There are five CalMac ships in the bay. Apart from ourselves there is the *Isle of Mull* which we pass very closely to port off Dunollie. Entering the bay at the other end is our next ship the *Isle of Arran* arriving from Colonsay. She berths at the pier to allow her foot passengers to disembark, leaving the linkspan free for our ship. The Lismore ferry *Bruernish* is sitting out waiting to load for her next sailing. Her place at the slipway is occupied by the *Raasay* which is refuelling from a tanker parked on her small deck.

We tie up and I take up my usual lofty position above the railway pier. The action continues below.

The *Raasay*, suitably sated, dances 'ring-a-ring-a-roses' with her sister, the *Bruernish*, as they swap places. The *Raasay* then heads out down the Sound of Kerrera – destination unknown. The *Lord of the Isles*, now loaded up for South Uist and Barra, leaves the pier and is immediately followed by the *Bruernish*, bound for Lismore. The *Isle of Arran* nudges forwards onto the linkspan and disembarks her vehicles. She then loads up with cars for her return trip to Colonsay and Islay – Gibbie's amongst them. Ian meanwhile is semaphoring perfunctory and disrespectful signals to me telling me to get back down to the pier.

We sail five minutes late, a result of the late appearance of two middle-aged ladies with strikingly blonde dyed hair. Ian refers to them rather unkindly as 'two old boilers'. Once they are up the gangway we can finally sail.

Squeezing down the narrow channel between the mainland and the as yet unconquered (in Island-hopping terms) Kerrera. Ahead of us we spot the *Raasay* squeezing into even tighter spaces east of the island Luing. Is she heading for the Crinan Canal?

As we are a bit behind time we sail inside the Garvellach Islands (as in 1989) which is a slightly more direct route than the more open channel normally navigated.

Up on deck, three moustached bird-watchers (and one of them is female) are relentlessly scanning the near horizon for sea birds, their binoculared eyes shifting in unison from side to side like the crowd at a tennis match. A few feet away, Gibbie, with a mug of steaming tea between his feet, is trying to tear the heart out of a Penguin biscuit wrapper. I feel that I have to chastise him about his sweet diet – a recently broken tooth is conspicuous by its absence at the front of his mouth.

'It's my age,' he confides, 'my teeth have got osteoporosis.'

More dental problems in the bar a short time later. Ian and I watch in mutual astonishment at the edentulous chap opposite us mauling an egg roll. His nose and chin come intimately close at each chew. Our silent wonder is broken when the two platinum-haired ladies who are responsible for our lateness enter from the door opposite.

'There's those two old boilers!' I loudly indicate. To my horror they come over to our table to join their husbands, who have been sitting next us.

At Colonsay there is the usual brief pandemonium on the pier. As the *Isle of Arran* has recently been re-painted with the black of her hull repositioned I decide to run around the bay to capture the new livery on film. I nod to the crewman at the gangway on the way off.

'Back in five minutes.'

'Better make it four, we're running late,' he replies.

I heed his advice. There are only three ships a week to Colonsay, and so take only three minutes.

On comes an assorted bunch of cyclists. They are heading for Jura (like us) to take part in the annual Fell Race up the Paps (unlike us). One of them is a lady well into her seventies. She has a tanned, leathery face topped by unruly white hair – like the head of a mop. She is wearing lycra longs with a knitted cardigan on top and is clutching a multicoloured woolly hat. We see her later in the restaurant devouring a huge plateful of macaroni and boiled potatoes; plenty of carbohydrate for the efforts to come.

Gibbie has noticed none of this. He has had his mouth full for the last ten minutes struggling over steak pie with his osteoporotic teeth. His efforts have not been helped by an altercation with a chirpy but belligerent two-year old, who insists on hanging over the back of Gibbie's seat and bellowing 'Hallo!' in his ear. Eventually Gibbie's nerve gives way and he turns and bellows 'Piss off!' at the toddler who gives him a stare of disbelief.

Up on deck to observe the side to side rolling of the ship as she makes her way between the islands of Colonsay and Islay. To our left, the twin peaks of the Paps of Jura have their tips modestly veiled by a curtain of mist.

The three bird-watchers are still at it. I side up to them, sufficiently curious to ask what interesting birds they have seen during their four-hour vigil.

'Oh, nothing in particular.'

I think I am more disappointed than they are.

If Colonsay was pandemonium then Port Askaig is total chaos. Lines of cars and lorries are straining to board the *Isle of Arran* for the remainder of the journey to Kennacraig. Bewildered passengers are trying the obey the directions of yellow-jacketed staff To add to the confusion the pier is roped off. Amidst all this we have to manoeuvre the car off one ferry and onto another – the *Sound of Gigha* bound for Jura. Gibbie reluctantly reverses aboard and we are on our way to our next island, which is a 'new' one for Ian.

Jura is a wonderful wilderness of an island with a surprisingly lush eastern shore. Almost thirty miles by six it is nearly two islands – being practically bisected by Loch Tarbert, a penetrating sea loch which pushes in from the west. There is only one road, which leaves from the ferry point of Feolin and runs to the only village, Craighouse, before gradually deteriorating into a rough track beyond Ardlussa. Eventually even this disintegrates to no more than a footpath. At the northern tip of Jura, between it and the neighbouring island of Scarba lies the infamous Corryvreckan Whirlpool. A few years ago a friend and I chartered a speed-boat to take us and our bicycles over to Jura's northern tip in order to watch this turbulent half-mile strip of water. For three hours it performed no more violently than a ripple in a garden pond. Apparently the wind direction and tide have got to be just right before it becomes fully animated. That afternoon, a scorching June heatwave, we cycled the rough route to Craighouse. A few miles from Craighouse we ran out of water and knocked on the open door of a farmhouse kitchen with our water bottles in hand. Nobody answered but despite our thirst neither of us could bring ourselves to cross the threshold to help ourselves from the tap.

Tonight we are staying at the only hotel in Craighouse. The ferry journey across to Jura takes five minutes and the hotel is an eight-mile drive.

It is a tranquil and peaceful scene at Craighouse. Even the Fell Racers, perhaps in anticipation of the rigours to come, have retired for the night into their multi-coloured tents in the field opposite the hotel. As if to complement the scene an indolent Border collie closes his eyes and rolls onto his side in deep repose as soon as I approach it. The only excitement around us is coming from Ian who is enthusing uncharacteristically about the polished stainless steel U bend under the sink in our room.

'Look at the beauty in that!' Once an engineer always an engineer.

Day Three – *A Stroll across Campbeltown Loch*

Up at 0730 for a specially arranged early breakfast. We have a ferry to catch surprise, surprise! Apparently there is an 0830 sailing over to Islay. This is essential for we have to depart from the far side of Islay at 0955 in order to get back to the mainland.

As we stand around at Feolin, looking across to Port Askaig, we are relieved to see some activity aboard the red-hulled vessel. Gibbie's joy is short-lived. He has just discovered his Jura hotel room key in his back pocket. There is no time to return it to its rightful owner. The discovery comes as a bit of a surprise, for the key is attached to an eight inch piece of timber that could have been pruned from a Giant Sequoia and Gibbie has been sitting on it for the past twenty minutes. The blond-haired ferryman, Donald, comes to

Gibbie's rescue. The key is sheepishly handed over with a promise in return that it will eventually be re-united with its door. Donald's shake of the head suggests that it is not the first time this has happened.

Donald is a familiar sight on the Jura ferry. His friendly face and patience with drivers who cannot reverse have been features on the *Sound of Gigha* since 1982. Not for much longer – Donald is staying but the ferry is soon to be replaced by a new one.

Surprisingly, this is the first time we have traversed Islay on one of our Hops. It will also be our first visit to Port Ellen. Previous visits to the island have been confined to the confines of Port Askaig.

On our way across the island we stop at the largest village, Bowmore. This is home to one of the seven whisky distilleries on the island (the number varies but at the time of our visit there were seven in function). The Bowmore distillery was founded in the 1770s and has been rebuilt in recent times. With some inspired planning, a public swimming-pool was constructed next door and by a process of heat exchange the pool is heated by hot water from the distillery. I believe that it is water in the pool, however, not whisky. A new shop and visitor centre successfully lures tourists and Island Hoppers inside. We are the first visitors of the day, it is only five past nine and receive a cheery welcome from the girls inside. They probably think we are a bunch of piss artists looking for a free dram – which we are not!

At the top of the hill leading out of Bowmore is the round church of Kilarrow, which pre-dates the distillery by a few years. It was supposedly built circular so that there would be no corners for the devil to hide in.

The church may be round but the road to Port Ellen is straight – as straight as a die. One stretch of it does not deviate for seven miles. At the other end of it is Port Ellen and the *Isle of Arran*.

Much as I love Islay, I have to admit that Port Ellen is a disappointing little village, partly redeemed by an attractive, curved sandy bay at its eastern end. Lots of whitewashed cottages here.

Behind Gibbie's car in the queue for the ferry is a hearse. It is empty apart from its driver. By ten o'clock the car, ourselves and the hearse are all aboard and we are heading out into the open sea. Once the ship has 'straightened out' I am off to the bridge to have a word with a cheerful Captain Fyfe.

I pose the question: 'Do the skippers of the various ships move around?'

He is quick on the response: 'Yes but only when they go for their lunch.'

He tells me that each ship has two and a half skippers. I am ready for the punchline but perhaps he is serious.

Captain Fyfe prefers the *Isle of Arran* to the *Isle of Mull* in heavy seas because he can step outside onto the open wings of the bridge when he feels queasy. The bridge of the *Mull* is all enclosed.

Today we are fortunate in sailing up West Loch Tarbert in daylight – we usually do it in the dark. The beauty of its still waters and the lush green countryside set upon the low hills around the loch make it look like an inland lake. A small red-sailed yacht tries in vain to catch up with us, the stiff breeze billowing her spinnaker.

We now have plans to finalise so drive off down the Kintyre peninsula for a working lunch at Tayinloan. There are two islands to reach this afternoon, Gigha, which sits just offshore from Tayinloan and, hopefully, Davaar Island.

Davaar is an 'Ailsa Craig-like' lump of granite which sits a mile offshore in Campbeltown Loch. It can be reached at low tide by a shingle causeway. This is no more than a narrow curving spit of stones and sand. This will be our only means of access to Davaar and our intended visit will naturally depend on the state of the tide. So before we jump on the ferry to Gigha I telephone the Campbeltown Tourist Office to check if the tides are favourable. We are in luck, low tide is happening as I speak on the phone. It is 1500. If we head down to Campbeltown now we will have plenty of time to stroll over to Davaar and back again without any fear of being stranded by the sea and having to spend the night in a cave. This even takes into account that the speed of our party will be dictated by the pace of the slowest – Gibbie!

So Gigha is abandoned and we continue our drive down Kintyre towards Campbeltown. We reach the town at 1600 and head off across the exposed causeway. Gibbie has been making grumbling noises. I have been telling him repeatedly and optimistically that the stroll to Davaar is only half a mile and will take a mere twenty minutes. Fifteen minutes into the 'stroll' has exposed my euphemism. My half mile stroll across the beach is really a two-mile slog across thick shingle. The spit of sand ahead of us looks just as long as it did when we set out. Not even the colourful sight of his favourite ship, the *Claymore*, can assuage his discomfort. She is entering the Loch ahead of us and our position on the beach offers us a shimmering, kaleidoscopic perspective. Her blue hull appears half buried in the shingle and the white of her considerable super-structure seems to glide silently through the dazzling green fields beyond the bay. For us she is tomorrow's ship – for CalMac she is yesterday's ship. This is our first view of her since her enforced sale.

Meanwhile, the stroll to Davaar is becoming a bit of a trudge. Above the noise of the cool north wind in my ears, Gibbie can be heard muttering something about 'yomping' and the 'Falkland Isles'. At the white buoy marking a change in direction in the causeway, he gives up and leaves Ian and me to continue over to the island. The causeway is now christened 'Gibbie's Spit'.

Just reaching Davaar (a 'new' island) is not enough. On the far side of the island (it would be the *far* side) there are a series of caves, one of which is home to a rock painting of Christ. This was painted by a local man by the name of MacKinnon in 1887 and has become a tourist attraction. We could hardly visit Davaar without seeing the picture. So we walk off around the southern shore of the circular island. The obscure path degenerates into a boulder-strewn beach. Above our heads the sheer cliffs rise, devoid of birdlife and hopefully devoid of any loose rocks also.

Apparently the painting is inside the fifth cave. But what constitutes a cave? By the time we find it, some twenty minutes after reaching the island, I've counted a dozen 'caves'.

Ian discovers it first. While I am exploring one promising cave with the enthusiasm of one of the Famous Five I hear Ian's voice echoing from an adjoining cave: 'I've found it!'

The painting is sufficiently interesting to have made our journey worthwhile. It is about five feet tall and depicts Christ on the cross. It looks as though it was chalked up yesterday.

Fed up with tripping over lumps of granite on the causeway, we decide to take a short cut back over the sands on our return journey to the car and a presumably sleeping Gibbie. When we are almost across the tide can be seen streaming in to cut off our route. Off come the shoes and socks and we paddle our way back to safety.

Gibbie is indeed snoozing but awakens with a start – and then gives us a start by suggesting that we retrace our way to Tayinloan and take that trip over to Gigha. We will have to move fast to catch the 1600 ferry.

Just north of Campbeltown our plans are close to being scuppered – by a herd of Friesian cows. They are being mustered by a harrassed farmer, ready to cross the road in front of us on their laboured way to the milking shed. Fortunately we scrape past before he signals the traffic to a halt.

A couple of miles from Tayinloan – with only five minutes to spare – we are less lucky. We succumb to the dreaded road-works traffic lights. Only about ten feet of road has been dug up, but someone in the Roads Department has decided that the traffic cannot be trusted to negotiate the short single lane without the guidance of two sets of traffic lights – ten feet apart. The result is that we miss the boat – not a common occurrence on an Island Hop. Not to be outdone, we hang around until the next sailing of the *Loch Ranza* at 1700.

This means one of those jump ashore and then jump back on again visits to Gigha but we go anyway. Below the sign reading 'Welcome to Gigha' we shake hands – it is the first time all three of us have been on the island at the same time.

We head back down towards Campbeltown again with the feeling that the day's agenda is now complete. We are now off duty. Past the farm with the cows. They are also now off duty and are randomly dotted across their lush green pasture, ruminating peacefully and no doubt feeling somewhat relieved.

Our hotel is one of the nicest we have experienced. We therefore decide to treat ourselves to a meal in its restaurant (the first dinner not aboard a ship since Morar in 1996) washed down with a bottle of Sauvignon Blanc.

Campbeltown is very much an end-of-the-road town, stuck at the south-eastern corner of the long Kintyre peninsula. South of it lie the lumpy cliffs of the Mull of Kintyre which hit the headlines with Paul McCartney's song and the 1994 helicopter crash which killed several of the Army's top brass returning from Northern Ireland. By coincidence that is our destination tomorrow. The ship that will take us is moored at the pier – heavily fenced off.

Our early departure necessitates the ordering of a continental breakfast and means that our evening visit to one of the town's pubs will be just a brief one.

Day Four – *The Irish Rovers*

0710 and three alarm calls are buzzing simultaneously in our three adjacent rooms. After croissants and jam we are down at the booking office of the Argyll and Antrim Steam Packet company trying to buy tickets for the *Claymore*'s sailing.

CalMac were denied to chance of operating this route from Campbeltown to Ballycastle and, as if to rub salt in their wounded pride they were forced to sell their beloved *Claymore* to the A & A SPCo at a knock-down price. The new owners were then given the privilege of operating the route that is hoped will bring much needed tourism and prosperity to the Kintyre town.

On entering the booking hall the overall impression is that of an airport. Behind her desk, a uniformed hostess in a pill-box hat of the same colour as the ship's funnels is tapping away at her keyboard, entering the details of intending passengers. A party of local primary school children are gaggling away in a corner, their anxious teachers trying to sort out their boarding passes with the minimum of fuss.

In front of Gibbie in the queue is a chap with a golden Labrador as a companion and a huge pheasant tail feather sticking out of the back of his hat, which is almost tickling Gibbie's nose.

'He's probably from Kilmarnock,' Gibbie surmises.

He peers over the chap's shoulder at the form he is filling in and spots his postcode. 'Yeah, he is from Kilmarnock,' he whispers back at us without the merest hint of surprise.

We are given the go-ahead to enter the Departure Lounge. Before doing this, however, we have to pass our bags through an X-ray scanner. We also have to empty our pockets of anything metallic and then step through the threshold of a metal detector. Two tall gentlemen, presumably from Special Branch, watch our every move with an unrestrained eye. The security is overt, but not without good reason. Today is the day of the Irish Referendum on the proposed peace plan. It is a momentous day to be visiting Northern Ireland.

Outside our Departure Lounge, alongside the most cordoned-off pier yet, lies the *Claymore*. No chance of a photograph from the pier here!

This is only the second year of the Campbeltown – Ballycastle service and so it is too early yet to assess the viability of it. No doubt it will attract tourists from Ireland who are planning a trip to the West Highlands, but just how many? I cannot imagine the route seriously challenging the traditional Stranraer crossings. With considerable investment in the new piers and pier buildings and in all the paraphernalia associated with such tight security, it may take a while for the Argyll and Antrim Steam Packet Company and the Development Agencies to get their money back.

Soon we are being escorted from the Departure Lounge through a gate in the steel perimeter fence by another uniformed hostess in a pill-box hat. Entry aboard is via the stern ramp and we are greeted by smiling faces all around. It all seems so different from getting onto the Arran or Islay ferry.

The *Claymore* is looking smarter than we have ever seen her. Her hull is a deep ultramarine blue and her super-structure white. The funnels are still red and black but the red now has an 'orangey' hue. Many of the smaller fittings such as ladders, door handles and some of the railings are picked out in blue. It all looks very fresh. This will be our first sail on the *Claymore* since 1991.

Before we sail, Captain McLundie comes around, smiling reassuringly and shaking hands with various passengers – including a couple of gentlemen in smart suits wearing CalMac ties. At 0800 he is steering his ship away from Campbeltown pier and across the famous Loch. As she heads out, the sun peeps through the grey morning sky and there is the promise of a fine morning's cruise ahead. We sail close to the Davaar causeway. The tide is in and there are only a few yards of exposed sand – Gibbie's spit – showing.

The ship seems alive with the party of school kids. So much so that Gibbie is referring to the ship as 'Weans-ville'. I have visions of them all throwing-up in response to the rough conditions of the Irish Sea. I need not be concerned, the notoriously truculent waters are behaving peacefully.

The *Claymore* takes a right turn around the southern cliffs of the Mull of Kintyre. On between Sanda Island and the village of Southend, which I have been reliably informed has the claim to fame of being the British mainland village that is furthest from a railway station. Wow!

Up on deck to view the cliffs. Paul McCartney's song is ringing in our ears, mainly because I am trying to sing it. The Mull lighthouse comes into view, above which the aforementioned helicopter crashed four years ago.

We are now out on the open sea but Gibbie's favourite ship and all the schoolchildren aboard her, are behaving nicely. Wish we could say the same for the weather. A huge dark cloud looms from the south-east and the sun perches above it, perilously close to becoming submerged in its dismal depths. The cold northerly wind is now strong – so we go below.

The main lounge of the *Claymore* has undergone a considerable tarting-up since our last trip. More trellises, flowers and pastel shades. The food is similar.

All of us have been to Northern Ireland before. I had a family holiday in County Antrim in 1968, when I was ten. That included a visit to Ballycastle. It is now forty years since either Gibbie or Ian visited the Province. I am now looking at the town thirty years on – and of course I don't recognise it. The ship is ahead of time due to a favourable tide as we near the pier – it is barely 1030. Just as at Campbeltown, a new Departure Lounge and a new security fence have been constructed at the head of a new stretch of concrete pier. The attractive town winds away from all this and further round to the left there is a lovely golden beach.

Another ferry is just leaving the pier. CalMac's *Canna* is departing with a car-deck full of people for Rathlin Island. CalMac have now served this island, which sits off the north-eastern corner of Ireland, for a couple of seasons under their own flag. Itis thus even more ironic that they were denied the opportunity to complete the link from Ballycastle back to the Scottish base of Campbeltown. The last time we saw the *Canna* was when she was operating the service to Scalpay – an island now shortly to be served by a bridge.

Ashore at Ballycastle arguing whether Northern Ireland counts as an island or not. It obviously must! It is eventually accepted as our thirty-fourth island (thirty-fifth if we count Eilean Ban) in ten years of Island Hopping. It is also the biggest – by quite a margin.

As we stroll out through the Arrivals Lounge a couple of security officers eye us benevolently and wish us 'Good Morning'. Just outside, chalked onto a wall is a poignant reminder of the importance of today's poll.

'Vote YES for peace.'

We wander around the shore road, looking for somewhere that is open in order to sample some local hospitality. We would settle for a half pint of Guinness – although none of us like it. We're out of luck in any case as the pubs don't open until 1130 – and it is only 1045. What's more, we only have fifty minutes.

The party of schoolchildren, whose visit will be just as brief, seem to have no problem in passing the time. They are snaking their way past us like a flock of obedient lambs, with their sheepdog minders scurrying around them issuing instructions: 'Come on, get a move on across that road. Don't drag your bag like that, Duncan. No, we're not going to the beach.'

We stop a young office girl out on an errand and ask her to say something to our camera so that we can record an Irish accent. She laughs off the request and replies in the broadest of County Antrim brogues:

'Oi chust spake the semm ash yoo!'

We find a cafe which serves us delicious apple pie and cream along with huge mugs of coffee.

Soon the flock of lambs is filing back, past the cafe. Our short visit has been worthwhile. The pleasant atmosphere and new hope for the future brings home to me that the thirty-year gap between visits has been too long and I should return soon to see more of Ireland.

Back to X-ray machines and metal detectors. This time all three of us are frisked by an apologetic security man. His regret seems genuine.

The *Claymore* sails on time at 1145, back to Scotland. We adjourn for our own version of a whisky-tasting session in the window-less bar. The timeless refrain 'Oh Campbeltown Loch I wish you were whisky...' comes to life in a glass in our hands. Gibbie reckons the aftertaste is like Mars Bars.

The tireless bunch of schoolchildren are now on a longer leash; playing 'tig' and roaming harmlessly about the ship. Their teachers are meanwhile enjoying a well earned coffee in a huddle in the lounge.

Off the Mull of Kintyre we are on the forward deck watching several flocks of gannets, 30 to a flock, circling round like squadrons of snowy white gliders. The Captain interrupts to apologise for the fact that we will be twenty minutes late into Campbeltown as the tide is now against us. We are in no rush. Out on the car-deck a crewman , attired in a white boiler suit which still has the CalMac logo sewn onto the front of it, checks some cargo.

We brave the cold wind out on the deck for the last part of the journey. Two of the teachers are also feeling the cold, for they are huddling ever more intimately together on one of the seats.

Claymore arrives back at Campbeltown at 1445 and we assemble below deck on instruction from one of the nice hostesses. The children are being rounded up prior to disembarkation. All is going well and they are all behaving themselves quietly until one of them farts and then mass hysteria breaks out.

Off we get, Ian is somehow ahead of Gibbie and me as we enter the Arrivals Lounge. I am boasting to Gibbie that even with dark shades covering my eyes I never get stopped by Customs Officials. There ahead of us is the man from Special Branch. It is a narrow corridor and I will pass right in front of his nose. I *know* that he is going to stop me. He does. His arm flies out in front of me.

'Excuse me sir, could you stop there please? Where are you from?'

I push the shades onto the top of my head and notice that Gibbie has wandered on ahead.

'Glasgow.' This causes confusion to the man and he responds with a string of questions.

'Are you alone?'

'No, I'm with these two gentlemen...' I point aimlessly, for Gibbie and Ian are nowhere to be seen.

'Are you with the schoolchildren? Where have you come from? Are you not from the other side?'

By the last question I presume that he means Ireland and not 'beyond the grave'. He presumes that as I am arriving off the first sailing of the day from Northern Ireland then I must have come from the 'other side', and he cannot understand how anyone would leave Campbeltown at 0800, sail over to Ireland and sail straight back again. He has obviously never been an Island Hopper. But at last the penny drops.

'Oh, so you just went for the sail?' He nods me on my way.

Outside, reunited with the car, Gibbie and Ian show no remorse for disowning me. I regain my composure and take the wheel for the drive up to Tarbert.

It is 'regatta day' in the Argyll town – it always is when we arrive here. A grill of sizzling beefburgers is irresistible before continuing onwards to the ferry slip. A new vessel for us, the *Loch Linnhe*, will take us over to Portavadie. We always seemed to miss this boat when she operated out of Largs but due to some re-shuffling of the smaller ferries she is now on this route. We sail across Loch Fyne at 1630 under a sky that cannot make up its mind whether it should be sunny or cloudy.

On the other side there is the drive round to Colintraive via Tighnabruaich. There is time to stop at the viewpoint above Loch Riddon and the Kyles of Bute. The view down the East Kyle, past Colintraive, as far as Largs, is one of the most impressive in Scotland. Far below us we can see our next vessel chugging across to Bute. Soon we will be there too. That vessel is the *Isle of Cumbrae* – another one displaced from her usual haunts. We are using Bute as a stepping-stone on our way home, as we have done before

Rothesay is quiet, very quiet considering the pleasant evening it is. We head for the best fish n' chip shop in town (recently given this honour in a newspaper poll). There we discover why the town is empty – everyone is in the fish n' chip shop queuing for haddock and chips. We sample the delights from brown paper bags up on the pier. For the record Ian insists that he had a salad-supper.

There are slight concerns on the pier. We are the only car in the 'queue' for the ferry. Does this mean that the next sailing will be a passenger only one – as some early evening runs have been recently? While we wait to find out I take off, with my video camera, to the Victorian Toilets recently restored to their former glory. I find the caretaker, Danny, positively glowing with pride as if he had single-handedly restored the ceramic urinals himself. Fortunately there is no-one there to hide in embarrassment as I pan the camera round.

'Do you let women in to see all this?'

'Oh, yes, they love them,' Danny claims.

'And what if some poor chap then enters, desperate to use the facilities?'

'I just direct them into the Ladies.'

We had thought that we might find the elusive *Raasay* at Rothesay but she is not there. Her disappearance beyond Luing remains a mystery. The *Jupiter* is soon arriving, however, which confirms that we will be able to get home with the car this evening.

The upper deck of the Clyde ferry becomes the scene of the Annual Toast. This time it is a special one as it celebrates our tenth trip. Gibbie gives a speech to camera as if addressing the House of Commons. '...I am the strategist who paints with a broad brush. The tactician makes the strategist's dreams become reality – in other words the tactician does all the hard work.'

This tactician can only agree – but can add that it has been a labour of love.

Over the ten years we have had so many memories and laughs. For the archivist we have reached thirty-five islands upon forty-seven vessels of all shapes and sizes; from the tiny Holy Isle ferry to the impressive *Isle of Lewis*.

We have sailed over one thousand nautical miles. What about the future – will we carry on Island Hopping till we drop? Perhaps the extension to beyond Scottish waters is portentious. Maybe Island Hops from now on will be in more far flung places, like the Greek Isles, the Caribbean or, even better, Polynesia – there are lots of islands there!

* * *

So what was the point of it all? Difficult to answer but when we look back on the memories, the anecdotes, the characters met *en route*, the beauty of the islands and the many hours peering out over the sea from the rail of a ship, it all seems very worthwhile.

* * *

Appendix I

Islands

(In order visited)

Arran	Islay	Jura	Colonsay	Mull	Iona
Staffa	South Uist	Benbecula	Grimsay	North Uist	Skye
Barra	Lismore	Gt Cumbrae	Bute	Harris	Scalpay
Lewis	Raasay	Ulva	Coll	Tiree	Holy Isle
Eriskay	Vatersay	Berneray	Gigha	Seil	Luing
Easdale	Canna	Eilean Ban	Davaar	Northern Ireland.	

Appendix II

Ships

(In order sailed)

MV Isle of Arran
MV Sound of Gigha
Fingal of Staffa
MV Hebridean Isles
MV Lochmor
MV Loch Striven
MV Jupiter
MV Canna
MV Isle of Cumbrae
MV Loch Riddon
MV Caledonian Isles
MV Juno
MV Canna
Easdale ferry
MV Rhum
MV Maid of Glencoul
MV Loch Ranza
MV Isle of Mull
MV Claymore
MV Kyleakin
MV Eigg,
MV Saturn
MV Suilven
MV Iona
Ulva Ferry
MV Loch Tarbert
MV Nordic
MV Brendan
PS Waverley,
Ossian of Staffa
MV Eilean Bernaraidh
MV Loch Linnhe
MV Glen Sannox
MV Morven
MV Lord of the Isles
MV Lochalsh
MV Coll
MV Keppel
MV Loch Fyne
MV Raasay
MV Loch Buie
MV Pioneer
MV Second Snark
MV Bruernish
MV Belnahua
MV Isle of Lewis
MV Loch Bhrusda